David Levell is a writer, journalist and television producer. In 2004 he helped WW2 commando Brian Walpole complete his memoir *My War*, and was contributing writer/editor for Ron Stephenson's *Victor Chang: Murder Of A Hero* (2005). His TV documentaries include *Wizard Of Love* (SBS-TV), about Puccini. David lives in Sydney with Josephine Pennicott and their daughter Daisy.

TOUR TO HELL

CONVICT AUSTRALIA'S GREAT ESCAPE MYTHS

DAVID LEVELL

First published 2008 by University of Queensland Press
PO Box 6042, St Lucia, Queensland 4067 Australia

www.uqp.com.au

Typeset by Bluerinse Setting
Printed in Australia by McPherson's Printing Group

Cataloguing-in-Publication Data
National Library of Australia
Levell, David
  Tour to hell
  9780702236860
  Convicts—Australia—History. Escapes—Australia—History.
  Penal colonies—Australia—History. Australia—History—1788–1851.
  944.02

For Josephine

You prisoners of New South Wales,
Who frequent watchhouses and gaols
A story to you I will tell
'Tis of a convict's tour to hell.

From *A Convict's Tour To Hell* (1839)
by Frank MacNamara, transported convict

Contents

NEW SOUTH WALES c.1791-1810

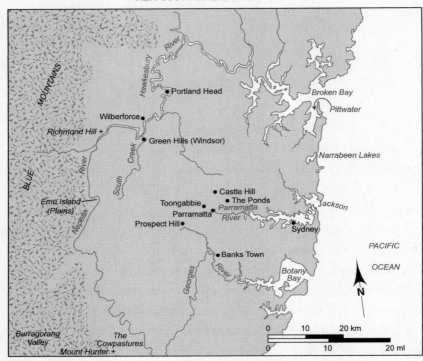

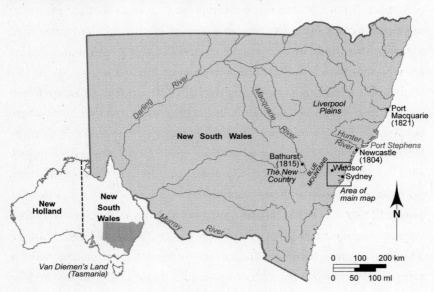

Introduction

> . . . an Irish convict, who had escaped from his work, and had been
> for some time missing, was brought in. He had wandered about for
> several days in search of a road which he expected to have found, and
> which was to have conducted him to China, or the new colony.
>
> David Collins, *Account of the English Colony in New South Wales*,
> January 1798

One of the strangest events in Australia's colonial history took place
in November 1791, when the first convicts sent from Ireland suddenly
began to flee the penal farms at Parramatta, sixteen miles west of Sydney.
It was the first mass desertion since the colony's foundation almost four
years previously, but the real shock was the fugitives' intention to walk
to China. Not only did they believe this vast, little-known nation was at
most an easy 150 miles to the north – it is actually some 5000 miles from
Sydney – they were also convinced of a welcome reception and asylum
from British justice, which to them was no justice at all.

Within a few years, Irish convicts were also sure that an independent
society of white people flourished a few hundred miles inland, somewhere
across the thickly timbered Blue Mountains. In this unseen realm the
land was better, the living was easier and hard labour was not required.
This went beyond escapist fantasy; it was an article of faith upon which
numerous runaways staked – and lost – their lives. The idea caught on
outside Irish ranks, and three decades later some convicts were still
seeking overland routes to other countries. As it formed something of
a sustaining myth amongst the convict underclass, I have adopted the
term *escape mythology* as a convenient umbrella for a fluid series of ideas

that located sanctuaries in the bush just beyond the grip of European settlement.

This is the story of what happened when the lowliest and most marginalised of our early colonists tried to make sense of their disorienting predicament on the other side of the world. Their outlandish conclusions reflect the bizarre beginning of colonial Australia on 26 January 1788, when a continent the size of Europe became an outdoor gaol for several hundred felons sentenced in English courts to transportation beyond the seas. The landmass was almost entirely a blank slate to the founding authorities, but this wasn't a problem at first. Until escape mythology swept through convict ranks, the bush made a very effective prison wall. Only a dozen First Fleet convicts went missing during the first six months ashore. Almost all of these absconded within days of disembarking at Sydney Cove, walking eight miles south to Botany Bay in the forlorn hope of joining two French ships which had arrived in the remote vicinity just a few days after the First Fleet. The commander, La Perouse, turned them away with gifts of food. By February 1790 Governor Phillip had reported only a further two convicts as 'lost in the woods', and the total missing for that year was just four.

The earliest convicts were not locked up or closely supervised outside working hours. At first they lived in tents, then rough wattle-and-daub huts. Some would occasionally hide in the bush nearby to shirk labour, but to abandon life in the settlement, brutal as it was, for the lethal freedom of the bush was hardly a risk worth taking. However, by the end of 1791 a reason to wander off had suddenly arisen. The wilderness wall was only as discouraging as its inmates believed it to be. For many, fear of the unknown was now dissolved by a liberating faith in the bush as a stepping stone back home.

The authorities were totally unprepared for this exposure of the prison-colony's Achilles heel. A succession of exasperated governors resorted to outlandish extremes in dealing with this unexpected development. They tended to dismiss it as a self-evident absurdity and its enthusiasts as deficient in rational thought. But there was some method to this apparent madness, and officialdom was not above nurturing an outback myth of its own – the inland sea – which had surprisingly close parallels with its convict equivalent.

Tour to Hell is not a general history of escape, although bringing to life the adventures of sanctuary-seekers is naturally a major part of the story. Other absconders, such as stowaways or those who connived to alter sentencing records, lie outside the scope of this book. Some individuals in these pages are well known, others find themselves emerging from the archival wilderness for the very first time. In re-imagining their curious actions in detail we can assemble a fragment of colonial and convict experience that has been rarely considered. In short, we can ask our runaways: what were you thinking?

Although much about the nature and genesis of escape mythology remains shadowy – as does its disappearance sometime after about 1830 – it can reasonably be considered European Australia's first folklore, the earliest informal body of belief that transportees developed and disseminated after arriving. But unlike most colonial lore, such as transportation ballads, escape mythology was not wholly European in conception. Its development depended heavily on Aboriginal input, which appears related to the vital problem of incorporating whites into their worldview. Conjured on both sides of the frontier, escape mythology was a hybrid creation, and the interaction that formed it represents perhaps the earliest intellectual exchange between the ordinary people of the two cultures. So while this book touches upon the imaginative life of our most reluctant first settlers, it is also a sort of prehistory of the contemporary Australian imagination which attempts to bridge European and Aboriginal traditions, however uneasily and imperfectly. That our first collective vision partly sprang from a determination to get away at all costs certainly highlights the sheer peculiarity of Australia's national beginnings.

The English colony in New South Wales followed centuries of

European dreaming about a great southern land. From ancient Greek reports (by Strabo and Ptolemy) of a vast landmass south-east of India stretching west to Africa, to 17th-century notions of Terra Australis Incognita filling much of the space between the equator and the South Pole, no other continent was ever imagined or anticipated as much as Australia was by the western civilisation that ultimately claimed it.

This dreaming didn't stop with the First Fleet. All colonies are built upon dreams; colonisation is a risky business and an act of faith. Visions of the future are projected onto the occupied land. For a willing pioneer, this is the hope of prosperity won by hard work. But the inner response of many convicts to their tough new environment was very different. Desperate circumstances made it impossible for many of them to envision a future – even a tomorrow – at Sydney Cove. The colony of their desire required immediate existence, and they grasped at any clue or chance offered by their new world to manifest it. Imagination was their only real freedom, the only part of their lives beyond the reach of authority and the lash.

Of course, accepting convict stories at face value, as colonial officials well knew, is problematic. Any prisoner telling a tale to their gaoler is likely to favour angling for advantage over telling the truth. Pondering what those advantages were to colonial runaways has recently prompted some historians to suggest that convicts only feigned belief in overland sanctuaries to mask other plans. However, the full weight of evidence – from administrators, informers, settlers, explorers, Aborigines, foreign visitors and sometimes the runaways themselves – indicates to me that stories of nearby mystery societies were widely circulated and believed.

Amongst the uneducated masses, travel was rare, global awareness negligible and knowledge often a product of gossip. Naturally, many of those dumped ashore at Sydney Cove were unable to accept or even comprehend just how far from urban civilisation they had been removed. They had little reason to trust the self-serving counter-arguments of hated overlords, whose ignorance of the new land appeared to match theirs. For many, the idea of never seeing home or family again was unthinkable.

Indeed, the unlikelihood of most transportees ever returning to Europe was one of the choicest pieces of bait that had first hooked the British Government into founding a penal colony in New South Wales. Several options for putting Cook's distant discovery to use had been argued ever since a public servant named James Matra first suggested exiling Britain's convict surplus to what was, for Europeans at least, literally the ends of the Earth. In 1785, two years before the First Fleet set sail, Alexander Dalrymple of the East India Company sneered that

> ... this project of a Settlement in that quarter has appeared in many Proteus-like forms, sometimes as a halfway house to China; again as a check upon the Spaniards at Manila and their Acapulco trade; sometimes as a place for transported Convicts.

He was mocking the indecision as to whether trade, military strategy or clearing the prison hulks should govern the form the proposed colony should take. But in the light of the escape myths that inflamed its first decades, his words seem oddly prophetic. Although the thief colony was the route finally taken — with the other benefits firmly in mind — for some of its forced pioneers, New South Wales did quite literally become a 'halfway house to China', and even more exotic destinations.

This is the story of how that happened.

CHAPTER ONE

The hopeful fraternity

The Botany Bay scheme is the most absurd, prodigal and impracticable vision that ever intoxicated the mind of man.

LETTER TO THE EDITOR, 'THE EDINBURGH BEE', OCTOBER 1791

April 5th, 1791, Cork Harbour, Ireland: From the dank, dark oaken belly of the *Queen*, a three-masted Indiaman at anchor, the following letter found its way to the senior British naval officer then in port. The anonymous author was locked below decks with over a hundred other convicted criminals, bound for the distant English colony at New South Wales, and the eloquent plea was all but vindicated by the high death toll they suffered in Australia over the following year.

Honourd Sir,

The deplorable state of the convicts on bord the *Queen* of London now in this harbour is perhaps the most dreadfull instance of cruelty you ever heard of. Each poor creature is to the allowance of ½ pound of beef & 6 potatoes in the twenty four hours nether bread or liqrs of any kind except bad water. The third of them will not survive the passage there. Letters are opend by the cruel Captn & Agent who are in favour of each other & of corse the poor wretches dare not complain. Adress them Worthy Sir as it is your character to be good & charatable & heaven may for ever reward you is the prayer of an unhappy convict.

Herded from various Irish gaols in early 1791, mainly from Dublin and Cork, the ragtag assortment included some two dozen women — some with infants — and four boys under fifteen years of age. The oldest prisoner was Patrick Fitzgerald, sixty-four, of County Limerick, a first-time offender who had stolen some clothes. David Fay, an eleven-year-old Dubliner, was the youngest. Over half were convicted in Dublin, many for street robberies, thefts and burglaries, such as Hugh Lynch, guilty of an armed holdup in Grafton Street. Catherine Devereaux had been sentenced to hang for highway robbery, but respited when she was shown to be pregnant. Other women such as Mary Ennis and Mary Whelan, convicted for being 'idle vagabonds', were probably prostitutes. Commuted death penalties were common; Felix Owen was to have been hanged and quartered for counterfeiting coins, while Francis McLernan, twenty, was the only man of a gang of five spared the gallows for a vigilante murder. A Dublin newspaper jocularly referred to Ireland's first transportees to Australia as 'the hopeful fraternity' — and with their future a forbidding uncertainty in almost unknown parts across the globe, hope was about the only resource left to them. Reports from this 'desert corner of the earth' had been grim. 'Famine is staring us in the face', a letter from Sydney said in the *Hibernian Journal*. 'Timber there appears not fit for building', another item ran, and runaway convicts had been killed and eaten by the natives they had tried to live with.

Public sympathy for the hopeful fraternity's plight took a dramatic turn one day in Dublin, when a mob stormed carriages taking sixty male and fifteen female convicts along Thomas Street. They broke handcuffs, unyoked horses and almost engineered a mass escape, but when order was restored only two men were missing, and soon recaptured.

Whisked by coach or boat to Cork Harbour under armed escort, the convicts soon found themselves aboard the Carolina-built *Queen*, a prize the British navy had taken during the American War of Independence. At 112 feet in length and thirty feet across, she was small for a convict transport and cleared just over five feet between decks. Some of the prisoners improvised little wire saws from smuggled springs, hoping to file their way to freedom. After one man was caught with one of these pathetic tools poking through the open sole of his shoe, a thorough search revealed others had them hidden in their shoes and hair.

A more pressing problem, however, was the extremely low quality — and quantity — of provisions. The twenty-seven soldiers on board were also affected, but the ship's captain, a ferocious salt named Richard Owen, fended off all complaints with ranting barrages of abuse. During one confrontation Ensign William Cummings, the soldiers' commander, went as far as to snatch the keys to the convict quarters from Owen, causing the convicts to start cheering him on sight.

Departure was delayed for weeks while arguments raged over the paltry and substandard provisions, and while Captain Owen busied himself making private deals with Cork merchants to trade various goods in ports of call. He was joined in this lucrative rort by the *Queen*'s naval agent, Lieutenant Samuel Blow, an official supposedly responsible for ensuring the voyage was conducted in accordance with the shipping contract. Things finally came to a head in early April, when Blow went missing for several days in Cork City. Growing worried the exasperated soldiers would assist a convict mutiny, Owen made peace with Cummings and turned on his crony Blow, blaming him for the holdup and demanding his replacement. The sacking was bungled, however; by the time the new agent reached Cork, the *Queen* was already at sea.

Finally weighing anchor on 16 April, the *Queen* set sail for St Jago in Dutch Guinea (Ghana). There Owen had been ordered to join eight

English convict transports and proceed to New South Wales as a part of the Third Fleet. Scattered by stormy weather in the Atlantic, the ships reached Sydney weeks apart. The convicts spent most of their time in barely ventilated darkness, manacled in tiny wooden alcoves. Many had spent a year or more in similarly dismal Irish gaols, but rough seas made a terrifying novelty, and seasickness an all-consuming misery. Added to this was the incessant gnawing of hunger and thirst, and the ever-present threat of fatal disease. Having left their home counties, in many cases for the first time, the only certain outcome of this living interment at sea, cramped in the fetid underworld below deck, was a Purgatorial afterlife in distant regions with no guarantee of seeing friends or family ever again.

At sea, a convict named John Martin was recruited to help dole out the convicts' food. In return for measuring flour rations a pound short — and for keeping quiet about it — he was allowed to live with the sailors and have as much flour as he liked. Meanwhile the rest of the convicts, half-starved, grew so angry and unsettled that Lieutenant Blow let them choose one of their own, Andrew Burn, to witness the weighing out. This, he hoped, would allay suspicions of short-rationing. Three days later, however, Captain Owen noticed Burn waiting outside the steward's room, where Martin and the mate Robert Stott filled the convicts' food bags. Owen exploded, saying it was 'a pretty thing for a thief and a robber to watch honest men'. Calling for a whip, he personally gave Burn a severe flogging, bellowing that he'd teach him 'to be an overseer'.

Things got worse after the ship left the Cape of Good Hope. Under pressure to cut rations further, Stott locked Martin in the steward's room and ordered him to scrape the lead weights. Two or three weeks out from Sydney, a troubled Stott approached Ensign Cummings on deck and admitted to cheating the convicts of their food allowance. Owen had forced him to do it, Stott whined, and wouldn't have been satisfied had rations been withheld completely. He also accused Blow of conspiring with Owen in the deception. A day or two before landfall, meals were improved in a belated attempt to get the prisoners up to strength, but it was too little too late. Seven men had died and the survivors, starved for six months at sea, were filled with bitter rage.

The *Queen* finally anchored in Sydney Cove on 26 September 1791, after creaking its way through the heads of Port Jackson in company with the English transport *Active*. The convicts were rowed ashore over the next five days — 126 males of the 133 embarked at Cork, and twenty-two females, with four infants between them.[1]

Europe's sole outpost on the Australian continent was less than four years old, just 'a few hundred hovels, built of twigs and mud', as the young marines captain Watkin Tench put it. Hungry and lonely, the colony was still struggling to feed itself, still heavily dependent on supply ships. Sydney itself, wrote Tench, was 'nothing but a few old scattered huts, and some sterile gardens'. The thin, sandy soil around the harbour had defeated all efforts at farming. The real strength was sixteen miles upriver at Parramatta, the colony's second town, where most convicts were either tilling the more fertile ground or clearing bush at nearby Toongabbie.

No land grants had been issued and few residents, if any, considered it home. The population was less than 3000, two-thirds of whom were male prisoners. Only thirty-five ex-convicts had settled on the land and the grand total of free settlers — three — was doubled by the number of Aborigines living voluntarily in the towns.

Like all newly arrived convicts, the human cargo aboard the *Queen* was fair game for the older hands, who relished the chance to move one rung up a brutal pecking order. To any indigenous Australians who saw them land, they were just more of the Bereewolgal — 'men from afar'. In fact they were quite different. Ever since the First Fleet anchored at Sydney Cove in 1788, New South Wales had included a smattering of Irish nationals sentenced in English courts. But the *Queen* imported the colony's first real ethnic minority, a new convict underclass further marginalised by their Catholic religion. In some cases this extended to language, too, as up to a third came from counties where Gaelic was still widely spoken.

To Lieutenant Arthur Phillip, the colonial governor, the *Queen* carried the least welcome of a most unwanted delivery — 'great numbers of the worst of characters,' he complained, 'particularly amongst those who came from Ireland'. Centuries of English–Irish turbulence guaranteed the *Queen* convicts would be dreaded as troublemakers. Ireland was then nearing the brink of upheaval. By the end of the 1790s, republican yearnings and the grievances of the impoverished Catholic majority would spark open rebellion. Meanwhile the enclosure of commons, rising rents and mass evictions were causing enormous hardships for the peasantry, who struck back by forming covert 'agrarian societies' — rural vigilante groups that toppled fences, maimed cattle and terrorised those who cooperated with hated landlords. Whiteboys, Peep-of-Day Boys and Ribbonmen were just some names these groups went by. Another name, Defenders, would very soon become a catch-all term for Irish troublemakers in New South Wales.

Despised and feared as the Irish were, there was still considerable shock at the emaciated condition they arrived in. Phillip was dismayed by how many Third Fleeters arrived too sick to work; a 'deadweight on the stores' he called them. David Collins, Phillip's judge-advocate who extensively chronicled the colony's first decade, branded the cruel treatment of those aboard the *Queen* and *Active* as 'offensive to every sentiment of humanity'.

Captain Owen wasted no time setting up shop, eager to line his pockets by selling the unused convict rations and other goods at grossly inflated colonial rates. The shipping firm was paid a flat rate per convict embarked, regardless of how many survived. As Collins remarked, this made the dead more profitable than the living. The earlier convicts died en route, the longer their rations could be drawn against their names fraudulently, and there was nothing to stop leftover provisions being sold to famished Sydneysiders at enormous markups on arrival.

For all this, the *Queen* was hardly a death ship. Most other Third Fleet transports suffered far higher casualties; the average mortality per ship was nineteen. The *Active* buried twenty-one men at sea. The *Albemarle* and *Admiral Barrington*, ravaged by smallpox, each lost over thirty, but the misfortunes on the Irish ship couldn't be put down to disease. Short-rationing had greater repercussions when Irish convicts were concerned, fuelling paranoia of an English conspiracy to starve them to death.

Stoking this fire was their absence of formal identity. The *Queen* convicts came unaccompanied by records of their names or sentences, papers which wouldn't arrive for another eight years — after many sentences had expired. This problem sometimes occurred with English transports, too, but with Irish convicts it amplified a sense of national injustice already keenly felt, bolstering suspicions that England intended them never to tread Irish soil again.

So vehement were the convicts' complaints that Phillip felt obliged to investigate. An inquiry into Owen's conduct convened on 17 October, with Judge-Advocate Collins heading a four-man panel of magistrates. A comparative test with other scales proved the *Queen*'s weights had indeed been scraped, and convicts such as John Martin described the abuses they had witnessed. Hugh McGinnis, a convict assigned to delivering the beef ration to the cook, claimed it was often less than half — sixty pounds for a 132-pound ration. Ensign Cummings, the only official who spoke against Owen, recalled seeing Stott short-weight the rations when he peeked through a crevice in the wall between his cabin and the steward's room. When Captain Owen came to the stand he blamed his mate Stott for everything, insisting 'it was his wish the ration should be issued according to contract'. Stott, who ventured he 'was liked by everyone on board, and never had a word with either soldier or convict', admitted that he 'received orders from Captain Owen to do justice' and had done just that 'to the best of his knowledge'. He was only following orders, in other words.

The court's decision was to avoid a decision. Although Collins and his panel found serious 'deficiencies' in the prisoners' treatment aboard, they ruled it was 'impossible for us to determine with any precision what those deficiencies are, so as to enable us either to redress the complainants or punish the defendants'. The court concluded by simply recommending Phillip act as he thought necessary.

Appalled as he was by Owen's conduct, Phillip was just as reluctant to act. Unsure of his jurisdiction, he had the court transcripts sent to the Secretary of State for the Home Department in London, making his own opinion quite clear by adding, 'I doubt if I have the power of inflicting a punishment adequate to the crime'.

Nothing was done. Owen was not punished for his cruelty — no transport captain ever was — but he was the first of the few called upon to explain it. Although significant for this fact alone, the trial also marked the beginning of Anglo–Irish conflict in the southern hemisphere, soon to take a new twist with the sudden appeal of overland desertion.

Before the *Queen* arrived, convicts generally saw little point in taking to the bush. Instead they preferred to exploit their gaolers' ignorance of local conditions. Watkin Tench described this opportunism:

> We found the convicts particularly happy in fertility of invention and exaggerated descriptions. Hence large freshwater rivers, valuable ores, and quarries of limestone, chalk and marble were daily proclaimed soon after we had landed.

Tench and other First Fleet officials were initially thrilled by these reports, but the scales soon fell from their eyes: 'perpetual disappointments taught us to listen with caution and believe from demonstration only'. Landing in unknown territory had launched a battle of the imagination, as the upper and lower orders each sought to impose advantageous perceptions of the landscape upon the other. Convicts cunningly appealed to their masters' fondest hopes for the infant colony, angling for rewards and pardons with false promises of much-wanted natural resources. Authority, on the other hand, emphasised the futility of running away, citing Aboriginal hostility and the difficulty of finding food in the bush.

The sudden onset of convict escape mythology at the end of 1791 brought the war of ideas to a peak. It also meant the authorities had to contend with genuine belief rather than conscious deception. But before then, the only thing generally believed about the continent was that it was a lost cause. The idea of entrusting your life to a one-way bushwalk had departed with the La Perouse expedition from Botany Bay almost four years beforehand.

The feeling of being swallowed by wilderness haunted the minds of early settlers. They could hardly have been further from home, perched on the edge of an endless, parched forest that seemed to hold such little hope for the British toehold. The harsh light, the apparent lack of edible vegetation, the oppressive heat that would erupt into savage thunderstorms — almost everything about this new country underscored its alien nature to European sensibilities.

After two years in the far-flung colony, the First Fleet chaplain Richard Johnson wrote to friends in England complaining how he felt 'buried alive' — and he, unlike almost all convicts, could at least seriously look forward to going home one day. David Collins, whose first, disconcerting impression of stepping ashore at Sydney was that 'every man stepped from the boat literally into a wood', confessed he was frequently 'struck with horror at the bare idea' of getting bushed in Sydney's thickly timbered maze of coves. 'It is certain,' he said of those unlucky enough to lose their way, 'that if destroyed by no other means, insanity would accelerate the miserable end that must ensue'. What could a runaway possibly hope to find out there? 'The westward was an immense open track before him,' wrote Collins, 'in which, if unfriended by either sun or moon, he might wander until life were at an end'.

A few officials, most notably Tench, took an interest in exploring this eucalypt abyss, but most quickly slid into apathy and despair. 'This country will never answer to settle in,' marines commander Major Robert Ross assured Home Under Secretary Evan Nepean after only six months. 'In the whole world there is not a worse country,' he wrote. 'All that is contiguous to us is so very barren and forbidding that it may with truth be said that here nature is reversed; and if not so, she is nearly worn out.' At the same time, Lieutenant Ralph Clark voiced the general sentiment that Sydney was already a failed experiment: 'it is the opinion of everybody here that the settlement will be removed to some other place, for it is not possible that this place can maintain itself in a century'.

Such talk probably helped to discourage desertion: why miss the chance of a relocation closer to civilisation? Fear of the unknown had other ways of keeping First Fleeters together, too. Few animals were seen, and nothing of any size, but at night the bush was a strange orchestra of unseen creatures, and in the third week ashore rumours flew of an eight–foot alligator near the camp. A couple of weeks later this bogey was reported again, apparently lurking just outside the tents, an embellished nightmare now fourteen feet long.

To abscond was to replace hard labour with a harder struggle for survival, plus the risk of sudden death by white scaffold or black spear. It was far easier to pilfer stores from inside the camp. The risk of the rope remained, but at least there was safety in numbers and a tent to sleep in. Even the toughest bolter of the early days, John 'Black' Caesar, a First Fleeter who ran several times over seven years, never lasted more than a few weeks at large. The first runaway to arm himself with a stolen gun, his method was to scare Aborigines from their camps and grab what food they left behind, but one day he staggered home, dreadfully wounded by spears. He only survived because he was careful to skulk fairly near the settlement; if the fight had occurred any deeper in the bush he would have bled to death. A more typical First Fleet runaway, Edward Corbet, deserted in June 1788 after stealing a shirt and almost died of starvation. He tried begging from Aborigines, who sent him away after giving him a fish. When he surrendered after three weeks, his skeletal appearance and sunken eyes shocked the colony; such sights were not yet commonplace. Corbet was promptly hanged, and likewise Thomas Saunderson, who went bush after a robbery later in the same year, was dangling from a noose within a month. The following May, a general muster found that only one convict (Caesar) was absent.

Relations with Aborigines were uneasy — if not always unfriendly — from the very beginning.[2] The Eora, as the people of the Port Jackson vicinity have since become known, had lived there many centuries. At first they avoided contact, leery of soldiers' muskets and bewildered by the frenzy of destruction as trees were felled and fresh water fouled around Sydney Cove. But competition for fishing grounds and mounting convict depredations soon provoked their retaliation. Accustomed to leaving their weapons, canoes and fishing gear lying about untended, they now found these essential belongings stolen by convicts, who sold them as souvenirs to departing sailors. Within four months of the First Fleet's arrival convicts began to feel the full effect of Aboriginal anger — a couple were speared, another was found with his head beaten to a pulp — and it became untenable for any European to venture unarmed beyond the settlement.

Phillip's orders included the impossible directive to peacefully reconcile the Aborigines to their dispossession, and he was well aware why they were angry. But he also saw antagonism between convict and Aborigine as helpful, turning the aggrieved locals into a de facto camp guard. Anything that increased the convicts' dread of the bush was to his advantage.

'Their attacking straglers is natural,' he wrote to London in 1790, 'for these people go out to rob the natives of their spears and the few articles they possess; and as they do it too frequently with impunity, the punishments they sometimes meet with are not to be regretted — they have had a good effect'.

By the time the *Queen* delivered the first Irish shipload in the following year, the colony's hopes had turned to Parramatta, where better soil whispered the first promises of self-sufficient agriculture. At the same time the hopes of the Irish newcomers also turned to regions overland from Sydney, dreaming of a way out the authorities could hardly have guessed at. With the coming of the *Queen* the bush barrier, so effective for the first four years of settlement, would never be the same again.

CHAPTER TWO

An evil which will cure itself

If, when the time for which they are sentenced expires,
the most abandoned and useless were permitted
to go to China, in any ships that may stop here,
it would be a great advantage to the settlement.

GOVERNOR PHILLIP, 9 JULY 1788

IF PHILLIP THOUGHT THE HEARING INTO OWEN'S CONDUCT WOULD placate the Irish newcomers, he was sorely mistaken. Just three weeks later the *Queen* convicts made their first, startling bid for freedom. On Tuesday, 1 November 1791, twenty men and a pregnant woman — the wife of one of the men — disappeared from their labour at Parramatta and took to the bush with a week's rations, bedding, clothes and some tools. Just after setting out, they encountered ex-convict settlers, probably some of the half-dozen farming at the Ponds district, a couple of miles north-east of Parramatta. They asked the Irish party where they were going.

'To China,' came the reply.

There was no persuading them of this grave error of judgment. The settlers tried several approaches, including ridicule, but as Watkin Tench recalled, 'neither derision nor demonstration could avert them from pursuing their purpose'. They were convinced sanctuary from British rule lay within walking distance, and were determined to reach it. The settlers made no attempt to detain them — just as well, perhaps, as they were armed with knives and tomahawks. Soon enough the runaways pressed on in pursuit of their fancy and the settlers observed they seemed to know enough about China's basic direction to head north. They soon veered east, however, as if hoping a coastal route would keep them on track.

Soldiers set off after them, tracing them eastwards from Parramatta until the trail went cold in the thick bush beyond Lane Cove. Sydney Cove was reached without incident; the Irish had seemingly spirited themselves away without trace. As it turned out, the expedition split up fairly quickly, some pushing north towards Pittwater while others got themselves bushed on the harbour's lower North Shore.

Days later, a boatload of men from the Third Fleet convict ship *Albemarle* encountered the 'wretched female', as David Collins described her, while gathering timber somewhere on the North Shore. She had been alone for three days after accidentally separating from her companions. Hopelessly lost, carrying an unborn child and without any food, her distress must have been enormous.

The following day more boats were sent out. Next to turn up was the woman's husband, suffering greatly from exhaustion, hunger and the debilitating November heat. He had been alone two days, perhaps leaving the others to look for his wife. Who was she? The most likely candidate is Catherine Edwards, a 29-year-old Dubliner then about six months pregnant with a boy, Thomas Driscal Edwards, who was born on 24 January. The father, named Thomas Driscal in the baptismal record, was either Tim Driscoll, 27, or the unfortunate Dennis Driscoll, 31, who died soon afterwards. Both were *Queen* convicts from Cork. If the runaway couple was Catherine Edwards and partner, a personal tragedy suggests the flight was a desperate gamble to provide a better life for their unborn child. Catherine's two-year-old son John, who sailed with her from Ireland, had died at Parramatta only a week before the doomed walk to China.[1]

Attempts to find the other runaways continued over the next few days, with boats scouting Middle Harbour and various inlets of Port Jackson. However, the next discovery occurred about ten miles north of Sydney near Narrabeen Lakes, where three convicts were spotted by officers on an excursion. At first trying to elude capture, when secured and questioned this trio declared they 'wanted nothing more than to live free from labour'. The soldiers returned them to Parramatta, but they bolted again as soon as they regained the strength to do so. Governor Phillip was astounded that men so narrowly saved from starving in the bush were willing to push their luck a second time.

The soldiers sent in pursuit failed to find them, but had the extraordinary luck of stumbling across another thirteen of the wayward Irishmen, Collins relates, 'in a state of deplorable wretchedness, naked, and nearly worn out with hunger'. They had managed to survive by sucking flowering shrubs and wild berries.

Aware they had become a laughing stock — Tench noted the 'merriment excited at their expense' — some of these men would only admit to wanting to escape from hard labour and harsh treatment, declaring 'they preferred a solitary and precarious existence in the woods to a return to the misery they were compelled to undergo'.

Many of their fellow Irishmen concurred with this sentiment. Despite the grim risks of spears and famine, desertions continued as the month wore on. A few who managed to struggle their own way back — some wounded by Aborigines — briefly described what they hoped to find. As Tench reports[2]:

> Upon being questioned about the cause of their elopement, those whom
> hunger had forced back did not hesitate to confess that they had been

so grossly deceived as to believe that China might easily be reached, being not more than 100 miles distant and separated only by a river.

By November 1791 Watkin Tench was also eager to leave New South Wales. He had voluntarily extended his tour of duty by three years shortly after landing, but now the entire marine battalion had been recalled, an event he hailed with 'rapture and exultation'. A sensitive and intelligent writer, his bestselling *A Narrative of the Expedition to Botany Bay* had already run to three editions in England, and as 1791 drew to a close he was diligently finalising material for a sequel, *A Complete Account of the Settlement at Port Jackson*. As such, one of his final tasks on Australian soil was to itemise the progress of the promising farmlands at Parramatta.

The convict bids for China engaged Tench's journalistic sensibilities and he decided to investigate personally. One of his first calls in Parramatta was the hospital, on 2 December. There he met four Irish runaways he referred to as 'some of the *Chinese travellers*', who had been wounded by Aborigines.[3] Parramatta Hospital was fairly makeshift, just two long tents with thatched roofs. A wave of dysentery had burst its 200-patient capacity — the sick list then numbered 382, and twenty-seven patients had died in the last month.

Chinese travelling may have been a great Irish joke for some colonists, but the story these Irishmen told Tench from their hospital beds was no laughing matter. After three days in the bush one of their companions died of fatigue. Near Broken Bay — the Hawkesbury River's Pacific outlet, twenty miles north of Sydney — all progress was halted by Aborigines, who killed one man and chased the rest away. The survivors, some wounded, reached Broken Bay's southern foreshores. With no way of crossing, they began combing the waterside for shellfish to ward off their hunger. At this point — injured, starving and unable to proceed north — some decided to go back to Parramatta, about thirty miles away through rough country, rocky and treed. On the return journey they came across a fresh expedition of six escapees pushing north, also hopeful of finding China nearby. After telling their disheartening story, the old group persuaded the new to give up and return with them.

However, the myth's pervasive appeal withstood individual disillusionment. At the time of Tench's investigation, some thirty-eight male convicts were missing in the bush. When he asked his 'Chinese travellers' if they really believed they could have reached China, they readily divulged the details — but not the source — of their conviction:

> They answered that they were certainly made to believe (they knew not how) that at a considerable distance to the northward existed a large river, which separated this country from the back part of China; and that when it should be crossed (which was practicable) they would find themselves among a copper-coloured people, who would receive and treat them kindly.

Three weeks after the first break, Governor Phillip summarised the bizarre business in his official dispatch to London. 'As these people work daily in the woods, the preventing such desertions is impossible,' he told his superiors back home, careful to assure them — lest anyone think he'd lost control of his labour supply — 'but this is an evil which will cure itself'. Far from curing itself, the 'evil' survived to become a fervent Irish hope and a longstanding disruption to the colony. The perplexed governor could hardly have imagined his successors grappling with essentially the same problem decades later.

Phillip's report of the imagined destination differs somewhat from Tench's. His informants described a slightly greater distance to travel, and had additional ideas about what might await them in the unknown north:

> Of those who have been received from Ireland in the *Queen*, transport, from fifteen to twenty have taken to the woods, and though several of them have been brought in when so reduced that they could not have

lived a second day, if they had not been found, some of those very men have absconded a second time, and must perish.

Such is their ignorance that some have left the settlement to go to China, which they suppose to be at the distance of only one hundred and fifty miles. Others, to find a town they supposed to be a few days' walk to the northward.

Phillip's journal of this period, taken to England on a departing ship in December 1791 and published about a year later, includes a similar description of the escape myth, but with some variation in detail:

Some of these people had formed an idea that they could go along the coast and subsist on oysters and other shell-fish, till they reached some of the Chinese settlements. Others had heard that there were a copper coloured people only one hundred and fifty miles to the northward, where they would be free. Full of these notions, three parties set off; but, after straggling about for many days, several of them were taken, and others returned to the settlement.

Collins, too, recorded his impressions of the beliefs inspiring the runaways: the 'chimerical idea of walking to China, or of finding some country wherein they would be received and entertained without labour'. As desertions continued into the new year he returned to the topic, describing the believers as

. . . ignorant and weak enough to run into the woods, impressed with the idea of either reaching China by land, or finding a new settlement where labour would not be imposed on them, and where the inhabitants were civil and peaceable.

This development — the concept of a sanctuary that would freely succour runaways — was also noted by Phillip in very similar terms: 'the idea of being able to live in the woods and on the sea-coast until they could reach a settlement, or find a people who would maintain them without labour'. Of course, the convicts may have meant nothing more than the hope that anonymity and a plausible sob story would buy them a fresh start amongst sympathetic strangers.

Tench had written of China and the northerly haven with 'copper-coloured people' as one and the same place, but these other reports suggest not all the faithful were convinced this happy place was literally China. Otherwise, Phillip and Collins may have simply deduced two destinations from the same — or similar — convict information, unable to reconcile China with a place presumed to welcome foreign criminals.

A fake colonial memoir published in the 1790s adds another possibility, although it may merely be the London-based ghostwriter's guess at the relief runaways could hope for on the scarcely imaginable coasts of Terra Australis. Falsely attributed to George Barrington, a famous ex-London pickpocket transported to Sydney, this account claimed the runaways sought

> . . . a copper-coloured tribe 150 miles to the northward, who were
> much more civilized than the natives they were with, and who trafficked
> with the Dutch from Timor, where they would be free.

Strangely enough, there was a tiny group of non-Aboriginal settlers almost exactly 150 miles north along the coast. They may even have approached something resembling 'copper-coloured' after five scorching years under the Australian sun. John Turwood, George Lee, George Connoway and John Watson were runaway convicts, the very first to attempt escape by sea. Hoping to reach Tahiti, 18th-century Europe's leading fantasy island, they had stolen a single-masted vessel from South Head lookout exactly one year before the *Queen* reached Sydney, on the evening of 26 September 1790. Heavy winds battering the coast and the boat's poor condition made it seem certain they had perished at sea.

But five years later, a Sydney-bound ship blown off course found them at the unexplored deepwater harbour of Port Stephens. A fifth man, Joseph Sutton, had died, but the rest remained welcome guests of the local Worimi people. They were the first convicts known to be adopted into an Aboriginal community.

Taken back to Sydney in August 1795, the surviving quartet related an extraordinary adventure to the enthralled colony. After tribal initiation, each man was given a wife. Some had fathered children. They claimed the Aborigines worshipped them as ancestors killed in battle. Collins found this frankly unbelievable, but it seems recognition as a reincarnated relative was often all that stood between a stray European and the sharp end of an Aboriginal spear. Turwood and his friends had misread the situation, too: returned ancestors were well cared for but not worshipped as gods. But there was no doubt they had found 'a people who would maintain them without labour' — and in a place very close to where the Chinese travellers located their more fantastical version of sanctuary.

Although Turwood pioneered the sea route, he was eclipsed six months later by an even more remarkable piracy, the famous escape by a transported Cornish smuggler, William Bryant, and his convict wife Mary. Their venture was unusually well planned. Taking months to stockpile materials needed for a sea voyage, the Bryants also had the sense to monitor harbour traffic for the best chance of a clean getaway. Their window of opportunity opened early in 1791, when no vessels capable of overtaking them were in port. On the night of 28 March, the Bryants (taking their two infant children) and seven male convicts stole a government cutter and spirited themselves onto the immense darkness of the Pacific Ocean.

Boats sent in pursuit never sighted them. A combination of brilliant seamanship and good luck took the tiny open boat up the east coast, around Cape York and onwards to Timor in just ten weeks. There they posed as survivors of a wrecked whaler, but the deception soon came unstuck and they were handed over to the next English ship along. Only Mary and four of the men reached England — the others died en route, including William Bryant and both children. Lauded by the press as 'The Girl from Botany Bay', Mary was eventually set free, thanks mainly to the author James Boswell, who campaigned to secure pardons for her and the others.

The Bryant escape also caused a sensation in New South Wales — for very different reasons. The authorities lamented that Mary was not returned to Sydney to face trial and severe punishment as a deterrent. But nothing could stop her landfall in Timor (let alone the pardons handed out to the survivors in London) becoming a beacon of hope for several decades worth of convict pirates. And yet, because where Timor was — and just as importantly, what it was — remained hazy, the placename would end up an equally potent target for overland adventurers.

Like Turwood, the Bryants met with Aborigines just north of Sydney. Two days after escaping they became the first whites to enter the Hunter River, where they rested, caught fish and befriended Aborigines with gifts of clothes. But at Port Stephens they were driven off by spear-wielding warriors, never learning that Turwood and company were enjoying a totally different reception nearby.

Did misunderstood Aboriginal accounts of the Turwood or Bryant parties help to spark rumours amongst convicts about some kind of nearby non-Aboriginal society? Add some shaky geographical rationalisations and wishful thinking, and a local pseudo-China (or Chinese colony) is not so far-fetched. News of Turwood could easily have reached the Sydney region via the Aboriginal grapevine. The Eora's interaction with neighbouring peoples tended to be north–south rather than east–west, and the Port Stephens language was known to them. A young man named Wurgun was just one notable Aboriginal traveller/interpreter between the two regions. Only recently, the convict Thomas Watling wrote home in December 1791, had such a messenger 'called this way, and held forth to some hundreds of his countrymen'.

In the wake of the Bryants' vanishing act, security was tightened at Sydney's waterfront. Guards were posted at night and all vessels barred from casting off without official clearance. Governor Phillip banned the construction of boats exceeding fourteen feet. The front gates to the settlement, Sydney Heads, were thus better protected. Only months later, however, the first Chinese travellers had shown that the back door to freedom — the bush — was also in need of serious attention.

CHAPTER THREE

Thoughts of liberty

Thoughts of liberty from such a place as this is enoufh to
induce any convicts to try all skeemes to obtain it, as thay are
the same as slaves all the time thay are in this country.

JOHN EASTY, FIRST FLEET MARINE, 1791

ONE DETAIL OF THE IRISH CONVICT DREAM ESPECIALLY DRAWS THE
eye — the idea of China separated from New South Wales by nothing
more than a large river to the north. Locating rivers was a colonial priority
in the very beginning for several obvious reasons: fertile soil, fresh water
and the chance of easily navigable routes to the interior. North of Sydney,
the Hawkesbury — known as the Nepean upstream where it curls south
— was the region's biggest, most promising watercourse. Would it lead
the way through the mountains to the west? If so, what sort of land was
there for the taking? While its headwaters would remain unseen for
many years, the rich soil of its floodplains proved a vital breadbasket
as the 1790s progressed. Similarly, did the Hawkesbury River tantalise

convicts as a possible signpost to somewhere likely to benefit them? And how did this somewhere become China?

The location of the imagined China has a curious resemblance to the then still-valid theory that the east part of Australia (New South Wales) might be separated from the west (New Holland) by a body of water. The idea dates to 1699, when the English pirate-adventurer William Dampier visited the West Australian coast. Observing 'great tides' near the Dampier Archipelago, he suspected they indicated a strait dividing the mainland, perhaps leading 'into the great South Sea eastward'. The notion gained such currency that a century later, one of the instructions given to the French explorer Nicholas Baudin was to find the waters dividing Terra Australis 'into two great and nearly equal islands'. Shortly afterwards, in 1802, Governor Philip Gidley King reported to London from Sydney that 'the conjecture of New South Wales being insulated from New Holland still remains undecided'. The idea that east and west were two large islands remained a possibility until the following year, when Matthew Flinders achieved the first circumnavigation of the continent.

Did the supposed New Holland strait help inspire the convict myth? The land across the hypothetical water may have distorted into China as it passed into the oral lore of the working class. The Torres Strait between northern Australia and New Guinea, known to Europeans since 1606, may also have helped to conjure an Asian river border. Either way implies an interesting paradox: that doubt about New South Wales being part of a larger landmass helped join it to Asia in the convict imagination. However, the opposite explanation is just as likely — remnants of outworn theories about a vast south land stretching from the tropics to the South Pole still feeding rumours in the general population. Cook's voyaging had disproved this notion some twenty years beforehand, although — to complicate things further — his mapping of the strait between New Zealand's North and South Islands lent weight to speculation that Terra Australis might also be divided in a similar manner.

However flawed, the convicts' reconstruction of China from hearsay was not wholly irrational. It was a practical attempt to make sense of an alien environment, and its crowning glory was the hope it gave for deliverance from British sovereignty. Even common criminals amongst the Irish were apt to consider themselves captives of a foreign power, and if China wasn't Ireland's enemy, then why shouldn't they be received civilly, and even allowed to return home? Uneducated men and women, many of whom had never seen beyond their own counties before, knew nothing substantial about the real China. Even the most educated Europeans knew very little. China was still a closed society in 1791; the ruling Manchu Dynasty scorned all foreigners as barbarians and only admitted their trade at Canton, restricting business to a handful of authorised merchants. The memoirs of British seaman John Nicol, who made three voyages to Canton from 1785 to 1794, recounted his modest attempts to penetrate this forbidden city: 'I was different times at the gate,' he said, 'but all my ingenuity could not enable me to cross the bar, although I was eight days in the suburbs'. More importantly, he described the powerful impression the very idea of China had on his unlettered imagination, and how his expectations were, at first glance, exceeded:

> I was as happy as any person ever was to see anything. I scarcely believed I was so fortunate as really to be in China. As we sailed up the river, I would cast my eyes from side to side. The thoughts and ideas I had pictured in my mind of it were not lessened in brilliancy, rather increased. The immense number of buildings that extended as far as the eye could reach, their fantastic shapes and gaudy colours, their trees and flowers so like their paintings, and the myriads of floating vessels, and above all the fanciful dresses and gaudy colours of their clothes — all serve to fix the mind of a stranger upon his first arrival.

China doubtless inspired this awe in many more sailors than Nicol. Those taking convicts to Australia must have spoken of their anticipation or prior experience of it, and Nicol himself came to Sydney in June 1790 as steward on the convict transport *Lady Juliana*. Along with the South Seas, the mysterious East was 18th-century Europe's epitome of the exotic. China's reputation rested largely on a handful of exports — chiefly tea, silk and porcelain — and the centuries-old writings of Marco Polo. It was a shadowy world, veiled to outsiders, an evocative neverland of pagodas and godlike emperors. But the recent revolutions in France and America had tremendous impact in Ireland, doing much to foster hope that foreign countries might sympathise with Ireland's aspirations for freedom from British domination. According to a later Irish transportee, the rebel leader Joseph Holt, 'the world is friend to me, not only England' — meaning of all nations, only England was an enemy to Ireland. Such sentiment may partially explain why a nearby China might more readily fire Irish rather than English convicts with the prospect of sanctuary.

Of course, the idea that there was somewhere — anywhere — beyond the bush would have been sufficient inducement for many to abscond. Most of Parramatta's inhabitants in 1791 would have rated it a very poor second to anywhere else, and it was no secret that the next ports of call for departing transports were either in India or China. Some convicts would have assumed such colonial 'neighbours' were not far — and their concept of 'near' would certainly have differed from a sailor's.

Later the author Herman Melville, drawing on his own Atlantic crossing in 1839, preserved the particular reputation Irish emigrants had for geographical credulity, even if their global ignorance must have been generally matched by that of the British poor. In his semi-documentary novel *Redburn*, Melville's narrator recalls: 'They seemed to have no adequate idea of distances . . . to them, America must have seemed as a place just over a river'. The idea that New South Wales was 'well calculated for an intercourse with China and Japan' was well known, and published in a Dublin newspaper in May 1789. The quote referred to the colony's potential for trade, but the capacity of this frequently discussed topic for fuelling geographical misunderstanding is obvious.

Sydney's remoteness was keenly felt through the infrequency of shipping. Excluding La Perouse and a handful of domestic trips, mostly to Norfolk Island, only eighteen shipping departures preceded the Third Fleet in almost four years of settlement. Nine of these were China bound, including eight of the ten convict ships comprising the First and Second Fleets. If they were sailing up the coast to trade in Canton, couldn't the same basic route be traced on foot? If China was a large Pacific country teeming with millions of gaudily robed 'Celestials', wasn't it possible the 'back part' of its expansive territory lay within reach? What else, indeed, was there to reach for?

For Governor Phillip, a disturbing aspect of the breakout was that the Irish had succeeded in empowering themselves, even if only in a roundabout, self-destructive way. The colony didn't have the resources to stop them acting on their own initiative. It wasn't set up to cope with minds so unintimidated by the surrounding unknown.

Concerned by continuing desertions throughout November 1791, Phillip ordered an assembly of Third Fleet convicts at Parramatta later that month. Returned runaways had told him that others were lurking in the bush nearby, too afraid of punishment to surrender. He now offered to pardon any of the forty then absent who came in within five days. In the future, he added, absconders would be chased and shot on sight. If taken alive, they would be marooned somewhere in the harbour where escape was impossible and left to fend for themselves, or else chained together and made to live on bread and water. Next, responding to rumours of a plot to steal arms and plunder the public store, Phillip declared that anyone attempting it would be summarily executed. He concluded by changing convict working hours in response to an earlier request, and offered to forgive some smaller offences if they went 'cheerfully to their labour'.

The trouble with this approach was simple: the convict working day gave very little to be cheerful about. A typical day at Parramatta and Toongabbie began at 5 am, when the ragged mass of male convicts shuffled into the dawn to commence their morning shift. There was usually no breakfast — stores were too low for that — although a fairly lengthy rest was permitted around noon to escape the peak of the heat.

The main task in the early days was land clearing. The men chopped down trees, dug up the stumps, cut and hauled timber and turned the earth with hoes. Yoked like oxen, they dragged the logs in gangs of twenty-five. By two or three o'clock they were back at work until sunset. At night they crowded into ramshackle huts with no beds or blankets. These two-room wattle-and-daub hovels were built to house ten men each, but often had up to eighteen squeezed into them. Tench describes a penal farm near Parramatta with 500 men housed in thirteen large tents. Female convicts were assigned to clean and cook while the men were at work. Dinner was usually a tiny portion of flour, sometimes with rice or salted meat. Meals were prepared with a single iron pot, with cooking utensils usually limited to whatever could be fashioned from local wood. Bowls, plates and spoons were almost unheard-of luxuries.

Life was a maddening, monotonous grind of backbreaking work, filth, sweat and the constant twist of hunger. The stifling summer heat caused a great deal of suffering, and arbitrary punishment at the hands of brutal convict constables was ever-present. As in all penal systems, physical and sexual assault was endemic. In such a hard environment the weak went under, and only the very lucky or the very strong didn't weaken. Toongabbie was particularly dreaded in its earliest days. Irish-Australian folklore enshrined its cruelty, invoked in 1879 when the famous Irish-Australian outlaw Ned Kelly reviled Toongabbie as 'a place of tyranny and condemnation' where Irishmen, 'rather than subdue to the Saxon yoke were flogged to death and bravely died in servile chains'.

Phillip's bark was usually worse than his bite; his proposal to shoot runaways on sight was never enacted. Such threats of dire punishment were neutered by his inability to prove the missing convicts hadn't reached those tempting 'Chinese settlements'. The best disincentive was the cadaverous appearance of the lucky few crawling back to Parramatta in defeat. As a colonial memoir recounted decades later, they returned 'so squalid and lean that the very crows would have declined the proffer of their carcases'. Such self-inflicted suffering left them too feeble to withstand serious discipline. The governor, as he put it, found himself

> . . . less inclined to inflict any punishment on these people than to punish those who had deceived them by the information of 'not being far from some of the Chinese settlements, and near people who would receive them, and where they would have every thing they wanted, and live very happy'.

In later years Phillip's successors, governors King and Hunter, would also denounce the escape myths as malicious lies. Whether or not this was true, it made a convenient divide–and–conquer ploy. We simply don't know whether the Irish posited the bush–China themselves, or were just the first to act on rumours already floating about the colony. But were the false prophets Phillip described mischief–makers — cynically employing their 'fertility of invention' — or believers themselves? If they were the former, Phillip never managed to distinguish or identify them. More telling, perhaps, is the refusal of Tench's 'Chinese travellers' to divulge how they had been 'made to believe', suggesting solidarity with fellow believers rather than any sense they had been gulled by outsiders. Chances are that their natural clannishness, intensified by fear and mistrust of the older convict hands, would have precluded a cruel prank about a walking route to China succeeding so spectacularly. First Fleet convicts, according to Collins, were 'never concerned in these offences; and of them it was said that the newcomers stood so much in dread, that they never were admitted to any share in their confidence'. He came to see the myth as a self–generated Irish infatuation, one that believers would unhesitatingly impart to 'all of their countrymen who came after them, engaging them in the same act of folly and madness'. Seen in this light,

Tench's comment that the Irish runaways had been 'grossly deceived' reads more like his astonishment at their goal than their repudiation of it.

Collins recorded a theory which held some sway before the extent of the delusion was realised. Disbelief led some colonists to decide China's proximity was only a smokescreen for a more prosaic scheme:

> It was generally supposed, however, that this improbable tale was only a cover to the real design, which might be to procure boats, and get on board the transports after they had left the cove.[1]

But how general was this supposition really? No other chronicler of the Irish 'Chinese travellers' mentions it. Even Collins himself afterwards makes numerous references to convicts seeking a bush–China. In fact, in every subsequent mention of escape myths, he is certain they were genuinely believed.

Collins is perhaps noting a cynical reaction to the China story which subsided as more information came to light. Governor Phillip must have known of it, as Collins was his closest confidant and secretary, but he omitted it from his official conclusions to London. Was Phillip really so completely hoodwinked by convicts playing up to stereotypes of Irish idiocy? Phillip's acceptance of the bush–China story strongly indicates it was a genuine belief. If stowing away was the real plan, then Phillip had naively fallen for an absurdity designed to manipulate prejudices of Irish silliness. But this is unlikely, especially since convict stories were generally distrusted and a mundane explanation was readily available.

Phillip did have good cause to reject the idea. He was no stranger to plots involving stealing or boarding vessels, and none of the first gang had attempted anything like it. Most had clearly attempted a northbound overland journey from the settlement. While the *Queen* sailed on 2 November, the day after the escape, it was only to run supplies to Norfolk Island penal station and return a party of marines. The *Salamander* left for India on the same day. But bids for China continued for months afterwards, and similarly wild enthusiasms resurfaced with future arrivals of Irish convicts over many years, regardless of outbound shipping schedules.

Perhaps Phillip found a party of twenty-one uneducated, disoriented and desperate newcomers believing they could walk to China no more incredible than such a large group imagining they could board a departing vessel undetected. Stowaways tended to operate in much smaller groups, and often singly.

If the tale of walking north was just a ruse to misdirect pursuers, or to draw attention from the boats, then it was very badly bungled, because the soldiers used the story to catch them. The first party walked in the very direction they told the convict settlers they were headed, and may not have expected fellow transportees to betray them. They behaved as if nothing but the heady prospect of liberty had loosened their lips. Also, the three of them who fled again after being arrested — near Narrabeen Lakes, about halfway between Sydney and Broken Bay — actually denied the fantastical destination when interrogated. This change of tune, coming from men still determined to escape, contrasts with those who freely confirmed the China story after returning in defeat, convinced by bitter experience the journey was too difficult. Wanting 'nothing more than to live free from labour' was likely the real cover story.

Even if the *Queen* Irish did have their eyes on snatching a whaleboat or stowing away, this does not negate belief in an adjacent China. If its borders lay north along the coast then a seaside hike or sea voyage were both likely travel options, each worth keeping open. They seem to have initially travelled east to orient themselves north once reaching Sydney Harbour, and may also have hoped to signal shipping along the way.

Boats could be useful to absconders of all persuasions. The Turwood and Bryant escapes sent many dreams of liberty wafting around the convict huts, and it didn't take long for some Chinese travellers to take to the water. On 4 December a convict collapsed with sunstroke outside Surgeon-General John White's house. He was dead within twenty-four hours, but as White tended him that evening, two Irish convicts were busy rowing the surgeon's boat across the harbour. Outside the heads they turned left, hopeful, Phillip mused, of 'finding a Chinese settlement at no great distance to the northward'. But the open sea was too much for them; the next day they ran the boat ashore a few miles from North Head and proceeded on foot. They may even have landed in a panic after sighting the *Queen*, returning to Sydney that same morning after its four-week charter to Norfolk Island. Worse luck was the presence of a group of marines on a shooting expedition, who spotted White's boat abandoned on a beach and the two fugitives running up the sand to take cover in the scrub. Tramping down to the beach, the marines knocked a hole in the boat's planks, then broke the rudder and an oar. Having prevented the Irish pair from reusing it, they headed into the woods to apprehend them. There they chanced upon another lone Irish runaway, so exhausted he could hardly walk unassisted. Missing for at least five weeks, he must have been among the first to take off. The two boat thieves were never found, but over the next few weeks survivors from other escapes struggled in from the bush, bringing similar stories of disappointment and hardship to Collins' notice:

> Of these people many, after lingering a long time, and existing merely on roots and wild berries, perished miserably. Others found their way in, after being absent several weeks, and reported the fate of their wretched companions, being themselves reduced to nearly the same condition, worn down and exhausted with fatigue and want of proper sustenance.

Phillip put some in irons, but not for long. He hoped in vain that the myth would soon die of its own absurdity. Naturally some absconders were discouraged by failure, but others continued to take to the bush, filled with hatred, false hope and a burning desire to escape the harsh life of the beleaguered colony.

They weren't the only ones. Tired and in poor health, Phillip himself had been angling to get out for some time. An earlier request to go home had been rejected by his masters in England, who assumed it was for reasons of private business. Virtually incapacitated by kidney pain, Phillip tried again on 11 November, begging that he was 'at times unable to either ride or walk' and was anxious to seek medical treatment in London.

As more and more First Fleet sentences expired, Phillip worried about losing skilled workmen, particularly sailors and carpenters, who also wanted to go home. New orders arriving with the Third Fleet meant he was no longer able to bar those who had served their time from leaving the colony. The China myth only made things worse — a convict fit enough to abscond was fit enough to work, and every man with the strength to work was needed. At first Phillip thought a surfeit of lonely deaths in the wilderness would prove the most effective remedy for absenteeism, the 'evil that would cure itself'. But the death rate in the settlement was equally frightening, and a full third of convict fatalities recorded for 1791 occurred in November, just as the China myth began to take hold.

On 5 November, four days after the first breakout, 626 convicts were too sick to work. Three weeks later some 200 were lining up for medicine in Sydney and the surgeon counted over 400 incapacitated through sickness, many even unfit for light duties such as collecting grass for thatching huts. There were forty-seven recorded burials of male convicts that bleak month, including up to six from the Queen.[2]

Almost every day saw burials of convicts, mostly enfeebled Third Fleeters — more than one in twenty died before Christmas. In the midst of this crisis, pressure on the stores forced Phillip to reduce the ration. Two pounds of flour was replaced by one pint of peas and one of oatmeal, and a further reduction occurred in December. As convicts often consumed their meagre weekly portion in three or four days, a daily issue was substituted. Outrage ensued. On New Year's Eve a mob converged on the governor's Parramatta house to protest. Phillip dispersed them with threats of making 'immediate examples' of the ringleaders. It was the first mutinous assembly of convicts the colony had seen, with Irishmen from the *Queen* and other Third Fleeters playing a prominent role.

Most male *Queen* convicts were dead within a year of landing, although one lived right up until 1860. Only eighteen when he came to the colony, Michael Lamb lived to see transportation cease and the first sizeable numbers of actual Chinese travellers arrive from the real China, lured by the goldrush of the 1850s. Many of Lamb's shipmates weren't so fortunate. Weakened by the stresses of their passage, which starvation rations couldn't counteract, they quickly fell prey to exhaustion, dysentery and malnutrition. The first to succumb was James Marshall, buried on 12 October aged about forty-one. As others followed him to early graves a world away from home, many of those strong enough to run off did so. They took off 'in numerous bodies,' Collins noted, 'few of whom ever returned'.

On 6 January 1792, the *Queen* finally left the colony for India in company with the *Admiral Barrington*. A total of seven stowaways, English Third Fleeters, attempted to escape the colony in the two ships. A muster later in the month counted forty-four men and nine women now missing — 'in which number,' Collins exclaimed, 'were included those who were wandering in the woods, seeking for a new settlement, or endeavouring to get into the path to China!' Even allowing for the stowaways, the absentee list represented up to a third of the surviving Irish convict population.

This first wave of Chinese travelling was remarkable for including women; evidence of female participation in later overland ventures is lacking. It underscores the clannish nature of the myth at its outset. Usually scattered singly throughout the settlement as wives and housekeepers, women were less exposed to the rumours and more closely observed. Degrading as their position could be, women were much in demand and an advantageous marriage to the right settler or official could rapidly turn their fortunes. Generally female convicts had far more to lose by taking to the bush than did the men in government labour.

As Irish desertions continued, Parramatta was hit by a mini-crime wave. By the new year gangs of famished convicts were plundering the ripening corn harvest nightly, and the hospital and public bakehouse were robbed of large amounts of food. Armed patrols were given orders to seize anyone at large, and to shoot if necessary. A man who caught two men robbing his garden was struck in the arm with a tomahawk, which severed a tendon. Fifty pounds of flour was offered for the capture of any one of a gang of four who vanished into the bush after a series of robberies, but only one was brought in.

Amidst this disorder another plot to attack the barracks and storehouse at Parramatta was uncovered. The authorities were alerted by other convicts, possibly First Fleeters, who despised the newcomers and had no part in these disturbances. The fact that returned Chinese travellers were involved raised fears of a bolder overland bid in the making. Collins envisaged a major assault on the colony's dwindling provisions:

> As there had been seen among them people silly enough to undertake to walk to the other side of this extensive continent, expecting that China would be found there, it was not at all improbable that some might be mad enough to persuade others that it would be an easy matter to attempt and carry the barracks and stores there.

Proof was lacking, however, and no floggings were meted out. Reluctant to punish one group of convicts solely on the word of others, Phillip doubled the guard on the barracks and stores without public announcement, hoping to contain rumours of the uprising as well as prevent it happening.

Outfoxed, the Chinese travellers dropped the plan but continued to take to the bush. Two of them chanced upon a lone convict near Toongabbie soon after setting off for the imagined country in January 1792. They robbed his rations and beat him up so badly that he died soon afterwards, but not before naming and describing his assailants.

No search party was ordered. Walking to China, it was decided, was as good a death sentence as any. And the bush did avenge the dead man, even as Judge-Advocate Collins was hoping the killers would return to 'receive the reward of their crime'. They never did. A third Irish runaway, returning in defeat after travelling with the two murderers, claimed they had already died of hunger and exposure, victims of their hopeless dreams of China and freedom. The same dream would claim many more imaginations — and lives — in the years to come.

CHAPTER FOUR

The greatest
villains on earth

If you render a heaven on earth a hell,
most foul and malicious murder it is.

JOSEPH HOLT, TRANSPORTED FROM IRELAND IN 1799

THE IRISH PRISONERS' UNOFFICIAL EMIGRATION PROGRAM CONTINUED into 1792, as life in the colony peaked in intolerability. One April day, a passing troop of convicts — 'mere walking shadows' — horrified the newly arrived magistrate Richard Atkins. 'Human nature is indeed degraded in this country,' he lamented in his diary. The year's death toll was 477, with March and April seeing a third of the mortality.

The mania for overland absconding petered out sometime before May, by which time more than half the men from the *Queen* were likely either dead or missing. Gaps in the burial record suggest that upwards of forty men — about a third of the male *Queen* convicts — may have disappeared in the bush within seven months of landing.[1] Others, of course, survived the quest, such as the fifteen or so men and one woman rescued from the initial bid for China.

Even though more convicts had vanished without trace in the closing weeks of 1791 than in the entire four years of the colony's existence, Collins only listed four 'lost in the woods' for the whole year. The figure, he noted, was 'exclusive of the Irish convicts who had absconded, of whom no certain account was procured'. Absence of identifying records made it difficult to keep track of them, but the confusion was also symptomatic of a tendency to lump the Irish together indiscriminately as a nameless, troublesome rabble.

And so, with its adherents either disappeared or discouraged, the China myth subsided — but only until the arrival of the next ship from Ireland. Governor Phillip didn't remain to witness the remanifestation. With permission to return to England granted at last, he made his own escape aboard the HMS *Atlantic* in December 1792, accompanied by two willing Aboriginal travellers, Bennelong and Yemmerrawannie. By the time his successor John Hunter took over in 1795, almost three years of interim rule by NSW Corps commandants had produced an insoluble administrative dilemma. An officer–based trading monopoly — particularly in spirits, the de facto colonial currency — was now an entrenched feature of colonial life. As governors Hunter, King and Bligh would discover, opposing it provoked the hostility of the very men whose loyalty was necessary to wield effective power.

The second and third Irish ships arrived in 1793 — the *Boddingtons* on 7 August, with 124 male and twenty female convicts, and the *Sugar Cane* on 17 September, carrying 109 men and fifty-two women. Many of those aboard the *Boddingtons* were from Ulster counties where Defenders and other agrarian vigilantes had been very active. Their voyage was relatively comfortable — there were five births, only three deaths, and remarkably, the convicts each had their own bed. Rumours of mutiny had come to nothing. The plan was supposedly to murder all the ship's officers, keeping the first mate and surgeon alive until they had helped the convicts to a safe port. But no one was punished and upon disembarking, the convicts gave Captain Robert Chalmers three cheers — unusual behaviour from would-be mutineers. If anyone deserved applause it was the ship's surgeon, Richard Kent, who tirelessly maintained hygiene in the face of Chalmers' utter indifference. The *Boddingtons* was small for a transport ship and crowded, with five men above full complement. Kent insisted he couldn't have coped with even one more prisoner aboard.

Relieved at how healthy this new batch of prisoners was, NSW authorities were still disappointed with the small amount of supplies landed, though this had undoubtedly saved many lives at sea. Overstocked hulls impacted badly on hygiene — the raised waterline of a heavily laden ship greatly reduced ventilation below decks. It was an irony not lost on the colonists that more convicts landed alive meant fewer stores arriving on the same ship, and thus a greater drain on existing stores.

If the authorities assumed the tailing off of the *Queen* convicts' bids for China had buried this unforeseen motivation for escape, they now had to deal with the *Boddingtons* Irish, who began running into the bush soon after being sent to Toongabbie. Collins was amazed that the second Irish importation should so readily imitate the first:

> It might have been supposed that the fatal consequences of endea-
> vouring to seek a place in the woods of this country where they might
> live without labour had been sufficiently felt by the convicts who arrived
> here in the *Queen* transport from Ireland, to deter others from rushing
> into the same error, as they would, doubtless, acquaint the new comers
> with the ill success which attended their schemes of that nature.

One group of *Boddingtons* men stole a boat belonging to a German settler named Philip Schaffer. It was feared they had hidden themselves in one of the harbour's many inlets, waiting to join forces with the bush absconders to steal a larger boat. As the colony pondered the fate of these latest disappearing Irishmen, the next delivery from Cork loomed on the horizon. The *Sugar Cane* carried mostly urban offenders; about three-quarters were petty criminals from Dublin and Cork cities. A fever had swept through the ship in port and after six weeks at sea, rumours arose that the convicts were plotting a seizure. Finding some had managed to saw through their fetters, the captain hanged a man that same evening, the sole fatality of the voyage. A round of floggings in the morning ensured the passage was completed without incident.

The first clue to the fate of the *Boddingtons* runaways was unearthed on 22 September. Returning from an exploration up the Hawkesbury River, Captain William Paterson of the NSW Corps chanced upon Schaffer's boat, abandoned by the runaways near Pittwater. A few days later some of the Irishmen in question struggled into Parramatta. Like many of their *Queen* predecessors, the fantasy of freedom had been frustrated by the reality of Aboriginal spears. Two had been killed, they said, and this was readily confirmed by Aborigines in town who already knew the other side of the story. The dead men were said to have been ringleaders of the aborted mutiny.

On 15 October, two days after the *Boddingtons* and *Sugar Cane* left the harbour, seven men and a woman from the newly departed ships made their escape. That evening four of the men, their faces and hands blackened as a disguise, raided a settler's house and bashed his two convict servants. They were captured soon afterwards. On the night of the 27 October, in the midst of driving rain, another seven Irishmen took to the bush with a stolen musket and ammunition. 'The two last ships from Ireland brought us upwards of 200 of the greatest villains on earth,' Atkins wrote in his diary, 'since which time crimes and riots have multiplied'. By Christmas, however, most of them had reluctantly settled to their situation, and escapes diminished. Collins noted they began to 'shew symptoms of better dispositions then they landed with, and appeared only to dislike hard labour'. By the end of 1793 just six men were counted as missing in the bush for the year, with a seventh found dead.

The starvation years gradually retreated, and death rates began to decrease markedly. Food stocks would still teeter on the verge of exhaustion, but time-expired convicts were increasingly farming small holdings and maintaining themselves off the government ration. Convicts were still, as ever, taking to the bush. Some absconded upon receiving their weekly ration and lurked in the bush until their next issue was due. Others simply wanted respite from labour, however brief, and others were probably still looking for the way to China. But with such a rumour prevalent, even runaways determined to live by stealing from farms had extra incentive to abscond — maybe they would learn of a route to China one day. Collins shows that bush desertions continued throughout this period, though their objectives were not brought to light:

> Numbers of the male convicts, idle, and dreading labour as a greater evil than the risk of being murdered [by Aborigines], absented from the new settlements, and, after wandering about for a few days, got at length to Sydney, almost naked, and so nearly starved, that in most cases humanity interfered between them and the punishment which they merited. They in general pleaded the insufficiency of their present ration to support a labouring man.

When the magistrate Richard Atkins noted on 11 February 1794 that eight Irishmen had 'absconded from the settlement and are gone into the woods', his assumption that they would lurk nearby to rob settlers shows that Chinese travelling was not then a serious concern. However, after a boat seizure by Irish runaways (seven men from the *Boddingtons* and *Sugar Cane*) the following evening, Collins wrote:

> Notwithstanding the success which had hitherto attended the endeavours of the Irish convicts stationed at Toongabbe and Parramatta to find a way from those places to China, a few of them were again hardy enough to attempt effecting their escape, and getting thither in a small boat which they took from a settler.

Atkins thought the gang was apprehended but Collins, a more reliable source, says they perished at sea. Three other attempts at piracy in 1794 involved Irish convicts. At first this suggests a dawning realisation that China was overseas — unless some decided a brief, coast-hugging voyage to an adjacent bush-China was a better bet than slogging their way north on foot. Laurence Davoren, a former Dublin lawyer, was one would-be deserter who may have scorned the unschooled escape myths of his less educated countrymen. In May he was caught plotting to take a boat to Batavia, a suicidal pipedream for a man with no maritime experience, but at least it wasn't a bid for a fictional north-coast sanctuary.

A rather more wild Irish outbreak in September involved a gang who took a six-oared boat from Parramatta. After rowing south into Botany Bay, they were tracked down and chased into the bush. Days later they were caught after attempting a robbery; one was shot dead. Believing they had rowed north to Broken Bay instead of south, the arrested men said they had no idea of where they would go, only that they wanted never to return.

In December, ten Irish and Scottish runaways drowned in a severe electrical storm after making off with two boats. Five survivors were picked up at an inlet outside the heads amidst torrential rain, but refused to discuss their intentions or motivations. They regretted only their bad luck, noted Collins, 'never attributing the failure to their own ignorance and temerity'.

By 1795, war with revolutionary France had brought convict arrivals to a virtual standstill. This wasn't just because of shipping disruptions; offenders due to be transported were now kept back to work in naval dockyards. After the *Sugar Cane* in 1793 there wasn't another Irish shipment for almost three years, during which time just three ships brought just eighty-five convicts from England. The Third Fleet proved to be the last big influx of immigrants for over two decades; afterwards an average of less than three transports arrived every year right up until 1814. Although a macabre clue later emerged to indicate that overland escapes persisted beyond the bids of *Queen* convicts, there was no outbreak disruptive enough to attract lasting official attention. The surviving dreamers of the first three Irish ships were reduced to dreaming. Without the enthusiasm of newcomers, the lure of overland sanctuary lay dormant.[2]

Escape mythology's second phase arrived in the wake of the next Irish transports — the *Marquis Cornwallis* on 11 February 1796 and the *Britannia*, on 27 May 1797. While the names of the believers are unknown, we do know they endured extremely violent passages to Australia, and were much more disruptive than any previous convict intake.

Of the twenty-eight English transports preceding the *Britannia*, only one had a convict mutiny, with betrayed or invented plots leading to floggings on four others. But four of the five Irish ships in the same period were alarmed by rumoured or actual uprisings at sea, and the other — the *Queen* — was spectacularly troublesome for other reasons. Punishments were far harsher on Irish ships. No English convict was executed for merely plotting (two were hanged for attempting to seize the Third Fleet's *Albemarle*), but on the Irish transport *Britannia* the captain flogged several suspected mutineers to death.

The *Marquis Cornwallis* was the first Irish ship in which ordinary criminals were outnumbered by agrarian Defenders. Governor Hunter called them 'as desperate as set of villains as were ever sent' and regretted they hadn't been sent to Africa instead. 'The refuse of sweepings of Irish jails' and 'the most horrid ruffians that ever left the kingdom of Ireland' are two other contemporary descriptions of this shipload.

One September evening in 1795, when the *Marquis Cornwallis* was nearing the equator off Africa's Guinea Coast, two convicts sought permission to see Captain Thomas Hogan. They warned him a revolt was being planned, and a third informer soon betrayed further details. The officers and surgeon were to be jumped during their regular examination of the convicts' bedding and their throats cut with their own swords. The convicts would then take the ship to America and freedom. Some disgruntled soldiers had joined the plot. Sergeant Ellis, who stockpiled six knives to cut the convicts' fetters, had been overheard complaining he was actually worse off than the convicts. 'Some of the convicts were only transported for seven years,' Ellis reasoned, but soldiers went for life, and were 'damned fools to be sold'.

Hogan flogged confessions out of accused ringleaders, but the mutineers went ahead anyway. After strangling one of the informers, they rushed the fore hatchway and stormed on deck. Hogan and his officers opened fire and, as one wrote to his brother shortly afterwards, there followed 'a scene which was not by any means pleasant'. Soon seven convicts were dead or dying and the rest screaming for quarter amidst the blood, powder-smoke and confusion. Sergeant Ellis and another mutinous soldier, Private Gaffney, were handcuffed, thumb-screwed, leg-bolted and chained together in the hold. When Ellis died nine days later he was thrown overboard and a convict ironed to Gaffney in his place. By the time they reached Sydney, the chains had bored a hole in Gaffney's leg. In all eleven convicts died at sea, with others requiring medical treatment upon landing.

The voyage of the *Britannia* was even worse. Sailing from Cork in December 1796, the ship was so poorly maintained that the original surgeon refused to embark. Continually swamped by icy sea water, many convict berths got so damp that clothes and bedding rotted away. Worse still, Captain Thomas Dennott was a self-righteous sadist whose vicious response to a thwarted mutiny was pure *Grand Guignol*.

After discovering the usual pipedream to seize the ship, Dennott had William Trimball flogged without respite until he named thirty-one conspirators. A search turned up a tiny cache of saws, knives, hoop iron and scissors. Furious beyond all self-control, Dennott visited a vengeance on the convicts that no one dared oppose. The full catalogue of horrors was revealed two weeks after the *Britannia* reached Sydney, when the poor condition and complaints of the survivors prompted an inquiry into Dennott's conduct.

Over several days in June 1797 the court heard statements from soldiers, seamen and convicts that exposed a hornet's nest of shipboard hatred and suspicion. Contradictory accounts of cruelty, embezzlement and neglect of duty flew thick and fast. Isaac Froome, the third mate, accused Dennott of stealing government stores and breaking up many of the ship's water-casks at Rio to make room for private trade goods. On the other hand he allowed that Dennott's behaviour was only 'sometimes cruel' — but this is the perspective of a man who beat a convict to death for being out of his bunk.

Dennott made all previous Irish transport captains seem angels of mercy. He ordered a total of 7900 lashes, by far the harshest punishment ever inflicted during a convict voyage. 'I'll not hang you, it's too gentle a death,' he told them, 'I'll cut you to pieces'. John Rutlidge or Relish, who had only his own urine to drink while recovering from 300 lashes, testified that even the soldiers said 'it was very hard to see such murder going on'.

The ship's replacement surgeon, Augustus Beyer, sometimes attended the floggings but mostly skulked in his cabin while the decks ran with blood. Already on his third convict trip, Beyer was a negligent coward who bullied the female convicts but was so afraid of the men that he only inspected their quarters about four times between South America and Sydney.

The *Britannia*'s master and surgeon hated one another to the convicts' utter detriment. Dennott ordered that the first mate, not the doctor, was to decide whether a convict could withstand his punishment. Too intimidated to insist on his duty, Beyer washed his hands of the affair and wouldn't even dress wounds. During one flogging he did attend, the victim pleaded he couldn't bear any more. Beyer simply shouted, 'You be damned!' and recommended eight more lashes. When Patrick Garnley died the morning after receiving 400 lashes, Beyer ruled he was a 'strong, muscular man' who couldn't possibly have succumbed to a mere flogging.

James Brady's pleadings for water during his 300 lashes brought a smile to the captain's face, but when Brady persisted, saying he'd die if he didn't get water, Dennott snarled at him to 'die and be damned'. How many died is uncertain because of discrepancies in the numbers embarked. Dennott was accused of six deaths, but the toll was at least eleven and could have been as high as nineteen.[3] The last shipboard fatality, Patrick Cassidy, died at Sydney Cove before he could be disembarked, and three others succumbed during the first week ashore.

Treatment of the female convicts was almost as abusive. Head-shaving was then a standard punishment for women, designed to humiliate, but Dennott turned it into a degrading torture. When Jenny Blake attempted to commit suicide to avoid punishment, Dennott personally cut her hair, gagged her, struck her in the face with a cane and shackled her so tightly, the court heard, that she was 'not capable of going to perform necessary occasions'. Mary Fane was locked in a neck yoke for an unnamed crime which 'decency alone induced her to commit'. Mary Cogan, mentally imbalanced and with a history of suicide attempts, jumped overboard to her death in fear of Dennott's rampage.

Beyer's attitude to the women was no better. Mary Bryan, who miscarried during the voyage, reported his only treatment of her three-month illness during the five months at sea was half a glass of wine. When another female approached him on her behalf, he 'damned her for a bitch' and threatened to kick her.

Francis Cox, who was 'flogged into a fit', described how Patrick Garnley died in chains just hours after being flogged, with second mate Wharton refusing the stricken man water, saying he'd give him poison first. After Garnley's death, cries for water amongst the convicts became so insistent that Dennott sent them seven or eight gallons, but then ordered them to their bunks after the ensuing mad scramble. When a convict named Connor was caught out of his berth, the third mate Isaac Froome struck him so hard across the loins he died overnight.

The next morning James Brannon and Richard Stapleton had a

second serving of 300 lashes. Brannon pleaded with Dennott that he was loyal to the King, but Dennott 'dam'ed his Majesty' and ordered the floggings to proceed with horse-skin leather straps. These were attached to a stick and knotted to improvise a more cutting whip. 'Damn your eyes,' Dennott told the two men, 'this will open your carcase'. Soldiers recalled that Beyer's sole contribution was to compare Brannon's 'hide' to a bull or buffalo. Apart from anything else it was a poor diagnosis, for Brannon died several days afterwards, and so did Stapleton.

Dennott told the court that although he believed that 'severity in some instances is lenity in general', in this instance 'very few were punished, and those but slightly'. If the mutineers had suffered unduly then Beyer was at fault: how could a ship's master be expected to know what constituted excessive punishment without medical advice? Beyer's response was equally absurd and callous, insisting that if Dennott chose not to consult him then he carried no responsibility. Beyer blamed damp conditions for the convicts' weakness, and attributed nine of the deaths to 'scurvy, flux and debilitation'.

Atkins and his panel of magistrates found that Dennott was 'imprudent and ill-judged' and 'bordering on too great a degree of severity'. Beyer wasn't tried, but he was censured as 'inexcusably negligent' and an 'accessory to the inhumanities he complains of'. Governor Hunter sent a trial transcript to England, where it was ignored.

These, then, were the Irish prisoners who, according to Collins, were refusing to settle into servitude and 'manifesting daily a propensity to desert from their work'. Worried that the Toongabbie harvest would suffer, the authorities assigned soldiers to watch over and coax work from the Irish arrivals. Hunter reported to London that they were

> ... so turbulent, so dissatisfyed with their situation here, so extremely insolent, refractory, and troublesome, that, without the most rigid and severe treatment, it is impossible for us to receive any labour whatever from them.

The *Marquis Cornwallis* and the *Britannia* injected an overpowering dose of Irish bitterness into a colony already bubbling with violence and unrest. The continuing absence of Irish sentencing records was in itself enough to guarantee trouble. But now, already chafing under foreign rule, they resented the barbarous conduct of the transport captains and regretted the failure of their thwarted mutinies. They burned for the merest ghost of a chance to extricate themselves from their predicament. And as they looked with longing to the horizon from the plantations of Toongabbie and Parramatta, they found one.

CHAPTER FIVE

The phantom white colony

In addition to their natural vicious propensities they have
conceived an opinion that there is a colony of white people
in some part of this country in which they will receive
all the comforts of life without the necessity of labour.

GOVERNOR HUNTER, 15 FEBRUARY 1798

THE BLUE MOUNTAINS WERE NAMED FOR A MIRAGE. SEEN FROM
afar, thin clouds of eucalyptus oil from the leaves of millions of gum trees
cast the slopes in a deep sapphire haze. This trick of the light hijacked
Governor Phillip's dreary decision to name them the Carmarthen and
Landsdown Hills, after a pair of titled British politicians. Despite the
official adoption of these names in April 1788, the popular colloquialism
soon prevailed, and Phillip himself was referring to them as the Blue
Mountains just over a year later.[1]

The foothills lay about twenty miles west of the penal farms
at Parramatta, and were only five miles from the outer bank of the

Hawkesbury River at Richmond Hill. Curving in a boomerang of ridges and chasms around the settlements' western fringes, the Blue Mountains form one of a series of natural barriers that separate much of Australia's eastern coast from the rest of the continent. They lie just east of the Great Divide between the eastward and westward flowing rivers. To the infant colony they were the blue wall that blocked the western horizon, turning the hidden inland into a *tabula rasa* onto which desperate dreams could be easily written, and not at all easily refuted. The very name of the mountains reflects the sense of mystery they inspired in the first Europeans to contemplate them. Even the appellation 'mountains' is illusive; it was later established that 'plateau' is a more accurate description. But for the first quarter century of British occupation, little more was known about them than a shimmery blue facade, beckoning to the prisoners as they sweated over their labour at Parramatta and Toongabbie.

The Blue Mountains seduced the convict imagination, moving escape aspirations from north to west. The overland escape plans of *Marquis Cornwallis* and *Britannia* arrivals were to prove even more outlandish than those of their predecessors. By late 1797, venturing inland became a trial that, once endured, might reveal China or other indeterminate destinations. Variations flowered from the seeds of rumour — roads hidden in the bush, inland societies of white people that promised release from penal labour and the chance of a passage home. The numbers of convicts tempted by such ideas would bring overland escape attempts to a peak.

For the origins of this curious development of convict escape mythology, we must look to the first white man to make the mountains his home. By some unfortunate quirk of history, the remarkable John Wilson is missing from many accounts of Australian bushranging and exploration. A dedicated practitioner of both trades, he was certainly one of the earliest success stories of either. By 1797 he had been living with Aborigines for several years, his chest scarified according to their custom. They even gave him a name: *Bun–bo–e*.

Convicted at Lancaster for stealing nine yards of cloth, Wilson arrived with the First Fleet with just under five years to serve of his seven year sentence. He went missing within days of landing, though probably returned soon afterwards. Always drawn to the bush, after his sentence expired he earned the reputation as a tearaway who preferred Aboriginal company. His lucky break was the friendship he formed with a Hawkesbury clan of the inland Darug people, known to colonists as 'the wood tribes'. Communicating through a mutually improvised pidgin, he forged a bond that was to make his reputation and ultimately, prove his undoing.

At the beginning of 1795 Wilson was living with Aborigines near the upper Hawkesbury River. With settlement along the river pushing Anglo–Aboriginal relations into open warfare, the authorities worried that he might offer his inside knowledge of the colony to help his Darug friends plan attacks. Wilson was asked to accompany a survey party to Port Stephens. Here his usefulness extended beyond bushcraft; he saved the government surveyor's life by shooting an Aboriginal warrior about to spear him. This was only a few months before the shock discovery of Turwood's gang at Port Stephens. They had been inland at the time, but knew the man shot by Wilson and were able to report his recovery.

Wilson soon went bush again, this time with William Knight, a Third Fleet runaway. In August 1795 they were arrested after attempting to abduct two pre-pubescent girls from one of the towns, but escaped almost immediately. Implicated in Aboriginal attacks on outlying farms, they were rumoured to have joined forces with the famous Pemulwuy, then the colony's most active and effective Aboriginal opponent.

Wilson was finally cornered in February 1797, in company with two runaways named William Barr and John Moss. He claimed he had captured them and was bringing them in, but was sentenced to another seven years. Again he escaped. Governor Hunter now proposed to outlaw him, issuing an order on 13 May that rendered him liable to execution without trial if he failed to surrender within a fortnight. Six months later Wilson boldly strode into Parramatta to turn himself in, wearing only an apron of kangaroo skin. This 'pest to the industrious', as Hunter described him, brought news of a world his countrymen knew nothing of. Wilson claimed to have ranged a hundred miles in every direction from the colony, regions alien to colonists and coastal Aborigines alike. He described wombats and lyrebirds, animals totally unknown to the colony, and said — quite correctly — that well-watered open country lay across the mountains north-west of the still-undiscovered head of the Hawkesbury River.

Impressed by the bushranger's knowledge of the wilderness, Hunter preferred to use rather than punish him. Wilson's most sinister information was his claimed sighting of more than fifty skeletons in the bush, some accompanied by rusty knives and mouldering shoes. Aborigines had assured him they were the remains of white men who had got themselves bushed. Early in the new year Hunter issued a public warning against absconding, describing the 'many dead bodies of men' that Wilson reported as 'some of those ignorant people who had left this place in search of some other, where they idly supposed and believed they would be more happy'. Wilson may have been scaremongering, making a sly bid to bolster the value of his own undeniable survival skills, but it's more likely he was telling the truth, as everything he said about unknown fauna and geography was later confirmed.

Wilson's body count matches the potential upper limit of missing *Queen* Irish, but it strains credibility to suggest they account for every skeleton in Wilson's bush closet. If his information was solid then 'Chinese travelling' had almost certainly continued beyond its first outburst, even if some of the dead had attempted permanent subsistence in the bush without inspiration from escape mythology. There must have been others, too; even the wide-ranging Wilson couldn't have seen the remains of every luckless wanderer.

As well as giving the authorities a lot of useful intelligence, Wilson doubtlessly discussed life in the interior with the lower orders. But did he acquaint them with the phantom white colony beyond the mountains? By the end of 1797, many Irish convicts were convinced of the existence of an inland settlement of white people. Although the precise origin of this rumour — escape mythology's strangest creation — is unknown, its full flowering certainly coincided with Wilson's surrender.

David Collins and Governor Hunter left us brief descriptions of this mysterious place. Collins, who had just returned to England, was now obtaining colonial information for his books from his friend Hunter, who had the advantage of speaking with convict believers directly. Collins recorded they believed

> . . . that there was a colony of white people, which had been discovered in this country, situated to the south-west of the settlement, from which it was distant between three and four hundred miles, and in which they were assured of finding all the comforts of life, without the necessity of labouring for them.

The south-west was already a land of surprises, having revealed the solution to the colony's first major mystery: the lost cattle of 1788. Four months after the First Fleet landed, the settlement's entire stock of cattle — four cows and two bulls — had gone astray, never to be recovered. Four years later Watkin Tench found the riddle 'so difficult of solution that I shall not attempt it'. No one expected the bovine bolters to travel as far as they did, or start a secret colony of their own. In late 1795, however, Aboriginal reports finally led to a vastly increased feral herd forty miles south-west of Sydney, in fine grazing land bordering the southern Blue Mountains region just beyond the Nepean River. This district was soon dubbed, naturally enough, the Cowpastures. Rumours of outback cattle had been circulating among the convicts for some time, and may have done a great deal to promote ideas of a white civilisation existing somewhere further south-west.

Hunter's description of the white colony is very similar, but he placed it somewhat closer without giving a direction. In 1801 he wrote to

Sir Joseph Banks, explaining there had been

> . . . a report which some artful villain in the colony had propagated
> amongst the Irish convicts lately arrived, 'that there was a colony of
> white people at no very great distance in the back country — 150 or
> 200 miles — where there was abundance of every sort of provision
> without the necessity of so much labour'.

Hunter remained certain that China was still considered an equally
likely overland prospect, regardless of the new stories coming in from
the bush. Perhaps the horizon's blue mountain wall reminded someone
of those blue-painted landscapes on China plates. The sole clue to the
origin of the new belief was preserved by Collins, who must have got it
from Hunter:

> On conversing with these infatuated people, it appeared, that the
> history of the supposed settlement had its rise from some strange and
> unintelligible account which one of these men, who had left his work,
> and resided for some time with the natives, had collected from the
> mountain savages.

If 'these men' was a general reference to the convict class, as it probably
was, then Collins surely meant the newly surrendered John Wilson. In
this event, Bun-bo-e was likely no more than an unwitting inspiration for
the subsequent escape attempts, even if he believed the stories himself.
The trust Hunter kept in him suggests he was not the 'artful villain' of the
governor's outraged imagination. Wilson's vagabond life may have been
enough in itself to conjure a white colony; garbled accounts of his bush
exploits could have drifted in before his surrender, to bolster and eclipse
ideas from the days of the first Chinese travellers.

However, taken literally, Collins' statement could conceivably
refer to an Irish myth-maker, a mystery man who had also been at large

amongst Aborigines. Collins himself made no such speculations. Instead he leaned towards a conspiracy theory, suggesting an anonymous 'wicked incendiary' wanted to destabilise Hunter's government by manipulating the supposedly gullible Irish to 'embarrass the public concerns of the colony'.

Absurd as the authorities found this gossip, they were unable to disprove it and before long it became troublesome beyond all expectation. Hunter was certain that this new crop were, like the last, 'some of those people lately arrived here from Ireland, and whose ignorance makes them the sport of more wicked and designing knaves'. The Defenders' woeful ignorance, Hunter assured his superiors back home by dispatch, left them vulnerable to 'improper persons in this colony who work on that ignorance to a dangerous degree'. Whether he literally thought they were the passive dupes of a malicious prank is uncertain; like the Chinese travellers of 1791 they seem more likely to have been fired up by a genuine infatuation. By 'wicked and designing knaves', Hunter could easily have meant Irishmen who spread an inducement to abscond that they believed themselves; the same sort of description was often applied to stirrers of more mundane Irish troublemaking.

But the governor never found such persons. All we really know is that the white colony rumours collided head-on with the frustration of the *Marquis Cornwallis* and *Britannia* Irish. Several Irish convicts deserted in late 1797 and were presumed to have perished in the bush, unable to find their way back. Some runaways targeted the colony's precious stock of horses, making several attempts on the government stables at Parramatta. Before long, two brood mares had been spirited away. This was considered a very serious blow, as there were only eighty-four horses in the entire country.[2]

Adding to the colony's woes was the irrepressible John Turwood, who escaped again. This time he hatched a plot to seize the *Cumberland*, the largest and best government vessel. On 5 September 1797, as it neared Broken Bay on a regular cargo run to the Hawkesbury, some of the convict crewmen suddenly rose up and threatened the lives of the others. Another boat pulled alongside, and the innocent men were dumped ashore at Broken Bay. Turwood took the *Cumberland* out to sea, this time never to be seen again.

Less than a month later, three of the men put out of the *Cumberland* participated in a piracy themselves. On the evening of 2 October, eleven convicts boarded a boat at Camp Cove (Sydney Harbour) owned by an ex-convict settler named John Ramsay. Forcing the crew of three to join them, the gang piloted the boat out to sea and set a southerly course. An armed whaleboat pursued them for about forty miles down the coast, but was blown ashore several times by a strong gale and returned without sighting them. It seemed that Ramsay's boat, apparently quite frail, had broken up and the fourteen men drowned.

These escapees included at least four Irishmen from the *Marquis Cornwallis* — Francis Royal, one of the informers who had helped defeat the shipboard mutiny; 68-year-old James Cunningham; Patrick Clark; and Patrick McCabe. A fifth Irish participant was John Whalan or Felan of the *Boddingtons*. But despite the bad reputation of the Defenders, the most ruthless characters in the gang turned out to be English: the leader Michael Gibson; Joseph Crafts, one of the few with maritime ability; Jonathan Burrobriggs, a recent arrival; and Henry Stamford, an old lag from the Third Fleet.

A third piracy was defeated in early November, when a party of armed constables and magistrates waylaid fourteen Irish convicts on the night of their intended departure. This gang had been stockpiling stores for a surreptitious sea voyage, but their scheme leaked and they were flogged and put to hard labour at Parramatta. Hunter now banned all boatbuilding without his permission, and ordered that any boat found improperly secured at night should be burned down.

Blaming the unrest on the bush sanctuary rumours, Hunter's first move was to scatter suspected ringleaders throughout various districts, but it backfired badly. Convicts still mostly worked in large government gangs; the relative dearth of settlers meant it wasn't yet possible to spread them thinly enough to stem the flow of rumour. To his horror, Hunter found he had only given them 'a better opportunity of irritating and inflaming the minds of those convicts who before such acquaintance have been found of better disposition'. As the myth gained momentum, plans for mass desertion by foot were drawn. In January 1798, Hunter was informed of

> . . . a far more numerous gang, who had provided what they thought necessary for their expedition, had fixed upon the place of general rendevouz, and were furnished with a paper of written instructions how they were to travel in point of direction from hence to this fancied paradise, or to China.

This myth–fuelled conspiracy — perhaps the largest ever assembled — originated amongst the Irish convicts at Toongabbie. The existence of written directions convinced Hunter that 'some wicked and disaffected person or persons' were making an Irish joke of the new arrivals, but despite having 'done all in my power to discover them', he was forced to admit failure to his superiors in London. Although other convicts would certainly have been quick to fleece believers with all manner of opportunistic scams, the governor unearthed nothing to suggest the enthusiasm was anything but self–generated. But he did learn that the conspiracy involved some sixty convicts, exclusive of unknown numbers who had already bolted. If they really were all Irish, they represented about a quarter of the males from the last two ships from Cork, or almost half the surviving men from the most recent, the *Britannia*.[3]

Hunter's first move was to send a Parramatta magistrate to Toongabbie and have him lecture an assembly of convicts on the danger and futility of taking to the bush. A few days later, however, considerable numbers were still planning to go 'in quest of the new settlement'. Fearing wholesale emigration to oblivion was about to take place, Hunter ordered an armed party of trusted convict constables to seize as many would-be deserters as possible. About twenty (Collins says sixteen) of 'these Defenders', as Hunter called them, were waylaid en route to their agreed place of departure and taken to the solid new gaol at Parramatta, a fenced structure with twenty-two cells, built with heavy logs. Several of the men were from Toongabbie, while others had absconded from a broad scattering of farms. What became of the other forty or so conspirators does not appear, but it's likely that some managed to slip away.

Visiting the captured runaways the next day, Hunter attempted to explain that resistance was useless; that there was little for them to discover in the wilderness except their own graves. Their response is revealing. If the vaunted 'paradise' was concocted to direct attention from other plans, such as seizing a boat, then why spurn this golden opportunity to gull the governor? But instead they refused to divulge their goal, probably still hoping to reach it.[4]

Hunter's visit unearthed a curious new aspect to the belief. Some were found to possess a paper illustrated by the figure of a compass, with written instructions on how to use it to reach their destination. Vague hints later emerged that these strange, talismanic drawings — none have survived — may have been intended to operate as some kind of sundial, with the carrier hoping to maintain bearings by travelling with the sun at a particular position relative to the drawing. If they expected to be pointed north then clearly the principle of magnetism was unknown to them. Possibly other convicts were cynically exploiting their hopes by selling them fraudulent escape aids. But it seems that after years of inconclusive results, believers were attempting to address the navigational difficulties of attaining their goal.

Amazed by the runaways' bizarre notions, Hunter found such apparent foolishness sat oddly with the resourcefulness and determination the same men had shown in planning their venture. And yet, as he informed the Duke of Portland, who was home secretary, the evidence seemed undeniable:

The ignorance of these deluded people, my Lord, would scarcely be credited if such positive proof of it were not before us, and yet (which seems to imply a kind of contradiction) it is extraordinary with what art and cunning they form their horrible plans of wickedness and villainy.

Exasperated, and ultimately seeing nothing but madness in their method, Hunter decided to wield the big stick of authority. 'Observing a considerable degree of obstinacy and ignorance about them,' he told the Duke, 'I conceived there could be no better argument used to convince them of their misconduct than a severe corporal punishment'. Seven ringleaders were removed to Sydney, where they each received 200 lashes. Other conspirators were punished at Parramatta and put to hard labour, strictly supervised. But the governor had only scotched the snake, not killed it. Hunter was no fool: he knew the delusion couldn't be simply flogged out of existence. The lash may even have exacerbated matters, increasing the desperation to get away. In any case, the convicts must have realised the cats would rain on their backs whether the bush sanctuary was real or not — after all, they were being flogged for escaping, not for their beliefs.

In the midst of the overland escape crisis came sudden news of the men who had taken off in Ramsay's boat. An English-dominated faction (Gibson, Crafts, Stamford, Burrobriggs and Whalan) had marooned seven of their accomplices — including all but one of the *Marquis Cornwallis* Irishmen — on an island in the still undiscovered Bass Strait, and returned to the Sydney vicinity. Two others had been spared to help work the ship, Ramsay's sailor Thomas Williams and a hapless Irishman, Patrick Clark, now demoted to slave. Early in the new year they raided two boats anchored in the Hawkesbury River, taking guns, ammunition and provisions. Letting Williams go, they headed off in one of the newly captured boats, armed with five muskets. When Williams came in a few days later, he revealed the gang had originally sailed south in fruitless search of a wrecked trading vessel, the *Sydney Cove*, hoping to salvage supplies.

There was little point in trying to rescue the marooned men, as Williams had no clear idea of their location. Instead Hunter sent a list of their names to England with the next government dispatch. He didn't separate the motives of the land and sea escapes, confident that addressing escape mythology would dissuade piracy as well as overland adventuring. Referring to believers in a 'a colony of white people', he noted that

> . . . a correspondence it seems has been carried on by these people from one district to another, and plans have been projected for their escaping from the colony, and a few have attempted by land, as well as by water, and for the want of our having early information they have succeeded.

Despite Hunter's generalisation it seems unlikely that Turwood, who had already tried to reach Tahiti, was now attempting to contact a bush sanctuary by sea. However, the governor may have been right in assuming escape mythology had encouraged at least some of the Ramsay's boat thieves. Differing goals contributed to the marooning of men who were, significantly, recently arrived Irish. Hunter learned that the gang broke up from 'finding it impossible to agree amongst themselves' as much as 'want of food'. Collins had no doubt they were from the subset 'prepossessed with the possibility of penetrating through the woods to China', the inducement of the wrecked *Sydney Cove* notwithstanding. Hunter saw Irish revolt all over the affair and unfairly blamed the 'lawless and turbulent' Irish for the complicity of Englishmen in the escapes. Their baleful influence had 'completely ruined' the English convicts, he wrote, who, 'although extremely bad, were by no means equal in infamy and turbulence to the others until mixed with them, which is impossible to avoid'.

For Hunter, a bid for Timor in a dodgy boat was as chimerical as a bushwalk to China, and just as troublesome. By now he badly needed to restore stability to the colony. There was already enough trouble with Aboriginal resistance along the Hawkesbury, the racketeering of NSW Corps officers, and the disaffection of settlers impoverished and bullied by the military elite. The last thing the governor needed was to lose control of the convict population. Two boatloads of pirates and upwards of sixty Irishmen straining for a Promised Land were enough for any administration. Hunter decided to act quickly, before their ranks swelled with imitators and converts.

CHAPTER SIX

Checking this
spirit of emigration

Of this wonderful country we have little or no knowledge,
except a small portion of the sea coast of a corner of it.
With two armed ships and a schooner, on purpose for
the use of the colony, no discovery has been attempted.
Such things are never thought of; and if a private
adventurer undertakes them, he is discouraged ...

REVEREND THOMAS FYSHE PALMER (POLITICAL EXILE),

14 AUGUST 1797

THE PROSPECT OF A MASS ESCAPE TO SOMEWHERE THAT DIDN'T
exist posed Hunter an unusual dilemma, and he came up with a suitably
unusual solution. Treating the white colony myth as the focus for the
unrest, he ordered the strangest mission of exploration Australia has
ever known — an expedition of anti-discovery, designed to demonstrate
an absence of mysterious Chinas and white convict sanctuaries just
beyond the settlements.[1] Here's how Hunter, writing in the third person,
described the plan in his General Order dated 19 January 1798:

His Excellency, from having understood that some of those people lately arrived here from Ireland, and whose ignorance makes them the sport of more wicked and designing knaves, have picked up, some how or other, an idle story of the possibility of travelling from hence to China, or finding some other colony where they expect every comfort without the trouble of any labour, has, to convince them of the folly and absurdity of such opinions, and also as far as possible to prevent that loss of life which must certainly attend every attempt to discover this fancied paradise, ordered from among those discontented people four men of their own choice, and on whose story they can depend, to be supplied with what provision they can take, and to travel into the country as far as they are capable.

Hunter expanded on his motivations in a subsequent dispatch to London. It shows how exasperation with an inflexible convict mindset convinced him that sanctioning an official search party was his only option. His concern touches upon the inconvenience of lost manpower but is mainly, to his credit, humanitarian fear for the deserters' lives. Unlike his predecessor Phillip, content for the myth to 'cure itself' through the accumulated suffering of its adherents, Hunter felt obliged to take active steps to save the deluded from themselves:

> In their schemes of desertion from the colony, their own death, if they succeed in getting away, is inevitable; but their minds have been worked up to such a pitch of folly, rashness and absurdity, that nothing but experience will convince them; if we suffer them to escape into the country they are lost, not only to us but to the world, for perish they must.
>
> For the sake, therefore of humanity, and a strong desire to save these men, worthless as they are, from impending death, I ordered four of the strongest and the hardiest of their numbers to be selected by the people themselves, and to prepare for a journey of discovery

for the satisfaction of their associates, in order that they might have an opportunity of relating, upon their return, whatever they saw and met with.

Two men were to accompany the four convicts. As the only real white bushman in the colony, John Wilson was the obvious choice as guide. No one else had anywhere near his knowledge of the regions the runaways longed to reach. Hunter had always intended to utilise his special skills, and Wilson had already offered to go after the convicts who had stolen the mares. His bushcraft would give the hopefully disabused Irishmen their best chance of returning alive to convince their countrymen of the error of their ways. As Hunter's order put it:

But to prevent their perishing, which would certainly be their fate if left to themselves, he has ordered two men, long accustomed to the woods and intimate with many of the natives, to accompany them, that in case of their repenting of their attempt they may be brought back to tell their own story.

The second man, who kept a journal of the expedition, was Hunter's teenage servant, John Price.[2] A Londoner, Price had sailed to the colony with Hunter in 1795 at sixteen years of age. Years later, Hunter explained in a letter to Sir Joseph Banks how the youth came to accompany Wilson. Clearly, the governor was not unmindful of other potential benefits the exploration might bring the colony, regardless of the conclusions the convict dreamers might draw:

As he grew up in that country and became pleased with traveling thro' the woods, he solicited permission to go upon the excursion then intended, and as he could write, he was instructed to enter in a paper the observations which their journey might suggest. He is an intelligent lad.

The Irish readily agreed to the peculiar expedition — not that they had a choice — but as usual they had their own agenda. Just before the expedition set out, a murderous plot came to light. The four convict representatives had arranged to meet up with a group of fellow conspirators somewhere in the bush. After killing Wilson and Price, this combined convict force would take their guns and provisions and at last make that much-dreamed-of dash through the bush to freedom.

Disturbed as he was by such 'wild and extravagant' news, Hunter regarded the expedition as too important to cancel. The 'necessity of checking this spirit of emigration', as Collins described the trip's purpose, was paramount. An armed escort of four soldiers was assigned to accompany the guides 'to the foot of the first mountain, with orders how to act if any others attempted to join them'. This was Mount Hunter in the Razorback Range. The highest peak known to the colony, it stood about thirty miles south-west of Parramatta, just across the Nepean River.

And so, with Wilson willing to lead the convicts toward their supposed utopias, Price able to document their progress, and four soldiers on the alert for a convict ambush, this odd party of anti-explorers set off from Parramatta in mid-January, 1798.[3] Unfortunately the surviving fair copy of Price's journal doesn't begin until 24 January, the day the expedition left Mount Hunter. Without knowing when they arrived there, we can only wonder how the first few days were spent. The leg to the mountain shouldn't have taken more than a day or two, trudging across gently rising hills and sparsely timbered land, with lush native grasses eventually giving way to swamps near the Nepean River. Perhaps the convicts were allowed to search in various directions en route, or make excursions once establishing their mountain camp. The only certainty is that the 'discontented Irishmen' quickly tired of the business and asked to go back after reaching Mount Hunter. Their mates had made no attempt to take on the armed escort, and they probably saw little point in a venture expressly designed to discourage them. They were not volunteers, and Wilson and Price were hardly likely to show them their sanctuary if it did exist — and even less likely to let them stay there. The presence of soldiers, who had a self-interest in convincing them to give up, would have made any journey unpleasant. Notoriously resentful of any form of convict guard duty, the troops must have cursed both the credulous convicts and the soft-hearted governor for landing them with what would have appeared a particularly pointless hardship.

Only one of the convicts, named Roe in Price's journal, wanted to persevere past Mount Hunter.[4] The other three turned back to Parramatta with the soldiers, who were doubtless relieved the farcical journey was over. Wilson, Price and Roe continued exploring to the south-west for another fortnight, travelling alongside the Razorbacks into land unknown to any of them except Wilson. A few miles from the mountain they re-encountered the Nepean River, which they had difficulty crossing due to steep rocks along the banks. The rest of the first day was spent beating into scrubby country. Price reported 'nothing strange except a few rock kangaroos with long black brush tails and two pheasants', which they shot at but failed to hit.

The next day the travelling was far easier over open ground. They saw many kangaroos and emus, and unlike the day before something strange really did occur. Price records that

> ... we fell in with a party of natives which gave a very good account of the place we were in search of, that there was a great deal of corn and potatoes and that the people were very friendly.

This Aboriginal news of the phantom colony must have been a welcome surprise, and perhaps something of a vindication for Roe. The travellers immediately set their sights on the supposed location of the mystery. 'We hearkened to their advice,' Price wrote; 'we altered our course according to their directions'. One of the Aborigines 'promised that he would take us to a party of natives which had been there'. They waited for him but he never returned to effect the introduction. Disappointed, the trio nevertheless continued travelling in the direction that the Aborigines indicated led to the mythical settlement.

This is a rare eyewitness account of the sort of exchanges between whites and Aborigines that brought such rumours in from the bush. Unfortunately Price recorded very little detail. Wilson must have done the talking, but how easily the parties understood each other is questionable. It appears the Aborigines were asked leading questions, so they may only have agreed with the nosy strangers according to the polite custom of many Aboriginal cultures.

However unlikely this news of indigenous white people must have seemed, it was a second and rather more mundane discovery that day which ultimately cost the mission its credibility. Price, filled with amateur enthusiasm, mistook a small encrustation for a 'great deal of salt', raising hopes of a mine which proved as illusory as any white colony filled with corn and potatoes.

On 26 January the explorers had trouble crossing another rocky river, either the Bargo or the Nepean again. It was the tenth anniversary of the First Fleet anchoring at Sydney Cove, and an auspicious day for the outside world's still scant knowledge of Australian natural history. Three animals which had eluded colonial knowledge for exactly a decade were described in writing for the first time. Wilson pointed out dung of a creature called a 'whom-batt, which . . . is very fat, and has much the appearance of a badger'. Then Price recorded the first European eyewitness account of a koala, an 'animal which the natives call a cullawine, which much resembles the stoths [sloths] in America'. Near the same location Price shot a colourful bird which struck him as a cross between a pheasant and a peacock. Collins described it as a variety of 'Bird of Paradise', a fitting discovery for a mission to the convict Paradise. These encounters with wombats, koalas and lyrebirds matched Wilson's previous accounts of unknown fauna.

On 28 January they broke into open country again, marching across a large expanse without a single tree. Somewhere near present-day

Mittagong they encountered more Aborigines, who fled. Wilson gave chase, hoping to take a prisoner who might supply more information, and caught a young girl. His pidgin proved useless. Wilson was now beyond familiar territory and the girl did not understand him — or else pretended not to. Nevertheless the travellers kept her all night. Perhaps this was only part of their attempt to communicate, as Price's diary implies, although Wilson's prior history of abducting young girls admits a less savoury possibility. Price's frank admission that she 'cried and fretted' over the night reveals little either way. Finding her too frightened to be of any assistance, in the morning the explorers gave her a tomahawk and followed her back to her friends, who were dressed in large animal skins that reached their heels.

Price didn't describe this encounter. Given the tensions of the previous day it's possible he only saw them at a distance. He next mentions climbing 'a fine hill' to see open land stretching to mountains which blocked the horizon to the south. Westwards a river sparkled its way in a north-westerly direction. 'We saw nothing very promising,' Price writes of this magnificent view, without telling us what he had hoped to see.

After marching a few miles on 29 January, the trio ran across creeks that seemed to feed the river they had seen beforehand. The ground became rocky again, and led to several waterfalls at the heads of the creeks. They switched to a northerly course to bypass these obstacles, but only found more, so they resumed their west-south-west direction of the last few days. The country ran timbered again, kangaroos and 'pheasants' reappeared, and they saw the droppings of an unseen animal 'as large as horse dung'.

By now the hardships of the journey were affecting Price. 'I myself was very sick,' he confessed to his journal, 'and wished myself at home again'. Roe was in even worse shape — he had hurt his leg and was unable to walk. In two days they had eaten nothing except a creature Price called a 'rat about the size of a small kitten'. Even so, Wilson seemed to be thoroughly enjoying himself. Price ended his daily entry by noting, perhaps ruefully, how only Bun-bo-e remained 'well and hearty'.

Continuing to struggle across rocky scrubland, the next day saw them meet the headwaters of a large river, possibly the Wollondilly near its junction with the Wingecarribee. They were now trespassing on the home turf of Gurrangatch, a fish-reptile spirit of the local Aboriginal Dreaming. Surviving mythology describes how the Wollondilly channel was carved out by his epic battle with Mirragan, the tiger quoll. Gurrangatch was said to lurk in trees, watching for intruders, and then slip into the water to drown and eat them when they came to drink. Although this mythic peril remained unknown to Europeans for another century, it seems appropriate that Price and Roe were in dread of crossing the river when Wilson suggested making a canoe:

> The other man [Roe] and myself were so faint and tired, having nothing to eat but two small birds each, we were afraid to venture on the other side of the river, for fear we should not be able to procure anything to subsist on; likewise our shoes was gone and our feet were very much bruised with the rocks, so that we asked Wilson to return.

This marked the journey's terminus.[5] Homeward bound at last, over the next two days Price and Roe continued to weaken, living off the occasional small bird. They made their way over open grassland (passing near present-day Bowral) and a series of lakes without any visible birdlife. After crossing a ridge of mountains they found a large mob of kangaroos. Wilson killed one, supplying their first full meal for days.

At sunrise the next morning they heard two shots. 'Do you hear that gun fire?' Wilson asked Price, who hadn't realised what the noise was. Price fired off five shots, hoping for a reply, but none came. Soon they entered country familiar to Wilson, but it proved barren with only roots and grubs to eat. Price was again haunted by fears of starvation, but Wilson kept his spirits up and foraged for the whole party as best he could.

For the next six days they passed through a succession of valleys strewn with rocks and bereft of sizeable wildlife. Price and Roe were so weak they could barely walk. Cramped with hunger, and having torn strips from their clothing to bind their bleeding feet, both were despairing of getting back alive. Only Wilson remained cheerful. Finally, on 9 February, they reached ground which was easier on their feet and, according to Wilson, only ten miles from the farms at Prospect Hill, which lay about five miles west of Parramatta township. Encouraged, they began to travel faster and reached the colonial outpost just before sundown. Price and Roe collapsed with exhaustion on arrival. Without Wilson's expertise they could easily have met the same fate as many of the runaways who had inspired their journey.

The trio of new animals certainly intrigued the colony, but what really piqued Hunter's interest was the salt, a vital commodity then imported at considerable expense. He sent Wilson out a second time on 9 March, hopeful of locating deposits that could be mined. Wilson's new companions also relied heavily on his bushcraft and knowledge of the country, which they marked by naming an imposing Mount Wilson in his honour. Leading a small party as far as Mount Towrang — seven miles north of present-day Goulburn — Wilson effectively sidestepped the mountain barrier without contemporary recognition. Unfortunately the salt sample returned was poor, which may have contributed to this achievement being overlooked.

None of the anti-myth expeditionary team featured further in colonial life. Roe's future proved as shadowy as his past. John Wilson returned to Aboriginal society to spend the final two years of his life as Bun-bo-e, deep in his beloved western wilderness. In August 1800 news came in that he was killed in a fight over a woman. Collins learned Wilson had 'appropriated, against her inclinations, a female to his own exclusive accommodation'. The abduction of women was not unusual amongst Aborigines, but neither was deadly reprisal from outraged relatives. Bun-bo-e found this dangerous game played to its conclusion when he was tracked to his camp one day and speared to death. He was about thirty-three years old.

Collins' misplaced scepticism about the occasional runaway being adopted as a reincarnated Aborigine resurfaces in his account of Wilson's demise. The bushranger had once boasted he had endeared himself to the 'wood natives' by persuading an elderly woman to accept him as her returned son. Collins couldn't resist joking that although Bun-bo-e had left his bush friends, they could now 'expect his return at some future period in any shape that their fancies might form'.

For all his faults, Wilson deserves acknowledgment as Australia's first white bushman, the first European to unlock the secrets of survival in an environment so unforgiving to the outsider. Naturally he owed this knowledge to the 'wood tribe' who accepted him into their community. He was almost certainly the first colonist to penetrate the Blue Mountains, up to two decades before the officially recognised achievement of Blaxland, Lawson and Wentworth in 1813.

Within a few weeks of Wilson's death Governor Hunter also left New South Wales, recalled to England largely for his inability to prevent the military's stranglehold on the economy. His servant Price and the precious expedition journal went with him. The incoming governor, Philip Gidley King, apparently knew little of the exploration, except perhaps the rumours of salt. Hunter and King had once been friends — both were First Fleet naval officers — but their fellowship was strained by King's eagerness to commence his rule in the face of Hunter's recall, and they were not on speaking terms when Hunter finally departed.

In retrospect, Hunter decided to downplay the expedition's major purpose to his superiors back home, emphasising its value as a conventional exploration. Although his first dispatch on the topic (19 January, when the expedition was in the field) plainly states that two guides accompanied four convicts, the next (dated 15 February, but sent months later) refers to 'three guides', whom he claims continued exploring after 'the whole of the men [convicts] returned with the soldiers'. With the convict Roe misrepresented as a third guide, all the convicts appeared to have been quickly disabused, leaving Wilson and company free to explore the interior without them. Hunter again referred to 'the three guides' in his next dispatch (1 March), claiming they were 'directed to proceed into and make what observations they could upon the country they travelled over' after the convicts went home. Here Hunter contradicts his February dispatch, which had reported the guides' orders were to escort the convicts home when they 'should feel disposed to abandon their journey'.[6]

Later in England, a nostalgic Hunter almost regretted not going on Wilson's trip himself. 'Old as I am,' he wrote to Sir Joseph Banks in July 1801, 'I was then both able and willing to make such journey, but I was too much annoyed with various matters of less real importance'. Hunter presented Banks with a fair copy of Price's journal and offered him an interview with its author, but the meeting doesn't seem to have taken place. Although Hunter reported to England that Wilson's journeys had revealed country 'in some places highly beautiful and fit for cultivation', there was no attempt to capitalise on the discovery. In the absence of any pressing need for colonial expansion, the exploration fell into obscurity and its significance remained unexamined until the twentieth century.[7] The major factor delaying settlement to the south following Hunter's departure was Governor King's wish to foster the large herds of feral cattle thriving in the Cowpastures.

There is no doubt that Wilson and Price achieved their objective of giving the convict believers 'an opportunity of relating, upon their return, whatever they saw and met with'. As a sop to convict superstition it was as far as Hunter was prepared to go. The trip had barely left Parramatta before he announced the matter was officially over on 19 January. The fate of the boat thieves was still unknown, which Hunter played to his advantage, stressing the likelihood that they had 'forfeited their lives by the ill-advised step they had taken'. He promised severe, unspecified punishment to any convict reckless enough to give him further trouble.

He had indulged the Irish as far as he dared, and now expected them to reciprocate by discarding their dream:

> The Governor judges it necessary now to declare, that after having taken so much pains and trouble to prevent those ignorant men from being misled by more wicked and mischievous villains, and to convince them wherein their real interest and happiness lays, that if his endeavours prove ineffectual, and any such wild and madlike plans are hereafter laid or attempted, that whoever are concerned shall receive such severity of punishment as may probably prove a stronger argument against such schemes than any other he can use, and he will find for such people a situation in which they will not have much time to employ in hatching mischief.

Despite Hunter's threats, such schemes easily outlasted him in New South Wales. The myth had imprinted too deeply on the convict imagination to be erased by a quick-fix bushwalk and a governor's lecture. Although no outback mystery society was located, its existence was hardly disproved. If anything, the expedition's Aboriginal tale of white farmers somewhere in the unexplored south-west was potent fuel for the rumour.

Although records of myth-inspired absconding temporarily subside after 1798, the belief itself lingered and spread throughout the increasing convict population. Thirty years later convicts were still taking to the bush in quest of a promised land that demanded no labour of them, a place where they could either live comfortably or which they could use as a stepping-stone to return to their homes and families. The plans inspired by the myth would be as 'wild and madlike' as ever.

CHAPTER SEVEN

The opinion of the common people

The colony had not been long settled, before it
was discovered that China was but a tolerable
walk from it; and many pedestrian attempts
have been actually made to reach the dominions of
'the brother to the sun and moon'; numbers of these
pedestrians having succeeded (the others plainly see)
in the attempt, – never having been since heard of!

PETER CUNNINGHAM,
'TWO YEARS IN NEW SOUTH WALES' (1827)

THE IRISH SHOWED LITTLE INTEREST IN HUNTER OPENING THEIR
eyes to his idea of 'their real interest and happiness'. To them, his
generosity was transparent and the results of his authorised bush
escapade not worth waiting for. Attempts to contact the imagined country
continued while the expedition was still in the field. Towards the end of
January 1798, while Hunter was inspecting public works at Parramatta,
a lone Irish convict was brought in with a familiar tale to tell. As Collins

relates, this man 'had wandered about for several days in search of a road which he expected to have found, and which was to have conducted him to China, or the new colony'. Travelling alone, with flour and water his only provisions, he carried written instructions on how to maintain a course and, like other recent escapees, he possessed a paper compass. After several fruitless days at large he gave up, and to quote Collins again 'had just sense enough to reverse the written instructions which had been calculated solely to carry him out, directing him to keep the sun on a particular part of his body, varying according to the time of the day'.

Now apparently travelling eastwards, the lone Irishman reached close to the head of the Georges River. One morning, racked by hunger and fatigue, he heard a gunshot. He spent all day trying to walk towards it, crying out for help, but was too weak to make much headway. Before collapsing into an exhausted sleep that evening he sprinkled the last of his flour with water and drank it. The next day he heard a man's voice, and this time his feeble but determined call was answered. He had reached Banks Town, a handful of new land grants about six miles south of Parramatta near the Georges River and Prospect Creek junction. The settler fed him at his hut and took him to Parramatta. Collins paraphrased the convict's answer when he was asked how he found his way:

> He said, 'that a paper compass which had been given him was of no utility; he therefore kept his face toward the place where the sun came from; but if the 'hord' [lord] had not been on his side, he should have been lost, for he had been two whole days without any food, except a little flour and water'.[1]

Meanwhile, Aboriginal reports that some of the feral herd had been killed led Hunter to suppose that other Irish bolters — 'nearly as wild themselves as the cattle' — were amok in the Cowpastures. A small detachment of soldiers spent a few days in February investigating, guided by Henry Hacking. They found neither convicts nor cattle, which had been frightened from their regular haunts by the passing runaways. Aborigines confirmed white men had been chasing down calves, and Hacking found sharpened leg bones of kangaroos that the convicts had used to fashion short hunting spears.

Another explorer active that year played a walk-on role in the drama. George Bass was already a veteran of several forays, including an unsuccessful attempt on the Blue Mountains in 1796 when he tried to haul himself up the ridges with grappling hooks. While Wilson, Price and Roe were busy following up Aboriginal reports of phantom corn and potato farmers, Bass was braving the south-eastern coast of the continent in a 28-foot whaleboat. His mission was to determine whether Van Diemen's Land (Tasmania) was part of the mainland, or separated by the strait that would one day bear his name.

Sighting smoke on a tiny island off Wilsons Promontory, Bass thought he'd come across an Aboriginal camp, but it turned out to be a bedraggled group of runaways — the marooned half of the gang who had taken Ramsay's boat. He could only fit two aboard, one of Ramsay's kidnapped crewmen and an elderly man, probably James Cunningham. Giving the others all the food and equipment he could spare, Bass ferried them to the mainland and pointed them towards Sydney, five hundred miles distant. It was little better than a death sentence and everyone knew it; as Bass gave his parting advice to stick to the coastline, tears were shed on both sides. Apart from a brief encounter a few days later, the unfortunate five were never seen or heard of again.

Towards the end of March the 'beings' who had marooned them — 'they do not deserve the appellation of men', a disgusted Collins insisted — were finally brought in. Sick of life on the run, they sent Hunter a note offering to surrender. In a curious aside, they furnished the lone (if hardly reliable) clue to the fate of John Turwood's final voyage, claiming to have seen the wreck of the *Cumberland* on their travels.

Michael Gibson, the ringleader, was hanged for piracy on 9 April alongside Jonathan Burrobriggs. Their comrades Stamford, Crafts and

Whalan enjoyed last-minute reprieves at the scaffold. Patrick Clark broke from gaol and eluded recapture for several months. When he was eventually tried in November, evidence that he had acted under duress won him a comparatively lighter sentence — fourteen years, with a recommendation for mercy.

Even though the two executed as the worst of the bunch were Englishmen who had left their Irish colleagues to die, Hunter remained adamant that the 'Defenders' were the real trouble. He railed generally against recent arrivals, not finding 'any others so wicked, so lost to a sense of their own comforts, as to be concerned in such mad and extravagant schemes'. This included English convicts like Burrobriggs, a relative newcomer, but Hunter saw the Irish as the corrupting influence and he wanted fewer sent out in the future. Whether London listened or not, his wish came true. Three years were to elapse between the *Britannia* and the next Irish transport. Myth-inspired escape activity slowed again, a lull coinciding with the absence of fresh arrivals from Ireland.

The unquenchable desire for deliverance began to take other forms. Later in April many Irish convicts became distracted by a rumour that the French fleet was coming to destroy the colony and liberate them. One Irishman at Toongabbie threw down his hoe and gave three cheers in front of his bemused workmates. The local magistrate had this 'advocate for liberty' tied up in the field and flogged on the spot. An elderly Scottish woman proved to be the rumour's unwitting source. As she explained to Governor Hunter, she had merely told someone her dream of a ship arriving. The story grew with the telling until the woman was surprised to find herself hailed as something of a prophetess.

The last known escape by the current crop of believers came to light soon afterwards. Beguiled by hazy weather, a boatload of colonists lost their way rowing up an unexplored arm of the Georges River. While trying to regain their bearings they were astonished to find a small party of 'weak and languid' Irish runaways stranded on a point of land between two waterways. Trapped there nine days, they were near starving to death.

One of the Banks Town settlers brought them into Parramatta on the afternoon of 2 May. These 'unhappy, deluded wretches' — all principals in the recent mass-escape conspiracy — had been at large for several weeks. 'From sad and powerful conviction,' Hunter assured London, with calculated optimism, they now 'promised to warn their countrymen against such wild excursions in future'.[2]

This escape is one of several known only because of a chance rescue; a 'miraculous event' as Hunter put it. The actual absconding passed without surviving comment. How many journeys to China and the white colony went unrecorded simply because the adventurers never returned? Attempts seem to diminish at this point, but the only certainty is that no large-scale conspiracies were brought to light. As dozens of *Marquis Cornwallis* and *Britannia* convicts left no trace of their presence in New South Wales, it seems likely that others vanished in search of the spectral China or white colony.[3]

Collins, heartily sick of describing exploits which to him were hardly removed from insanity, noted these latest travellers only as 'certain Irishmen, who had been for some time employed in searching for a road to China (that delirium still remaining unsubdued among them)'. He suspected them of stealing a bull-calf missed while they were at large. It was never recovered, but a few months after the excitement died down, men exploring towards the mountains from Richmond Hill brought in the skulls of the mares taken from the government stables. The convict thieves were already presumed dead: in April an Aboriginal woman had reported one starved in the bush and the other killed by Aborigines. 'They, no doubt, followed such route as their judgment was capable of pointing out,' Collins mused. 'But, unfortunately for them, they could not have known which way they went.' To Collins, the fate of foolhardy escapees was less important than the robberies they committed to support their ventures. Hunter buried his compassion when he assured the Duke of Portland that now, having indulged the convicts' myth-making, he would rule them with an iron fist:

Our flocks and our crops, my Lord, are all I feel any concern about; strict, rigid, and just punishment shall constantly hang over these delinquents, and this, I trust, they are already convinced of.

An unsolved arson on the first night of October 1798 may have been the final, frustrated outburst of this wave of Irish defiance. Between 7 and 8 pm Sydney's only church, a thatched building which doubled as a schoolhouse during the week, was set alight and razed to the ground within an hour. A recent government order had strictly enforced church attendance, a galling imposition to the Irish who were denied their own spiritual consolation, the Catholic Mass. Shocked to the core, Hunter offered thirty pounds, full emancipation and a place on a ship home for information leading to a conviction. Despite this astonishing reward, literally the chance of a lifetime, no one came forward.

The worst of Hunter's troubles with absconding were now over, but the associated myths did not die out. Instead, by the turn of the century they had spread to the English convict majority. The proof is in court records of English runaways from 1802 onwards, but the first clue comes from two literate English convicts, William Noah and David Dickenson Mann, who both arrived in mid-1799. Some time after landing, Noah wrote a letter to his sister describing the thief colony as he found it. He mentioned a curious convict mindset, of sufficient interest or importance to open his brief overview of life down under:

> The Situation and Extent of this Country is layd Down by several geo-graphers where they make it certain of being an Island of the lengh of 4000 Miles but is not the Opinion of the Common people & so Obstinate they are of Its Joining India that several have been Lost in Indeavoring to find it out but this they are Curtain that this part is the most Mount-anious & uncultivated abounding with nothing but rocks & Woods.

Noah found the essence of the *Queen* convicts' delusion widespread and well-entrenched, but not exclusive to recent Irish arrivals. David Dickenson Mann was also struck by its prevalence. Conditionally pardoned less than a year after landing, Mann worked his way through the tiny colonial bureaucracy to become Governor King's principal clerk in 1804, though he was sacked about a year later. After departing for England in March 1809, he wrote a book about the colony, *The Present Picture of New South Wales*, which included the following paragraph:

> An absurd notion had uniformly existed amongst the convicts that it was possible, by penetrating into the interior, to discover a country, where they might exist without labour, and enjoy sweets hitherto unknown. This ridiculous opinion had induced numbers, since the establishment of the colony, to desert their employment, and to trust themselves in forests which were unknown to them, and where they generally wandered until the means of supporting further fatigue had failed them, and they perished from want — until they became the victims of the natives who fell in with them — or surrendered themselves to the parties who were sent in pursuit of them.

Like Noah, Mann noticed nothing particularly Irish about the 'absurd notion'. His impression that it 'uniformly existed' throughout the convict class points to the phantom shedding its national colours. Well-educated and rapidly a part of civil authority, Mann ridicules the myth in a manner very similar to that of other officials. Noah, who rose no higher than lumberyard overseer, is more sympathetic and evenhanded, presenting it as an alternative geography — the 'opinion of the common people'.

Noah's letter is a fascinating insight into a tiny, insular society — still only about 5000 people — so sharply divided that the convict underclass refused to see the landscape as their superiors defined it. This was mistrust, but it was also a declaration of mental independence in the midst of physical captivity. It was as utter a rejection of hated authority as possible — even the government's perception of the country was invalid.

Noah's guarded comment on the Blue Mountains as obstacle — 'they say their [*sic*] is no passing' — suggests the interior's inaccessibility is an allegation he doesn't necessarily accept.[4]

Of course, many saw no need to actually seek sanctuary overland. Most convicts clearly accepted the unlikelihood of reaching adjoining colonies or countries, even if they suspected their masters were lying about the extent of their isolation or the scale of natural barriers. Actual attempts remained sporadic and usually prompted by particular, desperate circumstances. Outgrowing its status as an Irish joke, escape mythology proved its worth as a focus for passive, sublimated defiance. It is an early — perhaps the earliest — incarnation of that characteristically Australian attitude of bending to authority without respecting it, of conforming to its strictures despite an outward display of rebelliousness.

The colony's divides in perception ran very deep. The very word 'convict' was part of this demarcation; convicts considered it insulting and called themselves prisoners or 'government men'. Their tendency to use the 'flash' or 'kiddy' slang of the underworld meant that early colonial court hearings frequently required interpreters for witnesses and defendants.[5] A curious attitude that the convicts' lot was not particularly hard was widespread in the upper strata of officials, contributing to their confusion over the appeal of escape mythology. Governor Phillip was astounded that some early Chinese travellers declared 'they would sooner perish in the woods than be obliged to work' even though, he maintained, 'what would be called a day's work in England is very seldom done by any convict in the settlement'. Hunter wished Irish runaways would 'open their eyes to the comforts' this new country offered, 'certainly superior to any they ever possessed in their own'. And early in Hunter's term, Reverend Samuel Marsden's rave review of the colony to a friend back home flatly denied the dark underbelly:

> I think it one of the finest countries in the known world, and no people
> I believe will be more happy than the people of this island in a short

time . . . should you hear any reports of the sufferings of the people here, they ought not to be believed; such reports must in a great measure be false.

As most descriptions of the convicts' myth come to us via the prism of their rulers' accounts, Noah's connection of India to the outback is especially interesting. It implies a subversive geography more fluid than the official mantra of 'China or a white colony'. The drawing of India into the dream may have happened simply because Calcutta, along with Canton, was a frequent next port of call for departing ships. Otherwise, by India Noah may have meant something no more precise than the Indies, a vague catch-all term for South-East Asia that wouldn't necessarily exclude China. The East Indies, for example, were sometimes called the East India islands. In any case the sanctuary's name could withstand variation; more important was the underlying wish that Australia offered more than the mountains, that there were cultivated regions, alternatives to the limiting oppression of 'nothing but rocks and woods'.

Apart from the psychological appeal to a captive audience, there were more tangible lures. If stories sourced from Aborigines had helped generate the belief, they were always there to provide ongoing, compelling corroboration. The conduit for this trickle of rumour was the expanding population of escaped convicts roaming the bush, scratching an uneasy living from a little bit of hunting and a lot of petty theft.

In early 1796, Collins estimated that six to eight bushrangers were preying on the settlements, a rough headcount that would have included John Wilson and William Knight. Numbers increased as soon as vagrancy became a halfway feasible alternative to forced labour, around the turn of the century. Between 1795 and 1800 the number of settlers off the government store rose almost nine-fold, from 228 to 1978 (a shift from seven to forty per cent of the population). The most dramatic increase was at Hawkesbury, still the most remote mainland settlement, where 757 of a population of only 979 were self-supporting by 1800. With more and more outlying farms to raid for food, clothing and tools, life as a bush outcast became an increasingly likely proposition. In 1799 the colony was home to only 103 free immigrants, a net gain of just six people in almost four years. New settlers were mostly time-expired convicts, often willing to assist runaways. Apart from shared sympathies, they often found an extra worker more beneficial than the trouble of turning him in.

Another reason for an increase in bushranging was simply that a lot of sentences expired in the early part of 1799. Many had arrived with only a couple of years left to serve, and as Collins said 'there was no denying them the restoration of their rights as free people'. Without means of emigrating or interest in settling, many drifted into lives of vagrancy supported by robbery, often with the collusion of convict servants and housekeepers.

Dangerous as it was, the bush had appeal. Obvious hardships aside, it promised the joy of free movement to those who were, by their very presence in Australia, anything but free. It was the one place where authority was denied dominion over their bodies. The first person charged with an offence called 'bush ranging' appears to have been Colin Hunter, an English convict who faced the magistrates on 6 February 1802. Others quickly followed. The term 'bushranger' was sometimes used for those skilled in bushcraft, but more often specified a vagabond life outside the settlements. As theft was generally necessary to maintain this existence, the definition gradually narrowed to specify outback banditry.

An important part of escape mythology's appeal was its mockery of authority's insignificance before the might and mystery of the Australian landscape. Part of officialdom's rage at convict intransigence was frustration at their own failure to impose what they considered a commonsense attitude towards the unknown terrain around them. The enormous difficulties in establishing and maintaining the colony had given exploration a low priority in the 1790s. Convicts were free to do their own mental mapping, irrefutable in the absence of any hard evidence. They had little raw material with which to build an understanding of their surrounds, but they did not waste what they had. Whatever helped them transform dream into belief was seized upon.

For obvious reasons, oral accounts gleaned from Aborigines by poorly educated or illiterate bushrangers rarely made it to print. Two that did (see Chapters 9 and 12) mention 'white people, like the English, who dress in the same manner, and have large towns' (1802) and 'people whose manners and customs strongly resembled our own' (1803). Sometimes the authorities assumed bushrangers deliberately embroidered these tales. Sometimes the Aborigines were accused of dissembling for reward, but Aboriginal tales of the unexpected had a good track record. Only two years before the white colony emerged, for example, the same sort of hearsay led to the wild herd bred from the First Fleet's missing cattle — a most welcome discovery.

Although sheer disbelief meant authority rejected the white colony stories outright, the establishment nevertheless allowed Aboriginal reportage to guide its own infatuations. In 1827, Wiradjuri tribesmen of the Wellington Valley beyond Bathurst had the surveyor William John Dumaresq utterly convinced that

> . . . there exists in the western country, many days off, a vast interior sea, where the water is salt, and where whales are seen to spout! The manner in which they imitated the whale throwing up water was so completely satisfactory as to leave little doubt of the fact, and it is not likely these inland blacks could have known it but from actual observation.

The inland sea was officialdom's preferred vision of the interior in the colony's infancy. At the dawn of the 19th century, Governor King wondered whether the newly found but still uncharted Port Phillip Bay might be the southern opening of a strait reaching all the way to the Gulf of Carpentaria — a 'popular idea in this colony', he wrote. There were other rumoured gateways, too. In 1799 we find Hunter writing to Sir

Joseph Banks of his hopes that Queensland's Hervey Bay would 'shew us a large and extensive sea within'.

The white colony's respectable cousin, the inland sea or strait also depended upon misread evidence and wishful thinking. Each combined rational and emotional projections on the unknown inland. Sir Joseph Banks, an early devotee, wrote in 1798 that he found it 'impossible to conceive' that a continent so large lacked 'vast rivers, capable of being navigated into the heart of the interior'. Thirty years later the same certainty gripped merchant-explorer William Barnes after he sailed several miles into Western Australia's Swan River. He reported 'it quite practicable to pass from thence to Port Stevens on the east coast', which he proposed to attempt. In the same period a published map filled central Australia with a fantastic lake, hundreds of miles across and linked to 'The Great River or the Desired Blessing', a channel meeting the sea at King Sound (Western Australia). Its author, TJ Maslen, declared himself 'as assured of the existence of a great river as if it had already been navigated' — the same passionate lapse in reason that sanctuary-seeking convicts were routinely accused of.

But the relationship between the twin myths of authority and felonry had even closer connections: the inland sea was sustained and developed by the very same Aboriginal ideas that fired convict escape mythology. Flinders, describing his own idea of an inland sea or strait, wrote that it was

> ... countenanced by a tradition or report amongst the native inhabitants of Port Jackson. They said, that on the west side of their mountains existed a people, who planted potatoes and maize; and when asked of what complexion were these people, they shewed the inner side of their hands, of an olive colour. Now supposing the country to be intersected by straits, or occupied by a Mediterranean sea, it was possible that some Malay vessel had been lost there; and that the crew, finding a fertile country, had established themselves in the part specified by the natives.[6]

Flinders' interpretation is far too narrow. If these Aborigines really were denoting skin colour with their palms, they had done little other than signify a lighter complexion. A colony of 'white' people could be deduced from the same evidence. The shade of an Aboriginal palm may have helped create the 'copper-coloured' people 150 miles north of Sydney. If so, the frequent pairing of apparently different destinations as 'China' and the 'white colony' may simply reflect their common Aboriginal origin.[7]

    While perceiving that Aborigines may have been describing wayward travellers, Flinders didn't stop to consider convicts a more likely prospect than Malays. Desire to solve the riddle of the interior shaped his analysis, just as desire for accessible sanctuary ruled convict interpretation of similar Aboriginal information. But while no shipwrecked Malays ever emerged from the bush, runaways continued to be stranded in this manner.

During William Paterson's exploration of the Newcastle district in June 1801, one of his soldiers spotted a European in jacket and trousers amongst Aborigines. Thus raw material for a phantom white colony continued to seep into the colony — and in this case, just before the next major outbreak of attempts to reach it.

The renegade in question was from another shortlived north-coast convict 'white colony'. In November 1800, fifteen convicts had seized the Norfolk sloop in the Hawkesbury River as she ferried a cargo of wheat to Sydney. The runaways sailed north and ran aground on Stockton Peninsula near the Coal (Hunter) River estuary. This area was still virtually untouched by Europeans; low key exploitation of its rich coal and timber resources had barely begun. The gang's luck turned when they found a pair of boats anchored in the river. Under cover of darkness they boarded and ransacked both vessels. Continuing north in the boat of their choice, they soon split up, with some going ashore before the rest reached Port Stephens. Over the next three months, nine were returned to custody (two were hanged). One of the last to stand trial, found alone near Narrabeen Lakes suffering terribly from an inflamed stingray wound, gave a brief account of what happened. Seven or eight men agreed to settle at Port Stephens 'until something should turn up favourable', but the crop they planted proved meagre and all were afflicted with fever. Disgusted, several tried to walk back to Sydney. Others, including the leader Ismael Grace, vowed never to return. A few months later, Paterson reported from the Hunter River that he had 'no doubt of Grace's being in the neighbourhood', and concluded from Aboriginal information that the European seen amongst them was the last *Norfolk* pirate left alive. The man wasn't seen again. Whoever he was, he was Newcastle's first white settler, and he owed his life to the Aborigines who gave him sanctuary.

In 1805 Governor King recalled a short trek he once authorised in response to claims by men 'locally termed Bush Rangers' that they had visited a plain across the Blue Mountains. He sent them west of the Hawkesbury–Grose river junction for a follow-up investigation, but after twelve days in the field they reported nothing he valued. The governor was left with an impression of utter desolation: 'all rocky, gravel, and heath, with springs, and bogs', with rocks to the west presenting 'the most barren and forbidding aspect, which Men, Animals, Birds and Vegetation has ever been strangers to'.

King's bushrangers did, however, come across a curious 'heap of stones' that the governor assumed George Bass had erected as a marker during his 1796 exploration. Although now considered to be Aboriginal, these rarely seen pyramidical structures were always attributed to white men in the early days. Another, found in the Blue Mountains a few years later, was dubbed 'Caley's Repulse' by Governor Macquarie, who decided George Caley, a previous explorer, must have built it — even though Caley was never in the vicinity.[8]

Talk of these mystifying cairns amongst convicts may have added credibility to white colony rumours, but early bushrangers were undoubtedly triggers for the myth themselves. If some visited the interior, others attempted to settle there. An early colonial memoir describes one such establishment in an unsuspected valley fifty miles from Sydney — three women, and men known as Charles Fox, William Pitt and Edmund

Burke. Safely hidden away, the three runaway couples built a hut, kept livestock, grew vegetables and supplemented their unlawful domestic bliss by raiding legitimate settlers. The haven lasted several years, only coming to light when a dog stolen from a farm somehow found its way home. With Aboriginal help, soldiers or constables from Parramatta followed the dog's trail into the valley, laid siege to the convicts' fortress-like hut and arrested them after a gunfight. It was said the women were excellent shots. The men's names must have been satirical aliases — it seems too outlandish a coincidence that the founders of this little bush state should share the identities of the three most famous British statesmen of their era![9]

The convict escape myths provide a tantalising glimpse of some of the earliest casual encounters between ordinary, uneducated whites and Aborigines. Some bushrangers were prosecuted for crimes committed against them; in November 1798 William Barr and Joseph Smith went to the gaol gang for 'wantonly firing at & wounding a Native & being in the habit of associating with & herding amongst the natives & using them barbarously and indecently'. James Little was returned to custody by Aborigines with whom he sought sanctuary in August 1802. Sexual access to females was undoubtedly a lure, but nevertheless very few runaways sought or received acceptance into Aboriginal communities. Bun-bo-e's mate William Knight continued to be an exception. When he reappeared amidst the Darug in 1801 with a new offsider, James Warwick, thirty gallons of rum was put on his head. A larger bounty, dead or alive, was posted when he began helping the Aboriginal leader Pemulwuy attack farms that were blocking Aborigines from the Hawkesbury River. Knight was finally run to earth in early 1802 and shipped to Norfolk Island. Pemulwuy was shot dead later the same year.

During a short exploration south of Botany Bay in March 1796, Bass and Flinders befriended two Aboriginal men at Lake Illawarra who, Flinders wrote, 'amused us by the way with stories of some white men and two women being amongst them, who had indian corn and potatoes growing'. The Aborigines promised them the women — and 'plenty of black ones', too. Whether this was a tall tale or a real outpost of runaways, such a report was likely to foster white colony rumours.

While there is no doubt that the collision of European and Australian peoples played a vital role in the rise of convict escape mythology, just what the white colony meant to its Aboriginal co-creators is virtually irrecoverable. The belief's hybrid nature is steeped in obscurity, although an example of slightly later colonial folklore, the bunyip, may offer some insight into its formation.

The bunyip, Australia's fabled water monster, first surfaced in 1823 with reports of 'monstrous' and 'extraordinary' creatures glimpsed by whites in the Fish River and Lake Bathurst. The sightings were linked to Aboriginal stories of a child-abducting 'Devil-Devil' in the lake's marshes.[10] The word *bunyip*, taken years later from an Aboriginal language in an entirely different region, eventually became the most common name for what was at first considered a new type of large semi-aquatic animal, which naturalists anticipated would show up in Australia. Eager investigators rationalised and blended a variety of indigenous beliefs in water spirits and monsters to support this presumption. Through the distorting European prism, Aboriginal mythic concepts gave definition to the colonists' expectations in much the same way that misunderstood Aboriginal information boosted the phantom colonies. Scientific credibility didn't crumble until 1847, when a bunyip skull exhibited in a Sydney museum was identified as a deformed colt or calf. The following year, a bunyip drawing by a Murray River Aborigine highlighted the communication difficulties plaguing the hybrid's construction: it appears to be an emu. Another Aboriginal bunyip sketch from the same period closely resembles an ox.

David Collins knew first-hand how difficult it was to learn anything reliable about Aboriginal manners and customs. 'They conversed with us,' he wrote in 1792, 'in a mutilated and incorrect language formed entirely on our imperfect knowledge and improper application of their words'. Watkin Tench said that three years passed before anyone learned that *beeal*, wrongly assumed to be Eora for no, actually meant good. Misunderstanding naturally went in both directions; the Eora assumed *kangaroo* — an Australian word Captain Cook had picked up in faraway north Queensland — was English for any large animal, including sheep and cattle.

A more subtle communication barrier was also in place. Europeans were as yet unaware of a general cultural norm across many Aboriginal peoples to avoid open disagreement in a meeting. Hindsight suggests the confusion over *beeal* reflects this custom, which has been described in recent times by the writer Sally Dingo:

> Greeting was not a simple procedure, and yes can often mean no. There are rules you need to abide by, and signs you need to attend to . . . To openly refuse any offer or request is considered rude and insulting, and therefore highly shameful. The word 'no' could never, would never, be uttered in such circumstances . . . no-one is forced to take an action, outside those set down in Aboriginal law and custom, which they do not wish to take. It often leads, in interactions with non-Aboriginal people, to accusations of unreliability, vagueness and even of lying.

The tendency amongst Aboriginal people to agree with questions asked by non-Aboriginals has received enough attention to have its own name — 'gratuitous concurrence'. It partly relates to Aboriginal language structure, in which 'either–or' questions are rare, and also to the protocols of greeting outsiders, a situation where displaying amiability customarily took precedence over voicing opinion. Here then is a credible explanation for Aboriginal reaction to European interrogation, and why they might readily assent to all manner of leading questions, regardless of what they really thought. On top of this, it is easy to understand an inclination towards placating potentially aggressive strangers while finding ways to direct them out of tribal territory. Some Aborigines may have been angling for reward, as colonists often presumed, or even simply indulging a sense of humour.[11]

However, the decorum behind avoiding contradiction better accounts for the spread of the rumour than its genesis. While the existence of actual renegade white settlements remains the obvious solution to this puzzle, it is also possible that the 'white colony' was — initially at least — an entirely Aboriginal concept.

Turwood's sojourn at Port Stephens provides food for thought. When told of the existence of 'immense numbers' of white people living beyond their ken, his Aboriginal benefactors 'instantly pronounced them to be the spirits of their countrymen, which, after death, had migrated into other regions'. In this way, white bush kingdoms may have been presumed in response to European information, even before runaways fashioned actual prototypes by carving out secret lives in remote areas.

The idea that Europeans were the returned dead was practically universal amongst Aboriginal groups during the earliest phase of contact. Words used for whites frequently translated as 'dead men' and 'spirits'. The meaning of John Wilson's Aboriginal name 'Bun-bo-e' was never recorded, but it may be related to the Darug verb *boi*, meaning 'to die'. Tench noted that *boee* meant 'dead' in the similar Eora tongue, which is often considered a Darug dialect. Whites struggled to understand or accept the idea at first. Collins scoffed at Turwood's tale and assumed the adoption of Wilson was merely a criminal's rat-cunning exploitation of Aboriginal naiveté, rather than his unwitting incorporation into an existing belief system.[12] Turwood himself mistook pity for reverence, boasting that his rescuers worshipped him. But the returned dead were not divine, just demented by their afterworld experience. Unable to remember tribal customs, the simplest bushcraft or even their own kin, they required careful nursing and indulgence. Meanwhile the majority of whites were treated warily — and sometimes ruthlessly, if circumstances permitted — as the spirits of strangers, or even enemies.

The *Sydney Gazette* published an early acknowledgment of Aboriginal reincarnation lore on 29 September 1825. The article discussed the Wiradjuri, a major inland tribe:

> Though they 'barloo bungumba', tumble down, the expression they use for dying, they shall 'callionnah' jump up again, but it will be as human beings from this world.

The colonists' realisation of how well they fitted this cosmology came slowly. Their tendency to arrive from the sea, frequently an afterworld for coastal tribes, carried weight. Their white faces matched the pipeclay Aborigines painted themselves with for mourning ceremonies. The very presence of such strangers had significance. Who would take pains to travel such large distances without a sense of belonging to their destination? Why would runaways enter tribal territory if they had no business there, whether as friend or foe? It was far easier — even more logical — to think of whites as coming from the spirit world than unheard-of places that could neither been seen nor visited. For all intents and purposes, a distant land beyond the seas was hardly distinguishable from an imagined realm of phantoms.

Were Aboriginal stories of the white colony an offshoot of their afterlife, the abode of pale-skinned spirits? Perhaps the convict myth — a graveyard to so many of its believers — owed its beginnings to a misunderstood description of an Aboriginal land of the dead, or an otherworld newly imagined to accommodate the revelation of European society. When explorers and absconders asked about white people (or even just generally about the terrain) beyond the mountains, were they in effect asking directions to this shadowland? If so, a poignant irony raises itself. Although shaping an Aboriginal idea to their own purposes, convict believers saw the bush route to sanctuary in much the same light — the way back to a white homeland.

CHAPTER EIGHT

Their natural vicious propensities

The Irish peasant believes that the utmost he can
dream was once or still is a reality by his own door.
He will point to some mountain and tell you that
some famous hero or beauty lived and sorrowed there,
or he will tell you that Tir-na-nog, the Country of
the Young, the old Celtic paradise — the Land of the
Living Heart, as it used to be called — is all about him.

WB YEATS

HERE'S AN IRISH JOKE FROM AN EARLY COLONIAL MEMOIR, ABOUT
the only individual 'known to have positively reached China through
means of a footpath'. This proverbial Irishman, a transported convict,
escapes to spend three weeks toiling across the hills and valleys of New
South Wales. At last a crowing cock alerts 'Paddy' that he has made it:

With shouts of 'China for ever!' he hobbled onwards, eager to feast his
eyes with the beauties of a Chinese landscape, and hungry enough to
feast even on a raw Chinaman himself — Lent time though it was.

Soon the 'adventurous Hibernian' bursts upon a 'trim-built cottage'. Standing in the garden is a man in European costume — one Colonel Johnstone of the NSW Corps. 'Arrah!' exclaims Paddy, blissfully unaware he has trudged full circle back to the hated penal settlement. 'Long life to you, Colonel! And what has brought your honour to China all the way?'

Within the joke is a double meaning a more sympathetic teller might emphasise — that Paddy realises exactly where he is and uses his wit to make the best of a bad situation. A contemporary variation has Paddy cut a picture of a compass from a book and paste it on the crown of his hat, hoping to fix a north-westerly course. But a fortnight's hard slog through the bush comes to nothing. Poor simple Paddy puts his hat on backwards one morning — and follows his paper compass back to Sydney!

Paddy is not only Irish. He's an Irish criminal and, as the joke takes care to point out, a Catholic, too. In other words, in the eyes of Enlightenment Britain he is irrationality incarnate, the furthest from civilised — and the closest to a laughing stock — that a white man could possibly be. Overwhelmingly the religion of the so-called 'wild' Irish peasantry, Catholicism had dangerous associations with Jacobinism and other revolutionary movements. Its presumed opposition to the separation of church and state was a further stigma, and together these objections contributed to Catholics being legally forbidden to hold any British public office until 1829. In New South Wales, Catholicism and convictism were inextricably linked. Almost every Catholic in the colony during its first four decades was an Irish transportee. Even after large-scale free emigration got underway, a *Sydney Herald* editorial (26 August 1840) railed against the numbers of Irish arriving, scandalised that unwanted 'herds' from the south of Ireland were 'generally ignorant, indolent, vicious and priest-ridden, of disorderly habits, unmanly tempers and unskilful'.

The extent of this xenophobia is reflected in the continued identification of Irish convicts with the whimsy of escape mythology well after its documented adoption by other nationalities. The Irish jokes above, for example, were published some thirty years after this transition. Unfortunately, the nature of the belief suited contemporary prejudice, and the effect of Irish dominance throughout its earliest, most disruptive years proved indelible.

But did English convicts take up the enthusiasm earlier than the evidence attests? Even if the Irish were particularly desperate and marginalised, English convicts were desperate too — and similarly ignorant of global geography. Their early participation in myth-based escapes may have been masked to some extent by anti-Irish bias, as English believers are found as soon as the names of absconders appear in trial records. Yet all contemporary sources insist that the very first Chinese travellers were exclusively Irish, and Tench even took peculiarly modern pains to assure his readers that this was *not* a prejudiced generalisation:

> I trust that no man would feel more reluctant than myself to cast an illiberal national reflection, particularly on a people whom I regard in an aggregate sense as brethren and fellow-citizens; and among whom I have the honour to number many of the most cordial and endearing intimacies which a life passed on service could generate. But it is certain that all these people were *Irish*.

His contemporaries were rarely so sensitive or considerate. The fire-breathing Reverend Marsden, a holy terror to the Irish as Parramatta's chief magistrate, famously damned Catholic convicts as 'the lowest class of the Irish nation; who are the most wild, ignorant and savage race that were ever favoured with the light of civilisation'. David Collins found them 'ignorant and weak' in their enthusiasm for lands beyond the mountains, which revealed only their wickedness, idiocy and inability to come to terms with their rightful place in the imperial power structure. Governor Hunter similarly saw it as just more madness from lesser beings already lost to their 'natural vicious propensities'. The phrase contains all that he deplored in them — his presumption of their inherent criminality; his Presbyterian disdain for their rum and tobacco; and most of all, his horror at their proven capacity for revolt.

To the colonial authorities, it was only sensible for the convicts to accept their station in life as meted out by law. To do so was, in a sense, to demonstrate the ability to think rationally. Transportees were expected to earn whatever dismal comforts the colony could provide by enduring the hardships of their sentence. But the Irish fought the system harder than anybody. As much as English convicts resented their servitude, they weren't as apt to consider themselves beyond British jurisdiction. Of course, the Irish convicts' well-documented reputation for violence and troublemaking was a symptom, not the cause, of the turbulence in their country. This escaped the notice of Hunter and others, as did another aspect of their search for promised lands — the inclination to look on independent countries as allies against Britain's 'hostile crown'.[1] Unlike their English counterparts, Irish convicts could at least hope that other countries — real or imagined — would see them as victims rather than transgressors of British law. Another overlooked pressure was their forced removal from Catholic community. Exile to a place where the Mass was outlawed as a seditious assembly was tantamount to spiritual damnation. And so, as if reflecting a longing for familiar religious comforts — and the traditional role of churches in granting sanctuary to fugitives — descriptions of phantom colonies often emphasised places of worship. In 1802, an Irish overseer at Castle Hill (see Chapter 9) spoke of a nearby civilisation 'full of chapels and churches'. A year later the Sydney Gazette (3 July 1803, see Chapter 11) reported that believers thought their overland white colony was 'possessed of bells, churches, masted vessels, a sterling specie, and every other requisite that might seem calculated to convey the idea of civilization'.

Hunter and Collins missed the true depth of Irish despair, not seeing how the mad flights to nowhere articulated helplessness, homesickness, an urgency to shake off the intolerable and return to the familiar. Irish stereotyping is deeply ingrained in their assumption that believers were hapless dupes of more cunning and savvy prisoners, rather than victims of their own misguided initiative. Tench better understood an exile's agony, and openly sympathised with the Mary Bryant gang of absconders that rowed to Timor ('a heroic struggle for liberty'), confessing he regarded them with 'pity and astonishment'. But even he dismissed the first walk to China as 'an extraordinary instance of folly stimulated to desperation', when really the reverse was closer to the truth.

For all the officials' self-righteousness, however, they were not completely off the mark, because escape mythology clearly had a strong grounding in the non-rational. How far did subconscious and mythological associations intensify Irish response to transportation and help shape their perception of accessible sanctuary?

Britain's Age of Enlightenment had little time for spirituality outside conventional Protestant Christianity. Dead religions such as classical mythology were allowed refuge in literature and art, but living examples were supernatural fantasies fit only to be swept aside by the rise of rationalism. Such a worldview could only regard Aboriginal beliefs as primitive and childlike, evidence of a backward culture. Irish peasant lore was similarly deemed nonsensical. The Irish rebel leader Joseph Holt, who arrived in Australia in 1800, decried the superstitious nature of his less-educated countrymen when he uncharitably described Aborigines as 'afeared by night, like feeble minded people in Ireland'. Educated Irish convicts, it seems, could be as dismissive of bush-Chinas as their colonial overlords. Two known to resort to extreme escape measures (the lawyer Laurence Davoren in 1794 and Thomas Prosser in 1807) were willing to ape the Bryants by chancing a leaky boat to the distant East Indies, but left overland adventuring to the less-informed.

However it originated, the overland option was above all else a story. And Ireland has long boasted an especially rich storytelling culture. Late 19th century folklorists, rushing to record what they feared were dying traditions, were struck by how closely many Irish stories reflected, in theme and content, the great pagan myth cycles preserved (if Christianised) in medieval Irish manuscripts. Peasant fairytales in Ireland were often much more than idle fireside amusements. Frequently retaining the force of myth, they tended to be literally believed in by both the teller and the audience. This native tradition was naturally best preserved in the dwindling Gaeltacht, which still covered much of western Ireland in 1800 — a time when up to two in every five Irish people spoke Irish only. By comparison, England suffered a rapid and extensive loss of its oral folklore, the price of relatively early industrialisation and urbanisation.

In its promises of sanctuary beyond, and in the sincere belief this attracted, the phantom white colony could easily pass for an imported Irish myth. Perilous transformational journeys to mysterious places abound in Irish tales. Voyages to unknown countries also carried strong mythic connotations. We cannot know the extent to which the unlucky dip of 18th-century Irish transportees were steeped in their own folk traditions, but the possibility of havens hidden beyond deep woods and mirage-filled mountains clearly struck a chord. The manner of myth-making they took up after landing at Sydney suggests the legends of their homeland helped them cope with their displacement. More so, perhaps, than convicts from England, they were subconsciously primed to flee to presumed 'other-places' as the next act in the theatre of their snatching away. Furthermore, cancellation of the overlords' geography was a sublimated invalidation of their dominion over Irish bodies. Escape mythology offered a liberating redefinition of the new world on their own terms, one which gave shape to their desire to escape, to correct the inversion of their lives wrought by transportation.

Exile had been used as a punishment in Ireland for a long time. Until the American War of Independence, Britain had spent much of the 18th century sending convicts to its New World colonies, including some 13,000 Irish. But removal to somewhere as utterly distant as Botany Bay brought special terrors. A correspondent to the *Hibernian Journal*

(19 June 1789) gives some idea how this new place of exile was received in Ireland:

> Great Britain has adopted a mode of punishing reprieved criminals, more cruel than the death they have escaped. A desert corner of the earth, in the almost unknown terra Australis, far removed from converse, except with each other; surrounded by desperate cannibals, that devour men's flesh, whose territories, however savage, we have no right to invade, are considerations that should have struck the Minister with horror, at the cruelty and injustice of the proceeding.

The very name 'Botany Bay' is the convict era's most enduring myth of place. No convicts were ever landed there, yet the name is chained to transportation in popular culture even today. Phillip quickly rejected it in 1788 and took the First Fleet to Sydney Cove instead, but Botany Bay had been percolating through English and Irish minds since the days of Captain Cook; its appeal as an alliterative ballad lyric undoubtedly also helped immortalise it. In any case, accuracy of information was not on the authorities' agenda in 1791. What mattered was encouraging notions of the southern land as a place of unknown horrors, a vague hell to which miscreants disappeared forever.

Conversely, the happy other-place was a longstanding staple of Irish culture. During his boyhood in Sydney, the folklorist Joseph Jacobs (1854–1916) heard from his nurse a variation of *The Vision of MacConglinney*, an Irish tale which was by then at least five centuries old. The version in his *More Celtic Fairy Tales* (1894), written for Victorian-era children, describes travelling to 'a lake of new milk . . . in the midst of a fair plain' where a 'well-appointed' house is entirely made of delicious food. Michael Comyn's epic poem *Land of Youth* (1749) describes in more mature terms a similar haven of never-ending fruit and honey, a dreamland of plenty where pain and sickness are unknown. In another story collected by Jacobs, *The Dream of Owen O'Mulready*, the protagonist sets off for America with a mindset echoed by almost every white colony seeker:

> 'Where are you going this time of night?' says the boy.
>
> 'I'm going to America, with a letter from the master; is this the right road?' says Owen.
>
> 'It is; keep straight to the west; but how are you going to get over the water?' says the boy.
>
> 'Time enough to think of that when I get to it,' replied Owen.

That real places could be enmeshed in this mythologising is well-illustrated by the 88-year-old Fermanagh man who claimed in about 1911 that a man he knew well had been taken to America on Hallow Eve Night by the fairies some seventy years previously. After observing his expatriate daughter in her house, and a friend at another American location, the man was whisked home to Ireland by morning.

West across the North Atlantic, America occupied the space that tradition had once assigned to a host of Celtic otherworlds. The semi-legendary sixth-century voyage of St Brendan, reputed to be the first New World landing by Europeans, apparently began as a quest for the pagan Irish Heaven. But by 1791, when the *Queen* left Cork Harbour, America was a land of promise, not mystery. The war for independence was eight years past and the new nation was a shining beacon for republican dreams. 'Botany Bay' was the exact opposite, a hell still as shadowy as the heaven-worlds also somewhere across the sea. These dreamlands had many names and attributes: there was *Tir-na-nog* (Land of Youth); *Tir N-aill*, (The Other Land); *Tir-Innambeo* (Land of the Living); *Tir Tairngire*, (Land of Promise); *Mag Mar* (The Great Plain) and *Mag Mell*, (The Plain Agreeable, or Happy). Irish transportees were bound for an otherworld less esoteric, less familiar, and definitely less happy. Before sailing down the globe and then east across the Southern Ocean, the convict ships travelled west into the Atlantic, into the old sunset realm of myth. Doubtless some of the luckless Irish below decks made their own internal escapes, imaginative journeys into the realms of their fabled past. When it came time to assess their new world — and the chances for escape — those realms returned to haunt them again.

Hy-Brasil, the phantom island off Ireland's west coast, provides an especially close parallel to convict escape mythology. The island itself was more than a legend, although it never existed. Most probably a high-latitude (Arctic) mirage, it appears on various maps from the 14th century and was noted as 'Brasil Rock' on a British admiralty chart as late as 1850. Irish tradition filled its blanks. Like New South Wales, it was credited with a mystery civilisation, a prosperous and hospitable people whose buildings were plated with gold. Curiously, Hy-Brasil also boasted an inland sea of sorts, a semicircular watercourse at its centre. Sometimes it was represented as bisected by a river. And like New South Wales, its dimensions were uncertain. On his supposed visit, St Brendan had tried — and failed — to discover the island's limits on foot.

The crude 'compasses' and maps carried by runaways also deserve to be considered in the context of Irish myth. Outwardly the compass was a practical innovation, perhaps a misguided aping of navigational methods observed at sea. Some seekers may have been conned by unscrupulous tricksters who saw a ready market for such aids. But were symbolic, subconscious attractions at work? Another frequent Irish folkloric motif is the necessity of a special passport or key to the otherworld. In one well-known myth, a silver branch proves Cormac's entry to the Land of Promise, where there is 'neither age nor decay nor gloom nor sadness nor envy nor jealousy nor hatred nor haughtiness'. A similar talisman transported Bran and friends to the Island of Joy and the magical Island of Women. While convict runaways were not striving to reach literal fairy lands, traditions like these may have helped prime their faith in paper compasses as much as their ignorance of the principles of magnetism.[2]

The Irish enthusiasm may have received an additional emotional boost by aspects of Aboriginal white colony descriptions which superficially evoked the Celtic otherworlds, such as abundant crops and livestock, grand buildings and large bodies of water. Ultimately, Irish fairy lands derive from pre-Christian lands of the dead and, unlike the Judeo-Christian concept of Heaven, both Celtic and Aboriginal mythology located the afterlife on this plane of existence. This is not to say that Irish convicts enjoyed a special empathy with indigenous cultures. The convict workforce was at the business end of dispossession and, although relations were not relentlessly hostile, convicts were generally the Aborigines' worst enemies, regardless of nationality. And far from being partial to the Irish, Aborigines began making a curious generalisation about the colony's internal divisions, contemptuously referring to all convicts as 'croppies'. This term, in common colonial use by the early 19th century, was a nickname for Irish republican rebels, who cropped their hair short in the manner of French revolutionaries. Aborigines, unequipped to decipher the subtle tangle of English–Irish and convict–Crown oppositions, naturally assumed it referred to convicts in general, who certainly resembled a defeated enemy people within colonial society.

But no matter how deeply its appeal was rooted in Irish myth, the phantom colony was every bit as mundane as Botany Bay in the mind's eye of a believer. It was not a supernatural otherworld, but an everyday place without magical attributes. Prompted by Aboriginal evidence and geographical speculations, it was deduced as much as it was imagined. The dearth of detail indicates it tended not to be embroidered by conscious invention. The rational and non-rational both played roles in supporting the hypothesis of its existence, resulting in a lure that made sense to the heart as well as the head. Believers looked to a real world of possibility rather than a heavenly dream-world, a workable solution to a dire problem. And as the 18th century drew to a close, Irish problems seemed more dire than ever.

The Irish Rebellion of 1798 had dramatic repercussions for New South Wales. In May 1798, English artillery and cavalry had cut the Irish rebel forces to pieces at the Battle of Vinegar Hill near Enniscorthy. Some Irish leaders held out during a chaotic aftermath marred by numerous atrocities, but the uprising was effectively over before the year ended. Soon hundreds of prisoners were on their way to Australia. Some were shipped without formal trial. This technically made them exiles, not convicts, but few enjoyed any real distinction from transported criminals. Soon they would continue their struggle with an uprising that, while small by comparison, was the largest convict rebellion to occur in the colony.

The first news of the Irish rebellion reached colonial ears early in 1799. Thinking that British rule had been overthrown, some Irish convicts began insisting their sentences were no longer valid. Between January 1800 and May 1803 the colony absorbed just over a thousand Irish prisoners, about half the convict intake for the period. A high proportion is reckoned to have been the flotsam and jetsam of the scuttled Irish rebellion. The *Minerva*, the first of these rebel transports, entered Port Jackson one January dawn in 1800. A shipboard witness records the first sign of civilisation to greet them: the gibbeted skeleton of an executed murderer, Francis Morgan, three years dead but still creaking in the sea breeze on the harbour's Pinchgut Island. The macabre image would prove something of an omen.

The *Friendship* followed the *Minerva* in February. The arrival of the first real political prisoners from Ireland fanned the flames of paranoia. One of Hunter's last actions as governor was to initiate a court of inquiry into alleged Irish plotting. The investigation was held over nine days in September 1800, as the incoming governor, Philip Gidley King, hovered in the wings, eager to take on the colony's particular administrative nightmares. A much-vaunted weapon stash was never unearthed, but five *Minerva* Irishmen were sentenced to 500 lashes and four to 100 each. Some were accused of seditious conspiracy simply because they had been heard speaking Gaelic. Before the month was out, Reverend Samuel Marsden reported a similar 'horrible plot' amongst the Irish at Parramatta. Again the evidence was sketchy but presumed ringleaders were savagely punished, with some whipped in an effort to extract confessions.

On 21 February 1801 the *Anne* imported 137 of what Governor King called 'the most desperate and diabolical characters that could be selected throughout the kingdom'. An ill-starred attempt to seize the ship at sea occurred while the convict quarters were being fumigated with gunpowder. Rallied by the rebel cry 'Death or liberty!', some went for the master's throat as others, still in their irons, stormed the guard on deck. Two convicts were shot dead, one during the brief struggle and one afterwards by firing squad. More rumours of Irish plots followed the *Anne*'s arrival, resulting in more floggings and transfers to Norfolk Island. Governor King established a militia, but trouble subsided and by August he disbanded it, praising the 'regular and quiet behaviour' of the Irish prisoners. This lull was temporary, however; for many, exile only exacerbated their opposition to British domination.

The reappearance of escape myths came, like the outbursts of '91 and '97, in the shadow of a large influx of Irish prisoners rendered especially bitter and reckless by bad treatment. Between June and October 1802 the *Hercules*, *Atlas I* and *Atlas II* transports delivered 369 male and fifty-one female Irish prisoners. King was appalled to find the *Hercules* and *Atlas I* arrivals 'filthy beyond description'. Some were dead in their irons, and others died between the ship and the hospital. When the *Hercules* was a month at sea, some male convicts had burst free and attacked the guards on deck. It took several minutes of fierce fighting for the soldiers and seamen to force them back below. Thirteen convicts were killed. About an hour later, Captain Luckyn Betts strode up to the ringleader, Jeremiah Prendergast, and shot him through the head as he sat secured on deck. The other mutineers were closely confined for the rest of the voyage; this killed thirty of them. A further forty-three needed medical treatment upon landing, of whom eighteen died soon afterwards. King complained to London that the colony had to slaughter an extra ox per week to get the hospitalised survivors up to strength.

Betts was acquitted of culpability for the convicts killed during the fight, but the cold-blooded shooting of Prendergast attracted a 500-pound fine for manslaughter. At first King ruled this payable to his newly established orphanage, but had second thoughts. Aware that the Admiralty routinely overturned manslaughter convictions at sea, he suspended the sentence pending a final decision from England. This never came, so like captains Owen, Hogan and Dennott before him, Betts got away scot-free.

Even more vile was Captain Brooks of the *Atlas I*, architect of the highest death rate in percentage terms for any convict voyage. He crammed in so much merchandise for sale in ports of call that the ship sat too low in the water to keep the air scuttles open. Many prisoners were embarked with typhus and dysentery, and fifteen died before reaching Rio de Janeiro. Here the sick were allowed to recuperate on land, but only because Brooks wanted to reload the cargo to squeeze room for extra goods to trade in Sydney. Then, defying his orders on the pretext of a nonexistent convict mutiny, he stopped off at Cape Town to line his pockets with even more private commerce.

Ventilation grew so poor there wasn't enough oxygen in the convict quarters to keep a single candle burning. Brooks' murderous greed also extended to the old tricks of stealing convict rations through false weights and measures, denying them adequate water and refusing to air or clean the bedding, which was frequently soaked during heavy weather. Of 176 embarked, two females and sixty-three males died at sea, a death rate of thirty-seven per cent that outstripped even the typhoid-struck English 'fever ship' of 1799, the *Hillsborough* (thirty-two per cent). Another four *Atlas* men died in port. When the sails of the *Atlas II* were sighted above the horizon four months later Sydneysiders began taking bets on the mortality rate, so it came as a huge surprise that no lives were lost and the convicts were fit for immediate labour. After the master of the first *Atlas* was questioned by a magistrate for withholding provisions from both convicts and passengers, King wrote to London requesting clarification of the powers of colonial courts to redress such complaints.

As feared as the Irish were, the new governor's real opposition was the upper strata of colonial society. He had already antagonised them by reducing their total number of convict servants from 356 to ninety-four. Although fed and clothed at government expense, these prisoners worked only to enrich a handful of what King described as the 'vultures' of the officer class. King also made a concerted effort to break their monopoly trading in imported spirits. He even opened a brewery, hoping to coax the rum-sodden farmers into an alternative poison.

Hunter's term had finished with many settlers bankrupted by the officer-based trading cartel and dependent on grain doled out by the government. Much of this was imported at great expense. King's cost-cutting solution was to start a large government farm at Castle Hill, eight miles north of Parramatta. While waiting for the venture to find its feet, he rented 300 acres of Hawkesbury farmland called Cornwallis Place. The scheme was a success; by June 1803 the government had 710 acres under cultivation at Castle Hill, Toongabbie and Hawkesbury.

Hours of labour at Castle Hill were set from dawn to 3 pm, with a one-hour break at 8 am. The convicts were worked very hard but one concession was a pass system, where men who completed three weeks work in a fortnight were allowed to earn money by working overtime at private farms where extra labour was needed.

Many of the Irish arriving in 1802 were put to work at Castle Hill. Thick forests fell rapidly to convict axes; the sky filled with flame and smoke from the burning of deadwood in the hills and valleys. By early November a hundred acres were cleared and cropped.

The number of Irish arrivals now matched those from England for the first time, altering the colony's ethnic makeup. Eight ships had landed 735 men and 137 women from England between the arrivals of the Irish rebel ships *Minerva* and *Atlas II*; nevertheless by the end of 1802 a full quarter of the convict population was Irish. Most new English arrivals enjoyed relatively humane voyages: the *Royal Admiral* and *Earl Cornwallis* were disasters with a combined seventy-eight deaths, but the other six ships had only thirteen casualties between them.

Newly landed English convicts also made bids for the phantom colony, although the belief continued to be stereotyped as an Irish infatuation. Some said they first heard the tale at sea; court minutes suggest at least two ships from England — the *Perseus* (14 August 1802) and the *Glatton* (12 March 1803) — imported convicts already inspired by escape myths. Descriptions may have spread in England from the books of Tench, Hunter, Collins and Barrington, all of which were in print by 1798. However, as a natural topic for shipboard and portside gossip, the myth's dissemination was probably inevitable, given the steady trickle of maritime traffic between colony and mother country over several years.

By late 1802, Castle Hill had emerged as the myth's new capital. The large concentration of newly arrived prisoners facilitated the spread of rumour, unrest and ultimately, conspiracy. Fuelled by the gossip that disembarked with newcomers and found confirmation amongst older hands, the tale of a sanctuary across the mountains once again provoked enough disruption to require a governor's direct intervention.

CHAPTER 9

King of the mountains

The preservation of public tranquillity and frustrating
the Diabolical Schemes of the Ill-disposed is the first
and most imperious Necessity in a Colony generally
composed of felons, Rebels and Republicans.

GOVERNOR KING, 20 JULY 1805

ON 21 AUGUST 1802, A ROUTINE BENCH OF MAGISTRATES SITTING
in Sydney was enlivened by the extraordinary testimony of an escapee
named John Day. After making his way into the mountains, he reported
himself gazing upon nothing less than a completely unsuspected town!
The court recorded that he

> . . . had absconded from the gaol gang and pretended he went in quest
> of a New Settlement. Being interrogated as to his views, he fabricated
> a story of having passed five ridges of the Blue Mountains and
> discovered a town, which he did not go into, but [illegible; perhaps
> 'instead' or 'immediately'] returned.

Day stood charged with stealing goats and sheep in company with James Riley, an Irishman who had also fled the gaol gang. A third miscreant, Roger Bridgen, was charged as their accomplice in goat-stealing and 'other depredations on the public'. Riley and Bridgen were not specifically linked to Day's claimed mountain jaunt, but stock theft would have been an obvious way to provision such an expedition. Day and Riley were sentenced to 200 lashes, Bridgen 100, and all three went to the gaol gang in double-irons.[1]

Day's evidence was precisely the sort of traveller's tale that was igniting enthusiasm for a bush sanctuary. But he was more than just another wayward bushranger. His trip may have been prompted by the belief to begin with; Day is the first identifiably English convict claiming to have fallen under its spell. And as an eyewitness report his phantom settlement is doubly unusual.

The magistrates probably dismissed Day's excursion as a false alibi for the stock theft charges, or else considered his town a ruse to delay punishment. They may have been right, but it would be wrong to dismiss Day out of hand. The bush was apt to conjure such visions, even in the eyes of the most eminent colonials. In 1795, a legitimate Blue Mountains expedition noted 'a most picturesque and romantic view, the sun shining on rocks; they appeared to the beholder like towns and castles in ruins'. Years later, that indefatigable traveller Governor Macquarie was similarly enchanted in the bush by rocks of 'various odd shapes, isolated, and about sixty feet in height, some of the sides of these masses being quite perpendicular, and like the walls of an old castle'.

How the outback's faux-castles appeared to less sophisticated minds, especially those anxious to locate such sights, can be easily guessed. The mental and physical distress suffered by many runaways was obviously acute, their perception disoriented by hunger, exhaustion and probably hypothermia. Under the most trying conditions, it's no surprise that distant rock formations should seem to confirm those wondrous tales of hidden white towns.

To the court, however, Day was just another opportunist feigning an important discovery while at large. The best remembered of these charlatans was James Daley, the 'Goldfinder' of 1788, who enjoyed brief celebrity in the colony's first year by claiming to have located a gold mine. His deception was quickly exposed, but many convicts were sure he kept the real mine secret for future profit. Collins' haughty interpretation of this reaction — 'so easy it is to impose on the minds of a lower class of people' — was oblivious to the deep longing driving such fantasies, but it reflects the resilience of even the most unlikely rumours amongst the convicts, particularly ones pointing to wealth or freedom. Fourteen years later in 1802, the need to believe in a bush sanctuary was likewise stronger than rational arguments against its existence or accessibility.

Was Day exploiting convict rumours of nearby societies, banking on a chance to slip away should his captors ask to be shown this 'New Settlement'? Or was his town a bush mirage? Sunlight dancing on distant outcrops, a valley view warped with heat haze; all manner of natural phenomena could have led his strained senses astray. It is likely his time at large was unusually arduous. Three weeks after the trial, a convict named John Day was buried in Sydney. Had 200 lashes — savage punishment, but normally no death sentence — proved too much for his weakened constitution? If so, it's a shame he didn't at least live to be vindicated, because before the year was out a government expedition also saw what appeared to be houses in the Blue Mountains.

The leader of this mission, Francis Barrallier, was a 29-year-old French refugee. His efforts represented the first officially sanctioned bid for the interior since Wilson, Price and Roe in 1798. And like his predecessors, Barrallier's opportunity was directly connected to a governor's desire to quash convict escape mythology.

Evacuated from Toulon when it fell to Napoleon in 1793, Barrallier fled to Italy, but soon followed his father to England, where the elder Barrallier had used his aristocratic contacts to become a naval surveyor. Through his father, Barrallier obtained passage to New South Wales on the same ship as the incoming Governor King. A man of many talents, he hoped for a surveying or engineering position in the young colony. The only opportunity, however, was a shortage of officers in the NSW Corps, so he took an ensign's commission on 2 July 1800.

Barrallier was the only French officer in the Corps, and was atypical in other ways. Exploration was his passion, and he urged King to allow him to venture into the mountains and seek the longed-for crossing. His first bush venture came early in 1801, a short foray involving the accidental rescue of two runaways guilty of pirating the *Norfolk* sloop. Throughout the year his surveying skills were put to good use on three other expeditions — a mapping trip to Westernport, Victoria, and two explorations of the Newcastle district. He vividly described the 'terrible crash' of waves at the mouth of the Coal (Hunter) River where the *Norfolk* had come to grief, wild enough to 'make the bravest sailor tremble'. The journal Barrallier kept of his most significant journey, into the secret heart of the Blue Mountains, also brims with this wide-eyed sense of wonder.

Governor King was anxious to secure the continent from Napoleon with more settlements, but in 1801 the shipping lanes were the priority locations, not the interior. King was keen on the coastline of the Labyrinth (the Great Barrier Reef), musing that the tropical north might enable a thriving cotton industry for the China market. However, when King outlined this unrealised plan on 31 December 1801, he also announced that an officer would be sent 'to endeavour ascertaining whether there is a passage thro' the mountains'.

The idea was to establish a chain of depots to provision longer journeys, but when King wrote to England the following March it was still all talk. Three months later King sent a salt sample 'from a hollow in the mountains' to Sir Joseph Banks in England, adding that heavy rainfall had set in and would delay the mountain expedition until at least October. If the project had been allowed to lapse while Barrallier waited for the weather to clear, the landings of the *Hercules* and *Atlas I* gave it renewed urgency.

In the midst of a new outbreak of bids for the phantom colony — which we shall examine shortly — King reignited his scheme, depots and all. Sometime in late September or early October 1802, Barrallier completed several days reconnaissance for a likely spot to attempt a mountain passage. Travelling south across the Cowpastures and into the Razorback Range with four companions, he discovered the Nattai River and chose the site for his first depot — by a creek above the Nattai Valley, about forty-five miles south-west of Sydney near the present-day town of Oakdale.

At this point the NSW Corps' commanding officer, Lieutenant-Colonel William Paterson, suddenly put a stop to Barrallier's explorations. His reasons aren't quite clear, but they derived from a tangled spat involving Surgeon John Harris, a Corps officer employed as Sydney's harbourmaster. Harris was rather too conscientious in limiting liquor imports for the liking of his brother officers, who profited by the trade, and found himself court-martialled after informing Governor King of complaints they had made about missing out on brandy from the *Atlas I*. Paterson was not a trader himself, but found his subordinate's tale-telling 'ungentlemanlike', a violation of 'all discipline, command and respect' that was his due.[2]

During a heated exchange of letters with King over the affair, Paterson claimed to always put the colony's welfare first, even if this meant 'acting contrary' to certain Royal instructions. King demanded to know what he meant. Paterson revealed he had received orders from the Duke of York on 10 July — it was now 8 October — which forbade officers 'on any account whatever to engage into the cultivation of farms, or in any occupation that are to detach them from their military duty'.

Paterson named Harris as being 'frequently detached' from his duties — and also Barrallier, as roaming about the bush searching for mountain passes was hardly a regimental function either. He had accepted these illegitimate arrangements not just for the colony's good but also, Paterson said, so as 'not to frustrate your Excellency's wishes'.

Whether he intended it or not, his revelation left King no choice but to acquiesce to the Duke's orders immediately.

Had Paterson really schemed to remove the conflict of interest beknighting Harris? If so it was a deviously clever move. Or had he simply made a hamfisted, petulant expression of loyalty to King, not seeing its full import until it was too late? As he was a notably weak and compliant leader, it could also be wondered whether the liquor traders persuaded him to invoke the Duke's orders just to hobble their enemy Harris. They clearly weren't too troubled by rules which also banned military officers from farming, which they would continue to flout despite Paterson's orders to desist after the current crop was in.

King replied on the same day, requesting Paterson order Barrallier to his duty and asking what part of Harris's occupation he objected to. The letter carries a sting in the tail, grandly reminding Paterson that Harris and Barrallier had undertaken their 'zealous and highly useful duties' with his 'entire approbation'. Paterson now covered himself, as if worried he might get into trouble for ignoring the rules for three months. The next day he informed King he hadn't intended the revelation to cost the men their civil posts, but nevertheless would accept no blame for any fallout:

> When I mentioned those two officers I did not mean to deprive the public of their services; but from the unfortunate misunderstanding that at present exists between your Excellency and me, I must beg that you will take the responsibility of their holding any other occupations than their military duties upon yourself.

King was now ropeable. 'How could I agree to this,' he noted in the letter's margin, 'and subject myself to future humiliations?' He published a bitterly sarcastic General Order, stating that he,

> . . . being anxious to pay every deference and obedience to Lt–Col Paterson's Idea of that Instruction, dispenses in future with the

valuable assistance he has hitherto received from those Officers with
the Lt-Colonel's entire Approbation.

Following was a detailed summary of the many accomplishments and
abilities of Harris and Barrallier now lost to the colony, including the
Frenchman's 'advancement of the Geography and the Natural History of
the Territory'. Then, finding it 'necessary to anticipate any interpretation'
of the Duke's orders Paterson might make in the future, King replaced
his five-man military bodyguard with trusted convicts — a pointed insult
— and removed the Corps paymaster from magisterial duties.

He had lost his harbourmaster, but King was determined to keep
Barrallier. Over the next few days he dreamed up a countermove as
creative as it was bizarre. In order for the exploration to proceed, he
exercised his right to appoint a Corps officer his aide-de-camp, a
position vacant since March. In this capacity Barrallier could enter
the bush as official envoy to an entity the governor later described to
Sir Joseph Banks as 'the King of the Mountains'. The trip no longer
contravened Royal regulations; the governor was entitled to an aide-
de-camp and diplomatic representation was a legitimate duty of the
position. The secondment was announced on 18 October with — as King
triumphantly added — 'Lieut. Col'l Paterson's previous consent'.

I find it unlikely that the King of the Mountains was a hypothetical
Aboriginal leader, as some historians have speculated. That would have
invited a very easy refutation: why make ambassadorial overtures to people
already classed as Crown subjects? However, the ruse was watertight
if it implied a visit to a rival colony or sovereign state in the European
sense. Barrallier's involvement would then appear more consistent
with an aide-de-camp appointment than a forbidden detachment from
military duties. Most probably the King of the Mountains was a facetious
reference to a supposed ruler of the convicts' New Settlement, designed
to hamstring any objections Paterson might make or — unless King
dreamed up the phrase in retrospect — just to annoy the hell out of him.

It could even have been a pun; the (Governor) King of New South Wales sending his greetings to his mythical equivalent, the Philip Gidley King of the Mountains. It matches other instances of King's sense of humour, which tended towards a blunt playfulness with words. The success of the outré tactic delighted him, if his letter to Banks seven months later is any indication. Barrallier's journey, he explains

> . . . I was obliged to effect by ruse, as Col. Paterson had very illiberally informed me that officers being at all detached from regimental duty was contrary to the Instructions he had from the Duke of York. In consequence, I was obliged to give up his [Barrallier's] services after this unhandsome claim, but claimed him as my aide-de-camp, and that the object of discovery should not be totally relinquished, I sent him on an embassy to the King of The Mountains.

And so Governor King enjoyed a rare victory. Paterson was left with no recourse, however chagrined he may have been that his ensign was now playing the envoy to a fictional country. We can imagine the sour grapes of King's no-nonsense rivals in the Corps, thoroughly outfoxed — or at least Paterson, if he really didn't care how King resolved Barrallier's status, rolling his eyes at this outrageous piece of whimsy. Paterson couldn't categorically deny the existence of this apparent absurdity unless he was prepared to reconnoitre its alleged location. Which just happened to be against Royal regulations.

On 9 November, a few days after Barrallier set off, King wrote to Lord Hobart, Secretary of State for War and the Colonies. The dispatch contained his version of the Harris affair, but also outlined why it was high time the mountains were demystified:

> Many of the Irish Convicts lately arrived having been persuaded that a Settlement of Europeans, exists beyond the Mountains, I have sent an Officer to explore them, and convince those thoughtless People

of their Folley, and as the abilities of Ens'n Barrallier (who now acts as my Aid-du-Camp) points him out as the most eligible Person to send on that service, I have established Two Depots of Provisions in different parts of the Mountains, which will enable him to persevere, and obtain a more perfect knowledge of the interior of this Country.

Escape mythology's appearance as the trip's raison d'être at this stage is further evidence that it inspired the governor's King of the Mountains. But was Barrallier really sent to quash the convict belief? As King had mooted the exploration a year beforehand without mentioning convicts, the sudden need to combat Irish 'Folley' may have only been a calculated insurance against his sidestep of Royal regulations. If he had involved the myth in the local dispute, it was only sensible to be consistent when communicating with London. Certainly convict intransigence — particularly when it was Irish — offered King unique support. He may have grasped that Barrallier's activities presented well to London as a security measure for a destabilised prison colony, hoping to pre-empt any objection to the Frenchman's deployment by exploiting fear of Irish plotting. The whiff of insurrection lent the mountain venture a convenient military cast. Even so, his decision to cite the myth shows there was a credible need to disabuse convict myth-makers. He would hardly have risked an utter lie to Lord Hobart about the expedition's advantages; this would have been a gift to enemies who sought every opportunity to undermine London's confidence in his ability. Those 'future humiliations' were to be avoided at all cost.

On the other hand, if King was certain he could send his aide-de-camp into the wilderness as a de facto explorer without repercussion — which suggests his King of the Mountains was more joke than stratagem — then his citing of the phantom colony to Lord Hobart must be taken literally, as a follow-up ruse would have been unnecessary. Possibly the return of myth-inspired absconding had made King keen to find a way for Barrallier's long-intended expedition to go ahead.

And so, while escape mythology may not have prompted the proposed trip in 1801, its resurgence in 1802 supplied an urgency as well as the phoney ambassadorial pretext upon which to proceed. But whether it necessitated, inspired or just helped to enable Barrallier's journey, escape mythology played a major role. Barrallier himself treated the inland white colony as a useful Aboriginal belief, something to ask Aborigines about in the hope of being shown a passage through the mountains. For King it was (apart from a means to an end) an alarming empowerment of that section of the population whose lack of power was a keystone of social stability. It was a disease that a 'more perfect knowledge of the interior' might cure; its eradication would be a beneficial side effect of the young Frenchman's ambition.

The beliefs of the 'ignorant and weak' were now at their pinnacle of influence. Convict folklore was enjoying a brief leading role in the endless power play between governor and military, with the New Settlement's 'King' a handy pawn. In employing this personification of the unknown outback, Governor King had taken a cue from his convict charges: he had armed himself with imagination.

The governor had other subversive imaginings to contend with in 1802 — those of the French, whose supposed dream of Australia as *Terre Napoleon* gave shape to another colonial bugbear. After charting much of the southern coastline, Nicholas Baudin's two-ship expedition, ravaged by scurvy, had limped into port in late June. King received Baudin cordially, but there was an underlying uneasiness about Napoleon's intentions in authorising the voyage. Uncomfortably, the French visitors were intrigued by the proposed expedition of their countryman Barrallier. Baudin's naturalist Francois Peron wanted to accompany him, but King refused, not wanting to grant a rival power a glimpse of the interior.

King's suspicion was not misplaced. Upon returning to France, Peron wrote a recommendation that a French fleet overtake Sydney, arm Irish convicts and trade captured English troops for French prisoners. It is interesting that King did not cite the threat of French colonial rivalry in sending Barrallier on his way, as he so easily could have done. This is another indication that the convict myth was a real concern and not just an excuse for the trip.

Peron's covert reconnaissance preserved a valuable clue to the nature of the white colony myth. He understood it as an Aboriginal concept undiluted by European interpretation:

> They [the Aborigines] all agree in the impossibility of passing that western barrier; and what they relate of the countries which they suppose to exist on the other side, clearly proves that those countries are totally unknown to them. They assert that there is an immense lake, on the banks of which live white people, like the English, who dress in the same manner, and have large towns, with houses built of stone.

Peron concluded that 'the existence of this great lake, this sort of Caspian Sea', with no known sizeable rivers to feed into it, was 'as improbable as that of the white people and their civilization' thriving by its shore. Paradoxically, he dismissed the legendary Australian 'Caspian' for one of the very same arguments Flinders used to postulate its existence — the apparent absence of sizeable rivers. The thriving civilisation he rejected out of hand, but were these 'large towns' of the interior simply distorted accounts of an unsuspected renegade village? Long-lost runaway convicts may have managed to build a hut or two near an inland feature such as Lake George or Lake Bathurst — which are far from Australian Caspians, but reasonably large bodies of water when full. Peron regarded the inland white people as an Aboriginal idea of recent origin, 'inspired by the establishment of the English colony'. While this is feasible — the large town by a body of water certainly mirrors Sydney — the impetus behind such a creation remains obscure, and is probably now irretrievable.[3] Peron himself made no speculations. The belief interested him only as evidence that Aborigines knew nothing of the inland, which he ascribed to their 'religious terror' of the Blue Mountains barrier. In this he was mistaken: the phantom colony had already been confirmed by Aborigines who knew their way around the mountains better than anybody. Peron's notion that Aborigines considered the mountains impassable and 'are as little acquainted with them as the Europeans' only reflects coastal Sydney peoples such as the Eora, whose territorial limits tended to keep them east of Parramatta.

As King and Paterson bickered over Barrallier, convicts continued to take to the bush. Spiralling desertion prompted King to vastly increase the upper limit of lashes usually meted out to absconders. His order of 19 October 1802 read:

> Several Convicts having absented themselves from Government labour, Notice is hereby given that if they do not repair to the respective Settlements at which they were employed, and appear at their work on or before Monday next, the 25th instant, every person who may be absent after that date will, when apprehended, be punished with 500 lashes, and kept in double-irons in the Gaol Gang during the remainder of their Terms of Transportation.

Nine runaways happened to surrender before the deadline, though this can hardly have been deliberate. They appear to be survivors of various ventures to the 'New Settlement', although six denied that intention in court, and none described where they expected to find it. A bench of four magistrates — Paterson, Richard Atkins, Thomas Jamieson and James Thomson — tried them on 27 October. Despite King's statement that escape mythology was an Irish folly, its extension into the convict mainstream was now demonstrated by the fact that five of the nine were English.[4]

William Clarke, a sawyer at Castle Hill, said he first learned of the 'New Settlement' from a convict overseer named McAlister or McAlish, who 'frequently represented the place to be very like England and full of chapels and churches'.[5] Failing to locate it after a five-day solitary search, Clarke gave himself up to a man named Johnson at Pennant Hills. He claimed to know of fourteen or fifteen men who were 'indeavouring to reach this New Settlement'.

John Marsh, a lifer from Gloucester sent out four years previously, also admitted that he was 'induced from false reports to attempt to reach the New Settlement'. Making his break with others, Marsh gave himself up at Broken Bay after nine fruitless days on the run, and was taken from there to Hawkesbury where he was delivered into custody.

Next up was a trio of English convicts of only two months' residency in the colony. Reprieved from death sentences back home, they had done time together on the *Laurel* hulk in Portsmouth before reaching Sydney aboard the *Perseus*. Elbert Neale, forty-one, claimed he had 'heard something of a New Settlement on his passage to this country, but nothing of the kind since he came here'. Neale insisted his motivation was 'to avoid the hard labor at Castle Hill for which he was unfit by bodily infirmity', pleading that his overseer had kicked him. His complaint was borne out by an official report about 'fire-making' at Castle Hill just after his trial. Although each man was required to burn off sixty-three rods of timber per week, some barely had the strength to manage fifteen.

Neale was not entirely truthful in court. Despite his protestations, he seems to have been one of the myth's shadowy promulgators. Philip Poore, twenty-two, tried in Salisbury on the same day as Neale, had already heard 'general talk of something of a New Settlement' when the elder man suggested they desert. Neale proposed the expedition at Castle Hill during fire-making, but it was three weeks before they set out. Poore also complained of a regime that made a mockery of the set working hours, claiming he laboured 'from sunrise to sunset without any intermission'.

John King, thirty-eight, sent from Essex for life, claimed to have similarly 'consulted with Neale on the scheme' for three weeks. He had been 'deluded into this Expedition by false reports and was nine days in the woods' before surrendering to a fisherman who took him to Hawkesbury. King's account of Castle Hill echoed Poore's, a place where you worked from sunrise to sunset without any breaks, not even for meals.

Four Irishmen, who had travelled in pairs, were the last to be examined. All were from the most recent Irish transport, the notorious *Atlas I*. Edward Walsh, of Dublin, and Michael Byrne, from Meath, asserted they 'went into the woods for the purpose of relieving themselves from the hard labour which was more than they could accomplish'. At large for ten days, they ate nothing but grass for the last five, and finally surrendered at Tench's River (the Nepean) 'to a Kangaroo Man named Jos. Wild'.[6]

Daniel McCarthy from Cork and Dubliner James White, missing for twelve days, told a similar story about fending off starvation with grass. Although admitting they 'frequently heard general talk about a New Settlement', they were at pains to insist they 'had no idea of reaching it'. Again, avoiding excessive labour was the only excuse offered. They had also fallen in with 'Wild the Kangaroo Man', who gave them the hindquarter and head of (inevitably) a kangaroo, 'which they declare saved their lives'.[7]

Evidence that these Irishmen, amongst others, did have an idea of reaching their New Settlement survives in the records of a trial held two days earlier. The imminent departure of the Baudin expedition had prompted several attempts by convicts to spirit themselves back to Europe aboard the French ships. Most were Irish rebels, no doubt sure their former allies and fellow republicans would help them regain their liberty. Phillip Cunningham and Cornelius Shea (otherwise Connor Sheehan) were two of these hopefuls, arrested in Sydney after leaving Parramatta without a pass to seek surreptitious passage home.

On 25 October, Cunningham and Shea were asked in court 'if either of them had heard any of their countrymen express a wish or intention to find out some New Settlement on the other side of the Blue Mountains, and escape from the colony'. Both had spoken with survivors of such attempts — and the four Irishmen saved by the Kangaroo

Man were in custody by then. Shea claimed 'he had heard many of his Countrymen say that there was such a settlement and that they had been out with an intention of reaching it but were apprehended at Broken Bay'. Cunningham said he asked 'what had possessed them to go into the Bush on such an expedition'. While some 'did not admit it', others revealed 'they went with an intent to find out such Settlement' and now 'expressed some sorrow at having entertained so extravagant a notion'. The hard-headed ex-rebel captain clearly rejected his compatriots' reckless suppositions. But Cunningham's own extravagant notions, also aimed at escaping the colony, would soon cost a considerable number of Irish lives, including his own.

A final question may have concerned alleged maps to the New Settlement or paper compasses, as the court noted neither Cunningham nor Shea 'knew anything of any paper having been supplied by any of their Countrymen'. The interrogation at an end, Cunningham and Shea were ordered to receive 100 lashes at Castle Hill. The nine overland deserters received similar treatment. The bench unanimously decided they were 'highly culpable for leaving their Government Duty' and awarded them 100 lashes each, to be followed by hard labour in double-irons. Seeing no need to flog all of them, Governor King had them draw lots to select three for the lash, but the double-ironing went ahead for all nine.[8]

Elbert Neale, John Marsh and Philip Poore were the unlucky ones, with the added ordeal of being hauled before the Parramatta Bench of Magistrates to explain their allegations of cruel treatment at Castle Hill. Under the basilisk gaze of Reverend Marsden, Neale retracted his complaint about his overseer, now saying he had only been 'threatened to be kicked if he would not get up and work'. The others had nothing to say, and were ordered to their punishment. To have as many convicts as possible witness exactly what happened to deserters, Neale was flogged at Parramatta, Poore at Toongabbie and Marsh at Castle Hill.

As the nine tried were only those who either managed to surrender or were rescued, others probably made permanent their escape to nowhere.

The fifteen seekers William Clarke mentioned were never brought to trial. Disorientation rules the survivors' accounts, which show them scattering in all directions. The cold eye of authority remained blind to the harsh life at Castle Hill driving this desperation. Looking into complaints of overwork there that same October, Marsden and Paterson concluded that the convicts' labour was 'very inordinate, and not so much as they ought to have performed'.

The day after the trial of the nine overlanders, King issued a warning which emphasised their near-starvation and reiterated the various sticky ends of the *Norfolk* runaways. He appealed to reason and exploited fear of the unknown, but most of all he hoped against all precedent that another official denial would end this particular inducement to desertion:

> The Governor has for some time been informed of a Report, as wicked as it is false, and calculated to bring the believers of it to Destruction, that a Settlement of White People exists on the other side of the Mountains, &c., And that several of the Prisoners were so far deluded as to concert means for reaching that Settlement, in consequence of which, several have lately absconded from their Labour, Nine of whom have been apprehended, and on the Examination before the Magistrates, it appeared that some of them, instead of taking the course to the Mountains, had gone to the Sea-side, others had reached near the Nepean, whilst those less instructed than the latter, had wandered about near the place they had left, after being absent Ten Days, most of them nearly starved, and living on Grass for Five Days out of the Ten.
>
> Exclusive of former unhappy examples, the fate which befell those who took the *Norfolk*, the dismal end of the unfortunate Lime-burners, who were killed by the Natives on landing a few Miles from hence, and the folly of the late Land adventurers, joined to the punishment they have already received in being nearly starved, and the Corporal Punishment awarded by the Magistrates as an example, it is

hoped that what has occurred to those ignorant and infatuated People may have its effect upon others, and prevent such Schemes, as wild as they prove unsuccessful and destructive to those concerned in them.

A few simple and ill-informed People have been led into these ridiculous Plans, the consequences of which have been that those among them who pretended to a greater share of Wisdom than the rest have sacrificed the others by forcing them ashore, where they have been destroyed by the Natives, and a part of them executed for Piracy; Nor is there a doubt that if the present adventurers could have reached the foot of the Mountains, they must have languished and died for want of Food before they could have got a Mile into them.

Let those who are invited to such mad and inconsiderate undertakings reflect upon these things, and they will easily discover the risque attending such ill-judged enterprises.

King's other move was to finally give Ensign Barrallier his much awaited go-ahead. The decision to move may have been precipitated by the arrival of the *Atlas II* on 30 October, another shipload of embittered Irish rebels and potential gullible travellers. The governor afterwards described the sort of plans leaking from Castle Hill, visions of escaping 'by going to the mountains, or travelling to China and the Cape of Good Hope, etc'. South Africa is nowhere else claimed as a goal for runaways; perhaps King was punning on the misplaced 'good hope' inspiring the attempts.[9]

In another sense Barrallier also dreamed of transforming his situation by crossing the mountains. Unlike the convict dreamers, however, his effort was furnished with the governor's blessing and all the resources the colony could spare. At Parramatta a supply wagon was being provisioned for the historic excursion. On 5 November 1802, Barrallier, the first and so far the only New South Wales ambassador to the King of the Mountains, was ready to depart.

CHAPTER TEN

Almost super-human efforts

The air, the sky, the land, are objects entirely different from
all that a Briton has been accustomed to see before ...
the whole appearance of nature must be striking in
the extreme to the adventurer, and at first this will
seem to him to be a country of enchantments.

THOMAS WATLING, CONVICT, 1791

ENSIGN BARRALLIER WAS ACCOMPANIED ON HIS EXPEDITION BY
four soldiers and five convicts, but the Aborigines who volunteered
to accompany him played a much greater part in the story. They were
mostly Dharawal men, hailing from the southern district between Botany
Bay and Jervis Bay, bounded by the mountains to the west. The most
significant was Gogy, who had met Barrallier in his native Cowpastures
during the reconnaissance trip. A quixotic and rather violent individual,
he profoundly influenced the expedition's outcome.

Barrallier's journey would also broach the land of the Gundungurra,
traditional owners of the southern Blue Mountains and regions

stretching south-west to present-day Goulburn. Europeans knew little of them as yet. Barrallier found them 'shorter than the natives about our settlements, but very strong and well made'. A decade later the *Sydney Gazette* also praised the 'mountaineers' for their toughness, contradicting Barrallier's impression of their size:

> a much more athletic and hardy race than those of this part of the sea coast. They are taller, lighter coloured, much more comely in their persons and features, and wear their hair tied in a bunch behind.

Gogy joined the explorers at Prospect Hill. He seems to have conversed with Barrallier in English, a second language for both of them. After crossing the Nepean River, they camped by a swamp near the Cowpastures on 6 November. The next day brought them to the rich grasslands ruled by the feral cattle. Some herds numbered over 200 animals, and the belligerence of the wild bulls made for nervous travelling.

While crossing the Cowpastures, Barrallier met two more Aboriginal men. Bungin was a fugitive, having fled his clan over an unknown offence. In the manner of the inlanders, he wore a mantle sewn from various animal pelts. His companion was Wooglemai, whose name meant 'one-eyed'. Unlike Bungin he was familiar with Europeans and had often visited Parramatta and Prospect Hill. Barrallier presented them with a kangaroo head, eager to impress. Pleased, Bungin offered to exchange axes and built Barrallier a hut that evening, indicating the Frenchman was a welcome guest.

The journey to the depot site at Nattai took another full day. Early in the morning of 9 November, Bungin and Gogy brought two men into camp, Bulgin and Wallarra. Barrallier offered his hand but Wallarra, terrified by his first sight of a white man, could only shiver uncontrollably. The more experienced Bulgin was far more relaxed, and later that day brought his wife and child to stay at Barrallier's depot.

There was plenty of work to be done. Shelter had to be built for the expanding party, now including the families of Bungin and Gogy. In the evening the Aborigines brought portions of a koala into camp. Barrallier described it as a 'monkey', noting the locals called it a 'colo'. He hadn't seen one before and successfully bartered for its feet, which he bottled in spirits and sent to Governor King. Unfortunately he missed out on preserving a complete specimen — it would have been a colonial first.

On the morning of 10 November, after sending the supply wagon to Prospect Hill with Wooglemai as guide, Barrallier set out on his first exploration with Gogy, Bungin, Bulgin and three or four of his men. After crossing the Nattai River they hiked north along its west bank, where thick forest fringed a mountainous wall of stone towers. The alien nature of the land to European sensibilities was brought home to Barrallier that night, when he mistook the croaking of native frogs for the bellowing of wild bulls.

In the morning the party followed the river until its meeting with the Wollondilly, which they traced upstream, looking for a passage between the summits. A sudden thunderstorm terrified them with 'terrible detonations' and a thick mist enshrouded the mountains in grey silence. The rainfall and fog lifted by midmorning on 12 November. Passing a chain of mountains about four miles in length, and hills dotted with mobs of kangaroos, they decided to climb the most accessible summit (Tonalli Peak) to get their bearings. This proved far from easy. Sharp boulders rolled under their feet and they sank knee-deep in sand. They made it three-quarters of the way to the top, where Barrallier described 'immense overhanging rocks, which seemed to be attached to nothing, offered an appalling scene'.

After they descended to a hilltop near the base of the mountain, Bungin saw a fire. A small Gundungurra hunting party, including Wallarra, was camped nearby with their women and children. Motioning the others to be silent, Bungin approached the hunters, who rose with their spears as soon as they saw him. He told them the Europeans meant no harm and wished only to climb the mountains for rock samples. The hunters burst into fits of laughter at the idea of anyone going to so much trouble just to gather stones. After some parley they indicated it was all right for the Aboriginal guides to approach, but the whites were asked to keep back to avoid frightening the women and children. Barrallier had his soldiers light a fire and skin a wallaby for dinner while they waited.

Gogy was very tense and carried a gun into the camp. Only Wallarra would speak to him; the others argued about whether he should be allowed to sit with them. Barrallier noted how they 'threw terrible glances at him, biting their lips, which did not augur very well for him'.

The leader of the hunting party was named Goondel. His status made him the closest Barrallier came to dealing with an actual 'king' of the mountains. Goondel was hospitable to all visitors except Gogy, whom he refused to feed — a deadly insult and a sure sign of trouble ahead.

Barrallier had Gogy ask about the phantom white colony, explaining he intended to 'examine this new settlement when I knew its location and the number of days required to reach it'. Wallarra revealed that one of the hunters, Mootik, was 'the only one who could give any information about the new settlement which, he had heard, was on the other side of the mountains'. But the bad blood between Gogy and Goondel's party meant Mootik wouldn't answer any questions, even though Wallarra said it was Barrallier, not Gogy, who wanted the information. Rising to his feet and looking at Gogy with 'terrible eyes', Mootik stalked off to get some water.

By contrast, Bungin proved very popular indeed. Goondel offered him his daughter, a young girl named Wheengeewhungee, and asked him to leave the explorers. Barrallier readily agreed to Bungin staying with Goondel's party overnight. Meanwhile Gogy grew despondent and refused his share of the soldiers' wallaby. Fearing the worst, he said that if Barrallier cared about him he would abandon the mission. Wishing to avoid trouble and retain Gogy's goodwill, Barrallier decided to return to his campsite of the night before.

They retraced their steps, shadowed by Mootik and another man, both armed with spears. Gogy became highly agitated and the soldiers taunted him in his own language, calling him *gevenet* — coward. But Mootik retreated after an hour and the campsite was reached without incident. Gogy said that only the presence of the armed Europeans saved his life.

The next day, while tramping back to Nattai, Bungin caught up with them at the Wollondilly–Nattai river junction. His nuptials had hit a snag. Nobody's chattel, Wheengeewhungee fled upon learning her father's plans for her future. Goondel was busy trying to track her down, and so Bungin rejoined Barrallier while he awaited the recapture of his vanished fiancée. He showed them a shortcut back to the Nattai depot, a hard scramble up an almost perpendicular rise. They reached camp later that evening, where they ate a welcome dinner of kangaroo tail (and head) soup.

Thus the first leg of the exploration ended inconclusively, mainly due to Goondel's hostility towards Gogy. Barrallier had found no hint of a pass through the mountains, but the tantalising prospect of Mootik's knowledge being put to use remained.

After more than a week of heavy rain, Barrallier readied for a longer foray. He selected five of his strongest men and two new Aboriginal guides — a youth he dubbed 'Le Tonsure' because of a bald patch on his head, and Badbury, who had arrived in Wooglemai's company with the returning supply wagon. His first choice of guide, the dependable Wooglemai, was terrified by the idea and preferred to take the wagon on another supply run to Prospect, this time accompanied by Gogy. Barrallier was glad to be rid of Gogy, and not just because of the mountain incident. During the break he had tried to kill his wife, accusing her of sleeping with one of the soldiers. After knocking her unconscious and spearing her in the leg, he had almost succeeded in snatching a musket and shooting her.

The second expedition set off at 8 am on 22 November, descending the same gorge as before. By afternoon they reached the huts they had built on the first trip. Aboriginal hunting fires were burning along the creek. The heat of the day was suffocating and the explorers spent much of the day cooling off with refreshing swims.

The next day they spotted Goondel, Mootik and Wallarra resting beneath a tree across the creek with some women and children. Le Tonsure and Badbury went to parley and things went well in Gogy's absence. Goondel gave the two guides a kangaroo leg and sent them back with a message that he might visit Barrallier's camp for lunch. No doubt anticipating directions to a mountain pass, Barrallier selected a new axe as a gift and cooked a meal in advance. By 4 pm, however, storm clouds were gathering and Goondel still hadn't showed. Reluctantly, Barrallier moved on to make his next intended campsite before the skies opened. On 24 November, after passing the peak (Tonalli) they had attempted on their first trip, the explorers at last found an opening between two other summits.

Thinking he had unlocked the western door at last, Barrallier pressed on through a heatwave which burst into thunder and rain in the afternoon. Another hard day's tramping over rocky, scrubby hills brought them to a mountainside cave only half a mile from the passage. At 6 pm Barrallier sent two men forward to investigate. An hour later they returned to report the passage led to 'an immense plain'. So close to his goal, Barrallier couldn't bear to rest and used the remaining daylight to reach the mouth of the passage, a half-mile wide gap between steep, cavernous mountains. The ground was swampy but they found a dry hillock to camp on. Even a drenching thunderstorm failed to dampen the explorers' spirits. Barrallier's diary records they 'congratulated themselves with having succeeded in accomplishing the passage of the Blue Mountains without accident'.

Cooler heads prevailed the next morning. Barrallier got his little expedition moving by daybreak to verify the claim. Taking two men with him, he attempted the nearest mountain for another look. The climb revealed the plain about a mile below, stretching as far as they could see.

At the top it was excessively cold. Shivering on the sugarloaf summit, they were almost blown off their feet by a westerly wind that roared like 'the waves when breaking upon the rocks of the shore'. The trail behind them was veiled by fog, but beyond the plain a new range (Kanangra Walls) was now visible, higher than any they had yet encountered. With these distant peaks shimmering in his eyes, the convict myths may have returned to haunt Barrallier's thoughts, as he was granted a brief mirage of the impossible white colony:

> Some of these mountains appeared as if they were denuded of trees, and by the differences in the colours and shades I thought I could distinguish in the distance immense rocks which, by their juxtaposition, had the appearance of houses of different sizes.

In August, John Day had been dismissed as a liar for a more literal interpretation of such an apparition. The bushranger may have concocted his mountain town as a ruse to escape or delay punishment, but was he simply fooled by this sort of terrain during his own travels?

Barrallier's vision marked a turning point in the expedition. Having seen the halls of the Mountain King, he soon began to reflect on the unlikelihood of crossing their portals. It seemed all the hard work had only brought them to the middle of the ranges at best. Another day spent fighting their way through the passage — scrambling along the mountainside to avoid a river below — revealed that his 'open plain' was actually filled with ravines and cliffs, and that the heights blocking the western horizon were even more forbidding than the ones they had just conquered with the greatest difficulty. Barrallier reflected on the hardships his team were enduring: 'harassed with fatigue, our feet wounded and tumbling the one over the other on rocks which appear to have no termination'.

On 27 November, Barrallier sent two men to check out another nearby summit. They likened their situation to being amidst 'many pyramids by the side of one another'. The backbreaking effort of conquering one peak was rewarded only by the discovery of another. Provisions were almost out, and Barrallier's team had no mind to continue. A compromise was reached; Barrallier agreed to give up direct assaults on the heights in favour of following a west–flowing stream. This proved hard going as well; impassable banks often forced them to wade knee–deep in water, and rapids and waterfalls were constant obstacles. Finally they confronted a waterfall tougher than all the others, and if Barrallier needed any further confirmation that the mountain world was against them, that evening one of the men was attacked by a snake while cutting wood.

After some scouting the next day Barrallier decided not to bother crossing the waterfall. Marking the extremity of their progress with a St Andrews cross on a tree, the expedition caught some snakes for dinner — a meal the Frenchman found repugnant — and prepared to turn back. The collective mood was quite down, which Barrallier summed up in writing to King: 'I do not believe there can be so barren a desert in any part of Africa as these Mountains are'.

The return journey took five days. The weather swung between extreme, debilitating heat in daytime and some of the coldest nights they had yet experienced. A further inconvenience was the loss of huts they had erected on the outward route, burnt down by Aboriginal hunters. Back at the depot one of the soldiers was very ill, and food stocks were almost exhausted. Gogy returned from Prospect, having made peace with his wife, and other Aborigines also came and went as they pleased, sometimes joining the Europeans on hunting trips.

The third and final journey got underway in mid–December, this time towards the south along the course of the Wollondilly River. Gogy warned Barrallier against this, insisting the region was inhabited by cannibals. Barrallier laughed, though he had no real reason to. 'Well, master,' Gogy replied angrily in English, 'you will see that I am not a liar.'

Barrallier selected six of his European team to accompany him, and asked Gogy along too. Gogy's wife and child caught up with them on their first day in the field, not wanting to stay at the camp amongst strangers.

Barrallier grumbled in his diary, as they slowed down the travelling considerably, but said nothing. Later that day the expedition came within five miles of Goondel's hunting fires. Terrified, Gogy hurried his family back to Nattai in the morning, leaving the white men to fend for themselves amongst the phantom cannibals.

Gogy had good reason to fear Goondel; in the recent past he had abused his hospitality and committed a truly horrible crime. Fleeing his own clan over a killing, Gogy enjoyed Goondel's protection for several months before going home to face his punishment and earn forgiveness. But then he returned with one or more companions to abduct, torture and murder Goondel's sister. By Gogy's candid admission to Barrallier they tied her to a tree and raped her, and after putting her to death, cut off some of her flesh which they cooked and ate. The rest of the body was left hanging from the tree.[1]

The flesh-eating may have been bluster. At least we can only hope it was. Gogy seems to have been preoccupied by cannibalism, perhaps relishing the particular horror it evoked in Europeans. In 1814, when Goondel and others were rallying to combat European settlement in their territory, Gogy was still accusing his old Aboriginal enemies of cannibalism, this time from a new refuge at Broken Bay.

The day following Gogy's departure a violent wind erupted, felling many branches and almost uprooting several trees. They passed a wall of mountains seen on the previous trip, which now appeared so daunting that Barrallier ruefully concluded they 'could only be ascended by making almost superhuman efforts'. The river was similarly discouraging, continuing to flow south, though Barrallier was not to know that it eventually veered west. Even worse, it was barely accessible — the mountainous slopes ran down virtually to the banks. Barrallier decided enough was enough. By the time he got back to Nattai, Gogy had cleared out for the relative safety of Prospect, family in tow. The next day Barrallier started out for Sydney with three of his men, leaving others behind to arrange the removal of equipment and stores. They walked the entire way and arrived three days later, just in time for Christmas. Barrallier's head was filled with new plans to attack the mountains from Jervis Bay to the south, but he soon collided with an obstacle greater than any mountain — colonial politics.

On New Year's Eve, Governor King began writing a dispatch which summarised Barrallier's achievements. He did not reiterate the escape-inducing belief in bush sanctuaries — hardly surprising since the expedition found no antidote to the delusion. Although stories of Barrallier's hardships may have discouraged some convicts from staging their own amateurish journeys, nothing he accomplished suggested a white colony was not beyond the peaks. In fact, his encounter with Mootik had only added to the weight of anecdotal Aboriginal evidence that it was there, inviolate and flourishing. As it happened, Barrallier had given himself a sneak preview of an actual convict bush-sanctuary. Much of the terrain he struggled through was part of the rugged valley later known as the Burragorang, which would achieve infamy as a notorious bushranging hideout.

King's gloomy conclusion about the mountains — 'impassable to man' — may have seemed promising in containing convict aspirations, but it was of little benefit to long-term colonial development. King decided to promote the barrier as a handy container for the wild cattle, which he wrote 'secures them to the future advantage of the colony, unless they take a south route'. He went on to relate that follow-up expeditions to capture some of them ended in failure owing to the cattle's 'wild and ferocious state'. Sensibly, his report concentrated on the practical results of the expedition, the physical discoveries. How Barrallier had altered the convicts' mental landscape was less certain.

Some historians think Barrallier came much closer to his goal than he ever realised. His exact route is much disputed, but one theory says he got within two miles of the Great Divide on his second trip, and was only an hour's march from sighting the Abercrombie River, which could have led him through the final western barrier. A counter-claim says Barrallier would probably have ignored this route had he seen it, as the Abercrombie deceptively flows to the south-east before veering westwards beyond the ranges.

It's a curious coincidence that both Wilson and Barrallier independently discovered the koala to European natural history, a revelation unheeded both times. Five years after John Wilson showed Price and Roe the cullawines wedged in gum trees beyond Mount Hunter, the *Sydney Gazette* described the gumleaf-eating 'koolah' kept by Governor King, 'an animal whose species was never before found in the colony'. If His Excellency — who was fluent in French — had struggled through Barrallier's messy handwriting he may have recalled Barrallier's encounter with a peculiar — and tasty — native 'monkey', or its feet which had been sent to him. The incident was long-forgotten when the koolah came along. But by then Barrallier had already left the colony, his reputation in tatters.

It is hard to tell exactly what happened, but Barrallier appears to have fallen foul of the poisonous hatred between the governor and the military. A sudden new ingredient into this soup of paranoia and loathing was a rumour that the governor had forbidden his wife — 'under such threats as humanity shudders' — to visit the Patersons. When informed the rumour's source was his own aide-de-camp, King terminated the secondment immediately, returning Barrallier to the Corps on 9 May 1803. Disgraced, and unsupported by his military colleagues, Barrallier resigned his commission and left the colony little more than a week later on the returning transport HMS *Glatton*. King soon softened his stance, however, deciding the young officer was the innocent victim of his enemies' attempts to escalate his feud with Colonel Paterson. In a letter to Sir Joseph Banks he wrote how Barrallier

> . . . has been obliged to quit the New South Wales Corps, but I think he is not dishonoured by the impair imposed on him for a crime that is trivial, and levered from him by Art. How cunning of my friends and Col. Paterson.

Although not called upon to pay the governor's respects in the court of the Mountain King, Barrallier acquitted himself admirably as an ambassador to the Aboriginal groups he encountered. His journal is enlivened by perceptive descriptions and a sincere interest in a culture he could have barely understood. He seems to have delighted in cordial dealings with the local people. Without Aboriginal cooperation he would have had a much tougher time — he relied heavily on Goondel's restraint, Gogy's multilingual skills, and the superb bushcraft of Bungin, Wooglemai, Le Tonsure and Badbury.

The Cowpastures reached the inevitable flashpoint over a decade later. Goondel emerged as a resistance leader in 1814, when threats were issued to kill settlers 'when the Moon shall become as large as the Sun'. A sixteen-man party was sent to arrest him, but like the more esoteric Mountain King, Goondel was never found by his white pursuers.

Gogy's further adventures included another killing, for which he faced the spears (a traditional punishment) in March 1805. He deflected the first spear, but the second — thrown by the famous Eora man Bennelong — pierced his hip, and a third struck him in the lower back where it was lodged for twenty agonising days. Five years later he amicably met Governor Macquarie, who considered him the 'Native Chief of the Cow-Pasture Tribe'. While Goondel was fighting white intruders Gogy moved up to Broken Bay, wishing to retain European favour. By 1816 he was back on his home turf, listed as one of three 'hostile natives' that had been 'inspected' five days after the infamous Appin Massacre, in which some fourteen Dharawal were killed by a military patrol.

Barrallier was also fighting in 1814, serving with the British army in the West Indies against the forces of his countrymen under Napoleon. Shortly after Waterloo he briefly joined the French army, only to re-enlist with the British and retire on half-pay. In 1819 he married an Englishwoman and lived quietly in London for the rest of his life.

There have been various reconstructions of Barrallier's exact route into the mountains, but here we are more concerned with where he didn't go, with what he didn't see. For all the French ensign's brave efforts, the King of the Mountains remained undisturbed. This was only to be expected, for his true realm was human longing, beyond any mundane jurisdiction. The phantom colonies, undissolved by Barrallier, continued to beckon to the toiling masses at Castle Hill. In this concentrated environment, where 300 prisoners now laboured daily, rumours simmered under the surface of routine, and soon they would reach boiling point.

CHAPTER ELEVEN

Wild and madlike plans

> I am one, my liege,
> Whom the vile blows and buffets of the world
> Have so incens'd that I am reckless what
> I do to spite the world.
>
> WILLIAM SHAKESPEARE, 'MACBETH' III.I.

As TWILIGHT ENVELOPED CASTLE HILL ON TUESDAY, 15 FEBRUARY 1803, Mary Turley noticed something strange happening on the farm where she worked as an assigned servant. While bringing in clothes from bleaching on a line, she saw two men approach an outlying hut occupied by Patrick McDermott, the convict farmhand. When a third man appeared out of the dusk and walked towards the hut, Mary grew alarmed and locked herself in the main farmhouse, careful to fasten all the windows.

Mary had once enjoyed notoriety as a Dublin pickpocket nicknamed 'The Balloon'. But one day her bubble burst and she found herself bundled aboard the *Hercules* in Cork Harbour, one of twenty-five female prisoners bound for New South Wales. The *Hercules* women played a key role in quashing the bloody mutiny at sea; their terrified screams had alerted the crew to the male convicts bursting onto deck.

Things hadn't gone too badly for Mary in the year since her arrival. Assigned to the amiable Colonel Pierre Labourelle Verincourt de Clambe, a French chevalier, she made a new life for herself as his housekeeper and, in the colonial fashion, his mistress. De Clambe was a popular though reclusive individual. After military service in India he went to England to avoid the French Revolution, eventually seeking permission to settle in New South Wales. Stepping ashore at Sydney in December 1801, he received 100 acres the following February, a grant he called The Hermitage. De Clambe's countryman Francois Peron, who paid his respects when the Baudin expedition anchored in Sydney later that year, wrote how de Clambe 'shuns the world, and refuses the most pressing invitations of his best friends, in order to devote himself entirely to agriculture'. Something of a mad scientist, de Clambe spent much of his time experimenting with growing coloured cotton, of which Peron reckoned 'no European had hitherto been able to imitate, either by growing the cotton or dyeing it'. The Hermitage also boasted a vineyard and a coffee plantation. Unfortunately, it was adjacent to the Castle Hill penal farm, which meant the peaceful seclusion was soon shattered.

De Clambe went out on business on 15 February, and at nightfall was yet to return. Alone in the house, Mary Turley wondered fearfully what the men outside were up to. Soon there came a knocking on the door, followed by the distinctive (more on this later) brogue of her co-worker Patrick McDermott. 'It is I,' he said. 'Open the door, for here is a constable with a letter from my master'.

Lulled into false security, Mary unbolted the door. Nine men burst into the room and shoved her into the bedroom. She kept the presence of mind to demand her treacherous workmate produce his 'letter', to which one of the others replied, 'You'll have enough of the letter bye-and-bye'.

Mary looked on helplessly while the men ransacked the house, looking for guns and ammunition. She may have recognised some of them; at least two had arrived with her on the *Hercules*. The intruders threatened to kill her and she later complained that one of them struck her, although Mary had a sharp tongue and may have given a bit more lip than they were prepared to take.[1] As one man loaded a pistol, another ordered him to 'fire it down her throat if she says a word'.

They wanted a telescope and compass, but de Clambe only owned the former. There couldn't have been too much to plunder; Peron described him as 'an utter stranger to every sort of luxury'. Ranging through the house, taking whatever they could carry, the convicts soon broke into the Frenchman's store of wine and spirits and began drinking. One man grabbed some clothes from a trunk and wrapped them into a bundle. Before he left he had Mary fill two glasses of wine for him, a costly mistake as it turned out.

The raiders were Irish convicts who had taken off from Castle Hill earlier that evening. All thirteen had arrived in the last three ships from Cork. It soon emerged they wanted to reach the 'New Settlement' across the Blue Mountains, hopeful of eventually getting home to Ireland. Seven of them — John Lynch, Laurence Dempsey, Lachlan Doyle, Timothy Mulcahy, Patrick Ross, Michael Woollaghan (or Houlahan) and Francis Simpson — were from the *Atlas II*, transported for taking part in the Irish Rebellion. Patrick Gannan, John Morgan and Patrick McDermott had endured the hellish voyage of the *Atlas I*, while Thomas Shanks was from the mutinous *Hercules*. Two others — John Brown and James Conroy or Conway — elude identification. The only participant not in public labour, McDermott was nevertheless deeply involved in the venture. He had probably alerted the others to de Clambe's rare absence, an ideal opportunity to stage an unhindered raid.[2]

Liquored up, the gang left de Clambe's farm and travelled about a mile south-west onto neighbouring farms belonging to two of the colony's earliest volunteer immigrants, James Bean and Thomas Bradley. Both these men were doing it tough. After almost four years in New South Wales they still couldn't support their families by farming; Bean was doing carpentry jobs for food and the Bradleys were living off the government store.

Mary Turley had been very lucky her assailants had only been interested in provisioning their escape. It was a very different story at the Bean household. Emboldened by de Clambe's wine and the success of the first raid, two of the convicts now 'gave aloose to sensuality, equally brutal and unmanly' — they raped 17-year-old Rose Bean in front of her distraught mother. Another ugly incident occurred on the Bradley property, on the western boundary of Bean's farm about two miles east of the Hawkesbury road. Meeting some resistance from a servant, one of the convicts shot him in the face. The man recovered but was badly maimed. According to the *Sydney Gazette* the musket ball 'so shattered his face as to render him a ghastly spectacle, in all probability, during the remainder of his life'.

The runaways now disappeared into the night. Upon returning home later that evening, de Clambe scribbled the following note requesting assistance. His English increasingly faltered as he wrote, and it's easy to imagine the old soldier struggling to suppress his outrage and fear. It also betrays his concern for his terrorised convict de facto:

> Dear Sir,
>
> I am very sorry to inform you that this evening before I came from Parramatta many men did come at my house and did robb all my plate, cloth, linen, fire-arms and amunition, coutelas &c. &c., and struc and threat with pistol on the breast my housekeeper. Some men in employment at Castle Hill's settlement are very much implicated in it, but I fear for it to secure them; so if you would be so kind to come you self to-morrow mourning, I will not move noting so that you shall see the all by your one eyes.
>
> I am, dear Sir, yours truly, Le Chev. De Clambe.

News of the depredations spread quickly, and on the morning of

16 February a search party was organised to track down the offenders. The governor ordered a captain, subaltern and fifteen soldiers to be added to the guard at Castle Hill. At this stage it was assumed fifteen convicts were involved in the outrages as two others, Patrick Ward and William Ramsey, had gone missing from the plantation on the same day.[3]

The search party was a combined force of military and constables, led by John Jamieson Jnr and Andrew Thompson, chief constable of the Hawkesbury district. As they hurriedly prepared and loaded their weapons, one of the constables accidentally discharged his musket, killing an unfortunate convict who just happened to be nearby.

Undeterred by this ominous start, the party set off. Riding along the Hawkesbury road the next day, they had the extraordinary luck of catching two of the runaways literally napping. Gannan and Simpson had already left their companions. The day before, while tramping along the road, they had stopped a man named Joseph Willoughby, put him in 'bodily fear' and took a ha'penny worth of bread. Now Thompson and Jamieson found them asleep by the road near a group of Aborigines. They leapt to their feet but were quickly overpowered. Two muskets and other items stolen from de Clambe were in their possession, including some silver spoons found near where Gannan had been sleeping.

Thompson spent a couple more days in the bush, this time returning with three men who had ferried the remaining eleven Irishmen across the Hawkesbury River at Portland Head. He also brought in a bonus — a lone Irish runaway, John McCormick, apparently unconnected with the others.[4] The ferrymen may have furnished the first clue to the gang's plans. Upon Thompson's return, Hawkesbury magistrate Thomas Arndell informed Governor King that the chief constable had 'traced them to the mountains, over or around which they mean to go, under a false idea of finding a new settlement'. Perhaps mindful of the carnage they had already left behind, they 'declared their intention not to injure any person except such as may attempt to take them'.

Having found a convenient river crossing, the gang tramped west towards the mountains. With eleven mouths to feed, however, provisions soon dwindled, and late in the afternoon of 22 February they emerged from the bush to attack a fourth property.

Their target was the home of Thomas Neale, an ex-convict renting fifty productive acres near Richmond Hill. Brandishing a musket and a cutlass, Conroy, Lynch and a third man swooped on a neighbouring settler, John Kable, as he left Neale's farmhouse at around 4 pm. The trio told him not to be frightened, promising he wouldn't get hurt if he made no resistance. Forcing him back indoors, they asked for something to eat. Another visitor, John Smith, also found himself detained. Kable offered the famished raiders some 'cake'. They wanted meat instead, but made do with a peck of wheat. At that point a third neighbour, William Lane, arrived unawares with a bushel to grind at Neale's mill. The runaways commandeered the lot, ground it themselves and cooked up two pots of 'doughboys' (dumplings). When Neale returned home to interrupt the surprise party there was little he could do. Two runaways were grinding at his mill, and the other nine had taken over the house. They assured him he was in no danger, so he sat down to watch them finish their feast. Eventually, the eleven Irishmen bound their hosts hand and foot and grabbed the leftover wheat, a quart cooking pot and two muskets. John Lynch loaded one of the guns as they readied to depart.

As the closest settled district to the foothills, Richmond Hill was a logical place to begin a mountain journey. Stealing a final haul of provisions from there was a sensible strategy. But the gang fell far short of their promised land. Acting on information received from local Aborigines, a search party overtook them the next day between Richmond Hill and the mountains. The runaways gave their location away by lighting a campfire. As their pursuers closed in the gang dropped some of the stolen goods in panic, but none offered resistance. Seven were wearing de Clambe's clothes, with Dempsey especially well outfitted in a jacket, waistcoat, silver buckle and 'a pair of pantaloons'.[5]

Two days later, on Friday evening (25 February), the other Castle

Hill runaways blundered from the bush somewhere on Sydney's North Shore. Ramsey and Ward had hardly eaten during their ten days absence and were hopelessly lost. They were examined by the magistrates on the Saturday and committed for trial along with the larger gang.

Although they deserted on the same day as the others, Ward and Ramsey insisted it was only coincidence. This rings true; they were not seen at the farm raids and were picked up in a completely different district. Initially they must have been willing to risk the 500 lashes proscribed by King's draconian order of the previous October. But now, after ten days of starvation and exposure, they faced the prospect of capital charges for crimes committed by others. Making the best case of it, they pleaded an intention to return to Castle Hill by Saturday 19 February after enjoying some time off work, but were unable to find their way back. It may have been true, but if not they were hardly the first to deny an intention of permanent desertion. Their motivation for denial was paramount; they needed to distance themselves from the designs of the others as far as possible.

The fifteen captured 'delinquents' languished in gaol for almost three weeks until a panel of magistrates could be secured from amongst the Corps officers, who were continuing to undermine King's administration. Finally six soldiers were empanelled to join Judge–Advocate Richard Atkins on the bench, including Major Johnston and Ensign Barrallier, acting in one of his last official capacities in the colony. When the runaways were tried on 15 March, it was only for crimes against property. Rose Bean was spared from revisiting her ordeal in court. There was no need; the offenders would hang just as easily for stealing spoons and wheat.

Patrick Gannan and Francis Simpson were first to appear, charged with feloniously entering de Clambe's dwelling and having his 'seven silver spoons' upon or near them when arrested. Mary Turley, the Crown's chief witness, recalled Simpson tying up 'many things in a bundle'. Simpson's two glasses of de Clambe's wine now returned to damn him. When he challenged the convict maidservant, asking 'by what particular mark did you know me on that night?' she replied she had a full view of his face when forced to wait on him.

De Clambe followed by identifying his stolen cutlery. Three men of the arresting party — Thomas Jamieson, Andrew Thompson and Henry Lamb — described finding de Clambe's spoons with the defendants. Simpson and Gannan agreed they had been caught with de Clambe's property, but denied taking it from the house. After fifteen minutes' deliberation, the bench returned a guilty verdict and both men were given death.

Next, the eleven captured en route to the mountains stood charged with 'assisting the aforesaid felony' and taking de Clambe's property, including his sword, pistol and spy-glass. Mary Turley deposed that Woollaghan entered the house with McDermott, and that Dempsey had stolen a pair of razors. Dempsey asked to cross-examine her, wanting to know how she could identify him. Turley replied that she remembered him carrying a candle into the bedroom. 'You said "We may as well take all as not", and I saw you take my master's razors,' she said.

Dempsey stopped there, perhaps realising he was only tightening his own noose, and de Clambe again took the stand to identify his property. Matthew Lock and David Brown described the items found at the scene of capture. Andrew Thompson, who had taken charge of the prisoners when they were brought in to Hawkesbury, confirmed this evidence. All eleven defendants denied the charges. When asked for their defence, one of them offered that

> . . . he had embarked in this fatal expedition with no other view, than that of crossing the mountains, which the judicious and well-equipped have found impassable, and thereby returning to his family![6]

The court took longer to consider this charge before returning a guilty verdict and death sentence for McDermott, Dempsey and Woollaghan. The others (Lynch, Shanks, Morgan, Doyle, Mulcahy, Brown, Conroy and Ross) were acquitted but detained to face a second capital indictment at 10 am the next morning — feloniously entering Thomas Neale's house and stealing one bushel and one peck of wheat, valued at 10 shillings. John Kable outlined the particulars of the raid. He recognised Conroy and Lynch as the two of the trio who first bailed him up, but only identified Shanks, Ross and Morgan amongst those arriving later. Thomas Neale confirmed Kable's account, pointing out Lynch, Conroy, Brown, Shanks and Morgan as being present. John Smith stated that eleven men came to the house, three armed, but only recognised Lynch, Conroy, Brown and Shanks. William Lane added that one of the stolen muskets was his property.[7] Doyle and Mulcahy must have been the least forward; none of the eyewitnesses recalled them. They denied the charge, naturally enough, and so did all the others. This time only a few minutes passed before all eight men were sentenced to hang, with Judge–Advocate Atkins advising they ask Heaven to forgive their crimes.

Ward and Ramsey were discharged but may not have got off too lightly as they were detained for absconding, which meant up to 500 lashes. The lone runaway John McCormick was also discharged but not detained further — had he earned this leniency by assisting Thompson's search party?

After a few days' deliberation, Governor King decided only three of the condemned men should die. Strict as he often was, King was a reluctant executioner and a full year had passed without a capital punishment. His soft–hearted penchant for last–minute reprieves actually disadvantaged the condemned, some argued, by encouraging them to withhold those soul–cleansing confessions of guilt. In this case, however, King felt an example had to be made of at least some of the offenders.[8]

Patrick McDermott, who had betrayed his master de Clambe, was one of the unlucky ones. Gannan and Simpson were also slated for the gallows, which, considered with their early separation from the others, raises the strong possibility that they were the rapists. Perhaps the gang expelled them for violating Rose Bean. They may even have attacked the

Bradley and Bean properties without the others; certainly the raid they missed was much less violent.

Those spared by King had their sentences converted to life. This meant little, as most had been transported for life anyway. The condemned trio went upriver to Parramatta on 22 March and stayed in the watchhouse overnight. At 8 am the next morning they were marched the eight miles to Castle Hill, 'near to the spot on which they had committed the offence for which they were about to atone'. Here a temporary scaffold had been erected and a cart waited underneath the 'fatal tree' to launch the trio's aerial choking. Their arrival at 10.30 am was witnessed by a crowd of convicts, mustered from Castle Hill penal farm. Reverend Marsden urged penitence from the doomed men during a half-hour sermon. Gannan and McDermott were subdued, but Simpson masked his fear with false bravado. The *Sydney Gazette* wrote that Simpson, 'as if insensible to the terrors of his situation, had conducted himself with unbecoming levity until near the approach of death, when he listened with much attention to the exhortation of the Minister'.[9]

When Marsden was done the prisoners were brought up to the scaffold. Nooses were fitted around their necks and the cart readied to be moved out from beneath them. Suddenly, with a twist worthy of a Georgian melodrama, proceedings were halted and the chance of a reprieve offered to either Gannan or McDermott. Apparently Governor King now considered two deaths sufficient, as long as one of them was Francis Simpson. George Caley, the explorer and naturalist, described the macabre lottery that followed beneath the dangling nooses:

> At the gallows two were permitted to draw lots for a reprieve; but the one that was reckoned most notorious was not allowed the indulgence of such a chance, which appears to me quite novel as well as singular.

However peculiar this struck Caley, it was not an isolated incident. It was King's way of extending an impartial mercy while proceeding with the example of punishment. The method had been used to reprieve six of the nine runaways sentenced to 100 lashes the previous October. Caley related how on another occasion King had two convicted thieves each choose a folded piece of paper at the gallows, one containing a written reprieve (the victim had petitioned for either offender to be spared). Why Simpson's death was non-negotiable is unknown. The most obvious guess is that he had shot Bradley's servant in addition to raping Rose Bean. King all but acknowledged Simpson was punished for untried offences by reporting to London that he

> . . . caused two of the most wicked and desperate to undergo the sentence of the law, and have since granted a pardon to the rest conditional to their remaining here for life which I trust will have a good effect and remove the necessity of my exercising the most painful part of my duty.

The judicial Russian roulette ended with McDermott escaping the scaffold. Gannan and Simpson were hanged without further ado. No last words were recorded, although in the end Simpson, noted the *Gazette*, 'we feel the highest satisfaction in adding, also died a penitent'. Later that day King issued a General Order which he seems to have intended as the final word on convict escape mythology:

> The Governor trusts that the dreadful example made this day at Castle Hill, by the Execution of Two out of the 14 Malefactors that were condemned to die by the last Criminal Court, will prevent the obnoxious acts that rendered that Judgment necessary. After the repeated Orders, Advice and Warnings given by the Governor and his Predecessor, and the little effect they have had in preventing those under the Sentence of the Law (that have lately arrived) from being imposed on by the artful, designing knaves, who have no other pleasure than enjoying the mischiefs they occasion, the Governor only

hopes that the Convicts at large will be assured that their ridiculous plans of leaving public labour to go into the Mountains, to China, etc. can only end in their immediate detection and punishment; and that they will take warning from the fate of the unhappy men who have this day expiated with their lives the atrocious and vile crimes they committed.[10]

John Lynch, however, was far from finished with 'ridiculous plans'. Gathering fresh compatriots, he ran from Castle Hill a second time in July. This time one of his fellow travellers was James Hughes, a man of exceptional size and power said to have been a captain in the Irish rebel army before he was sentenced to life transportation in 1801. The rest of the gang came out on the *Hercules* with Hughes. Thomas Dowling (or Doolin) was from Kilkenny, Matthew Hoey hailed from Louth and the fifth man was James Tracey of Westmeath, colourfully nicknamed 'The Key of the Works'.

At 6.30 pm on 24 July, this gang burst into the hut of a Hawkesbury settler named Samuel Phelps, knocking him down and throwing a blanket over him. They tied up his wife Elizabeth, snatched two rings from her fingers, and began stripping the hut. The raid was efficient enough, but their swift downfall lay in a curious aftermath. The booty included the deeds to the property, which the next morning Lynch asked another Irish prisoner, Patrick Mulrain, to stash for him. Mulrain concealed the papers in the loft of a Toongabbie hut, but pretended to have lost them when Lynch and Hughes asked for their return soon afterwards. Even offerings of Phelps' silver teaspoons and gold watch failed to jog his memory.

The escapees' anxiety for papers seemingly useless to them is puzzling. The pains Lynch and Hughes took to hide the deeds separately from the other stolen items implies they saw special value in them. Yet they didn't trust Mulrain with the more readily disposable plunder. Possibly they realised that, although hardly likely to turn a profit within the colony, the deeds provided an excellent false identity — even an asset to sell or borrow against — should they reach the New Settlement or beyond. Mulrain's involvement may have been a means of hiding this intention from the other runaways. Their actions may simply have been the random product of stress and ignorance, but it does seem they wanted the deeds for something in particular. If Lynch intended another overland adventure, he was going to start out better equipped. Mulrain later claimed he feared Lynch and Hughes would silence him permanently after he handed the papers back, and was particularly afraid of Hughes. Equally he may have intended to cheat them of something he imagined was valuable. Either way, Mulrain soon regretted his complicity and revealed the hiding place to a Parramatta constable, who found the deeds bound by cords from Lynch's hammock.

The gang were rounded up in the bush a few days later. Despite being handcuffed, the burly Hughes overpowered the two arresting constables and fled into the scrub. His strength and cunning were especially worrisome to the authorities. Richard Atkins, acting on King's instructions, issued a proclamation dated 14 September warning that Hughes was 'to be OUTLAWED if he shall not appear in three weeks next falling to Date hereof'. Anyone guilty of harbouring or not turning him in would be liable to the staggering fine of fifty pounds.

Lynch, Tracey, Dowling and Hoey were tried on 20 September, along with Bryan O'Brien, another Irish convict arrested in their company. Dowling turned Crown's evidence and named Lynch, Tracey, Hoey and Hughes as his accomplices in the Phelps robbery. O'Brien was exonerated but detained on suspicion of another theft. The others were sentenced to death, with Hoey offered a reprieve of life imprisonment.[11]

The double execution was set for 27 September. Lynch and Tracey also went to Parramatta by boat and were marched to a gallows at Castle Hill. Lynch did what was expected of him as he stood on the cart, acknowledging his guilt and urging the crowd to take his fate as a caution against falling into 'similar vices'. But a sullen Tracey protested his innocence to the last, even shouting down Lynch's last minute show of penitence. As the *Sydney Gazette* put it, he 'harshly desired him not to gratify the spectators'. It made no difference; there were no last minute reprieves this time. The cart was driven off and both men launched into eternity.

During the mutiny on the *Hercules*, Tracey had been badly wounded and, thinking he was dying, blamed the instigator Jeremiah Prendergast for leading them all to ruin. Captain Betts seized on this comment (along with Tracey's admission that Prendergast would lead a second mutiny if the first failed) as a defence when he was tried for killing Prendergast. The *Sydney Gazette* twisted these facts to infer 'The Key of The Works' was despised as an informer. Lack of real evidence aside, it is rather at odds with his spectacular nickname, which suggests some degree of convict kudos, at the very least someone resourceful or influential. The real object of hatred was Dowling. After Tracey and Lynch were in their coffins, an Irish convict named William Gorman attacked Dowling with a knife, reviling him as a 'hangman dog' for shopping his mates.

The fate of the elusive Hughes remained a mystery — and a topic of rumour — for over two years. Finally, in January 1806, an Aborigine led an emancipist settler named John Tarlington to the bones of a white man in the bush 'under the first ridge of the mountains'. A tin kettle and a musket lay on the ground nearby. The great size of the skeleton pointed to it being Hughes, and the *Sydney Gazette* didn't hesitate to speak ill of the dead when offering the following obituary:

> Hughes was an able active man; well known in Ireland during the rebellion that existed in that country for his abominable depravities; and it is hoped his miserable end will warn the thoughtless, inexperienced and depraved against an inclination to exchange the comfort and security derived from honest labour; to depart from which can only lead to the most fatal consequences!

The report also confused him with Lynch's first set of associates, mistakenly noting that he was the last unaccounted-for Irishman who fled Castle Hill in February 1803 'on the ridiculous pretext of finding a road to China, but in reality to commit the most unheard of depredations'. The newspaper may have preferred to think they were motivated by plunder alone, but amongst other evidence Governor King was sufficiently convinced of the visionary objective to describe it in a Government Order and two dispatches to Secretary of State for War and the Colonies, Lord Hobart.

Patrick McDermott made no more escape attempts, but pushed his luck too far by bailing up another farmhouse three years later. Arrested the day after raiding the property of Joseph Pearce at Seven Hills, McDermott was taken straight back to the farm for identification purposes, which the *Sydney Gazette* reported went very badly for him:

> . . . his voice (which is particularly remarkable) was immediately recognised by an infant in an adjoining room, who, without facing him, exclaimed, 'here's the man that was here last night come back to kill us.'

At his trial McDermott tried in vain to prove he was five miles away at Castle Hill when the robbery took place. He was hanged at Parramatta Gaol on 20 May 1806. The rest of his old gang were fortunate by comparison. King didn't send them to Norfolk Island and, as no other penal outposts then existed for colonial offenders, they were returned to labour within the existing system. In later years they would have been retransported to designer hellholes like Newcastle, Port Macquarie or Moreton Bay. Instead, within three years most were assigned to various settlers and despite their colonial life sentences, they were ultimately treated no differently to other convicts of their generation. Some were freed during Governor Macquarie's administration, such as Lachlan Doyle, who settled at Liverpool in 1816. In 1814 Michael Woollaghan, working in a Parramatta road gang, was wrongly convicted of a double-murder and only escaped the gallows by the narrowest of margins when one of the real killers, a bushranger also under sentence of death, confessed the truth before hanging. Woollaghan was released and two years later finally pardoned for whatever crime had seen him shipped to New South Wales. He ended up a farmer at Campbelltown, married with six children.[12]

Timothy Mulcahy and Patrick Ross were among the 167 convicts pardoned by Macquarie in 1815. A quarter of them were being rewarded for building the first road across the Blue Mountains, but it's unlikely Mulcahy or Ross appreciated the irony of gaining their freedom alongside men who earned theirs by such a venture. Mulcahy didn't use the road to start a new life in the interior, if his King Street, Sydney address in 1825 is any indication.

These escapes from Castle Hill are usually only mentioned in passing — when they are mentioned at all — as a prelude to the convict uprising of 1804, an early warning that Irish discontent was soon to break out into overt rebellion. But in another sense the 1804 rebellion can be seen as the bloody aftermath of the failure of the bush sanctuary bids of the previous two years. When summarising the de Clambe–Bean raids to Lord Hobart, King advised that 'excepting this instance, which would not have occurred but from the infatuation of their infamous advisers, the conduct of the convicts has generally been quiet and obedient'. The governor garbled some details of the case, attributing the outrages solely to 'the mutinous Irish who came in the *Hercules*'. He also made the extraordinary claim to have known of 'their intention and ridiculous schemes' in advance, either a general reference to leaked rumours or maybe just indicating that previous escapes had typecast the myth's adherents as Castle Hill's prime troublemakers. King also followed his predecessors with the suspicion that escape mythology was the work of 'artful, designing characters with which this colony abounds'.

The escape myths were still sublimating rebellion into absenteeism, but open revolt was not far away. The disaffected still yearned to escape the colony, but continual disappointment began to alter their focus. Instead of looking outwards to China and the white colony, they began to increasingly look inwards. As if deciding a colony in the hand was worth two in the bush, they dreamed less of reaching their 'fancied Paradise' and more of seizing control of the Purgatory that held them.

CHAPTER TWELVE

The fatal excursions of John Place

And some dark night when everything
is silent in the town
I'll kill the tyrants one and all;
and shoot the floggers down;
I'll give the Law a little shock;
remember what I say,
They'll yet regret they sent Jim Jones
in chains to Botany Bay.

'JIM JONES AT BOTANY BAY', CONVICT BALLAD

JOHN PLACE DESERVES A SPECIAL PLACE IN THE CONVICT VALHALLA. After chance, timing and survival against all odds won his failed walk to China unprecedented contemporary coverage, he cemented his notoriety with a second ill-starred escape and a leading role in the biggest convict uprising the colony would ever see. His single, action-packed year in New South Wales not only encapsulates the close connection between convict dreamers and rebels, it serves as a vivid reminder of how ignorant many Europeans in Australia remained, even as late as 1803, of the strange new world around them.

An Englishman from Yorkshire, Place began his downward spiral in June 1801 when he entered York's Ousebridge Gaol on suspicion of 'feloniously stealing thirteen yards of ribband', the property of one Bransby Turner. On Monday 20 July, Place heard himself sentenced to death at York's Guildhall, although the sentence was commuted to fourteen years transportation before the Assizes closed a week later. The following year he was embarked on the HMS *Glatton*, a 56-gun frigate newly outfitted as a convict transport.

The *Glatton* had recently seen action at the Battle of Copenhagen, captained by none other than William Bligh. But the Treaty of Amiens had ushered in a short-lived cessation of the war against France, and England's fighting ships were being put to other uses. The HMS *Calcutta* would also take convicts to Australia, but in September 1802 it was the *Glatton*'s turn. The arrangement had two presumed benefits — the navy wanted to return a cargo of timber for shipbuilding, and naval expertise was thought to stand a better chance of delivering prisoners in good health. But the voyage was overcrowded and sickly. Seven men and five women died during a six-month passage via Madeira and Rio de Janeiro, and a quarter of the convicts were scorbutic upon arrival. On 11 March 1803, the day before the *Glatton* anchored in Sydney Cove, a hundred 'weak people' were ferried ashore; half were hospitalised. Even Captain James Colnett suffered from diarrhoea and had every one of his teeth loosened by scurvy.

John Place was one of many *Glatton* men sent to Castle Hill, where 300 acres were now under cultivation and work had recently commenced on a two-storey stone barracks. Chances are he arrived in time to witness the hanging of Gannan and Simpson. Their example did nothing to dampen his similar dreams of freedom. A few weeks later Place took to the bush with a small group of fellow *Glatton* newcomers.

On 26 June, the *Sydney Gazette* published a detailed account of their doomed flight, headlined 'FATAL EXCURSION'. Place's companions — Joseph Cox from Buckinghamshire, William Knight from Southampton, and Philip Philips from Brecon — were all lifers.[1] According to the newspaper, three of the quartet were married men anxious to rejoin their families. Their hopes had been raised, as Place confessed, 'in consequence of having heard people on board the *Glatton*, and while at work at Castle-hill, that they could get to China, by which means they would obtain their liberty'. His testimony suggests they conceived a short overland trek would meet this goal: they 'resolved to pass the Mountains, and took with them only their week's ration'.

The escape was from Cornwallis Place, the government's Hawkesbury farm, where they had been sent for the wheat-sowing season. While travelling along the Hawkesbury Road to this new posting, the four men agreed to abscond into the Blue Mountains together. Three days later, on Saturday 7 May, they slipped into the bush after receiving their weekly ration. By Wednesday the food was gone and they were grubbing around for wild currants and sweet-tea leaves. Seventeen days of freedom brought nothing but exhaustion and frustration. They got into the thickly wooded foothills easily enough — possibly in the vicinity of Kurrajong Heights — but like better equipped expeditions before them, found no way to penetrate any further.

Tormented by the spectre of starvation for almost a fortnight, the runaways finally realised they had to get back to Hawkesbury or die. The Welshman Philips, who was the strongest, went to gather berries for the return journey while the others rested. He disappeared into dense foliage, never to be seen again. Place recalled hearing him cry out several times, so he must have collapsed or met with an accident fairly close by. No one had the strength to go to his aid, and soon he was heard no more.

For the next twenty days the three others, oppressed by hunger, dehydration and chill winter nights, trusted to their befuddled senses and struggled on. When they had reached within five miles of Richmond

Hill (by Place's estimation), Knight collapsed and couldn't get up. Place and Cox pushed on to reach the Hawkesbury River later the same day. They tried fording the river near some rapids, and were separated by a strong current. Swept to the other side, Place scrambled ashore by gripping the branches of overhanging trees. The less fortunate Cox was washed backwards, and Place last saw him lying drenched on the far bank, wearing only his shoes and shirt.

Exhausted, Place also collapsed by the river. The next morning brought the luck that saved his life and enabled the *Sydney Gazette* to preserve his story. A kangaroo shooting expedition — a lone white man and several Aborigines — chanced upon him as he lay on the verge of death from starvation and hypothermia. The Aborigines assisted him to shelter. He was unable to tell them about Cox, whose body was not found. The next day (about 13 June) Place was taken to Hawkesbury, and then to Parramatta Hospital in an extremely weak and emaciated state.

Interrogated from his sickbed during the next fortnight, Place claimed his little expedition had 'travelled the whole of the seventeen days with the sun on their right shoulder, and found great difficulty in ascending some of the Mountains, and also attempted to return by the direction of the sun'. They had reversed this practice and kept the sun to their left when all hope was lost. Such slapdash navigational methods make his reappearance after more than a month's absence all the more remarkable.

After detailing Place's disclosures in its 26 June issue, the *Sydney Gazette* made him the subject of a lengthy editorial the following week. Even though Place's 'melancholy account' suggests he was technically a Chinese traveller, the paper took the opportunity to decry escape mythology in general. It's a rambling passage, but unique descriptions of the white colony makes it worth quoting in full, especially since it also reveals how the authorities imagined these ideas were spread. A concept later seriously propounded by Flinders, that unknown castaways had founded a mystery settlement, is rejected out of hand as absurd. But the article has its own absurdities, clearly aimed at discouraging runaways. These include an assertion that the Blue Mountains are separated by large lagoons, and also a bald denial that officialdom had ever sanctioned searches for 'chimerical establishments':

The dismal consequences that have invariably resulted from the rash project of crossing the Mountains, have proved, upon the most fatal evidence, the impossibility of its accomplishment, and the certain wretchedness and destruction of those who ignorantly presume on the attempt. From the numbers that have at different times fallen victims to the dangerous desire of emigrating and who have absconded from the several Settlements under an illusory persuasion that an Establishment exists on the other side of these immeasurable heights, it becomes the duty of every well-wisher to his fellow creature, by reasonable argument to point out the impracticability of performing such a journey and the egregious absurdity of fostering the idea of an imaginary Settlement.

It had been reported, by persons who were careless whether they asserted facts or falsehoods, that the natives of the interior have made mention of a set of people whose manners and customs strongly resembled our own; and others, willing to give a still more improbable colour to the imposture, affected in addition that these distant inhabitants were possessed of bells, churches, masted vessels, a sterling specie, and every other requisite that might seem calculated to convey the idea of civilization. The natives, upon whose verbal testimony this suggestion is pretended to have been founded, have too frequently convinced us of their ingenuity in dissimulation, to obtain the most distant shadow of belief where a doubt possibly could subsist; and we are also well aware of their readiness to acquiesce in every thing, however absurd, that may obtain them encouragement, or administer to their immediate wants. That such chimera may have so originated we cannot altogether question; but nevertheless venture to affirm, that were two or more of these reports compared, the delusive supposition must vanish into nothingness, and this establishment prove indebted for its existence to the fertility of a romantic brain.

To suppose that a body of civilized people should assemble on a coast, by shipwreck or other possible cause, and although possessed of the means yet entertained no desire to communicate with or return to their native country, would be as unreasonable as to imagine them set down in secret, and never after become a subject of enquiry, as no tradition has ever hinted at a circumstance that could possibly have given birth to so truly unreasonable, so preposterous a conjecture.

Were it therefore possible that an individual could make good this journey and safely pass the numerous and large Lagoons by which these Mountains are intersected, no other reward awaits this fatal curiosity than death under accumulated miseries.

Missions, well directed and equipped, have indefatigably endeavoured to explore them, not in pursuit of a chimerical establishment, but upon useful discovery; and they, altho' provided with every necessity for the long and laborious travel, have been successively convinced to abandon the design, after an absence of many weeks: what then must be the portion of the rash and inexperienced few, who unconscious of the difficulties they are unprepared to encounter, yet dare to venture on the project? Sorry we are to say, the consequences have already been too manifest — three out of four have LATELY fallen victims to their rashness, and too late repented of the credulity to which they were about to become the most wretched victims.[2]

His lost companions may have repented of their credulity as they succumbed to the elements, but Place certainly didn't because he ran again only a few months later. When his strength recovered he was put to work at Parramatta[3], where he gathered a new set of willing companions for a second escape bid in November.

Accompanying him this time was fellow Yorkshireman Edward Hill and someone Place claimed to know only as 'Dick the Waggoner'. Hill was another of Place's *Glatton* shipmates, but their association went back a little further. In April 1801, then aged forty-five, Hill was charged with breaking into a house in the Yorkshire village of Ecclesfield and stealing various items, most notably seven silver teaspoons. Tried and sentenced to death at the York Assizes on the same day as John Place, Hill was also reprieved later in the week.

The three men took a bushel of wheat as provisions, but again the food lasted less than a week. Hungry and exhausted, they pressed on until, as the *Gazette* reported on 18 December, 'convinced that the project unhappily set out upon was all vanity, and a vexation of body as well as spirit the sole reward of their romantic expedition, they had jointly determined to return'. For some reason they separated after this group decision, with Hill turning himself in at Hawkesbury and Place surrendering to the gaoler at Sydney.

Edward Hill's trial seems to be undocumented, although he re-appears in the 1806 convict muster as an assigned servant. The return of Dick the Waggoner — if he ever did return, or even depart — has similarly escaped record. John Place, however, was tried for absconding on 17 December 1803, about a week after his surrender. The *Gazette* reports a new goal for this second expedition. They intended

> . . . to cross the Mountains, and, if not so fortunate as to establish the existence of the imaginary settlement, a chimera to which several had already become the most miserable sacrifice, that they had entertained no doubt of arriving to a sea-side (although their route was diametrically opposite to such an object), where they trusted they might obtain some relief from shipping that might chance to pass.

The indeterminate nature of Place's destination may be another clue that what some runaways called China and what their interrogators dismissed as 'the imaginary settlement' were essentially the same mirage. His back-up plan is especially interesting. The newspaper mocked what it presented as an ignorant bid to reach the Pacific Ocean by travelling west, but Place's certainty of finding a sea there was fully supported by the current state of knowledge. The idea of New South Wales and western New Holland as a pair of large islands was tenable until Matthew Flinders accomplished the first circumnavigation of Australia — just days before Place was found dying by the Hawkesbury River.

Far from repudiating an inland sea, however, Flinders pondered whether a landlocked sea washed against the inside of the coastal cliffs along the Great Australian Bight. It was a reasonable reaction to the apparent lack of major river outlets; he had missed the Murray delta by the smallest of margins. And he didn't rule out an undiscovered channel that might connect a new 'Mediterranean' to the ocean. This dream-sea held an appeal for Flinders remarkably similar to the vision sustaining Place and other convicts:

> In the case of penetrating the interior of Terra Australis, whether by a
> great river, or a strait leading to an inland sea, a superior country, and
> perhaps a different people, might be found, the knowledge of which
> could not fail to be very interesting, and might prove advantageous to
> the nation making the discovery.

As the inland sea remained credible speculation and the topic of debate for several decades, it's not surprising that offshoots should fire false hopes amongst the lower orders. Gossip in the wake of Flinders' achievements as much as convict confidence in the imaginary settlement may have spurred Place on to this second effort. While a long shot, his scheme was not without logic: runaways hoping to be rescued from an uncharted coast overland to the west could at least assume little risk of being found and brought in by colonial sea traffic. A phantom colony with access to a phantom seacoast could promise not only sanctuary but also the chance to sail home undisturbed by British shipping. The civilised people 'on a coast' and the masted vessels described by the *Gazette* as elements of the 'imaginary Settlement' across the Blue Mountains further suggest how convict mythologising may have drawn upon the inland sea. At the very least, Place was eventually vindicated in rejecting the certainty of his superiors that the Blue Mountains were impassable, a view which held official sway for another decade.

This time around the magistrates — Paterson, Atkins and Jamieson — were understandably suspicious of Place's 'undebilitated appearance', a sharp contrast to the half-dead state his first flight had reduced him to. Considering that 'no man in existence had the hardihood to make a second experiment of this nature', they decided his story was concealing an attempt to find work at a remote property where he could pass for a free man — or where a settler was more interested in a man's labour than his legal status. They don't seem to have wondered why Place turned himself in so soon after absconding — an unusual move, especially if he was not in physical distress. Dick the Waggoner's permanent disappearance lends some credence to Place's story in hindsight, although the court could only assume he was still at large — or never existed. Either way, Place had good cause to forget his full name.

A likely scenario is that, bamboozled by the mountains a second time, Place turned back before the going got too rough, convinced by his first hideous bush experience — and the sympathy the ordeal generated — that this was the safest course. But if he assumed another heartrending tale of delusion and privation would keep the lash at bay, he had a bitter pill to swallow. A severely debilitated runaway might be excused punishment on account of his self-inflicted injuries, but sob stories alone were not enough. The bench, 'after serious consideration', decided to make a savage example of him in accordance with the governor's anti-absconding order of the previous year. His trial minutes read:

John Place accused of absconding from his labor at Parramatta a month ago. He says that himself and two others left the Settlement with some provisions, and proceeded towards the blue Mountains intending to make the sea-coast, in the Expectation of being taken up by some vessel, or to fall in with a Settlement he had heard was to the W.ward or N.ward. To receive 500 lashes.

He may not have copped the full 500. Flogging was often curtailed according to the victim's ability to bear it on the day, assessed by attending officials. But Place's desire to escape was beyond this manner of cure. Sent back to Castle Hill, he nursed his wounds and grievances, adding his groans to the rumbling groundswell of rebellion that gained momentum in the opening months of the new year.

The convict uprising of 1804 was largely an Irish affair, but men of other nationalities were involved and some, like John Place, were leading players. At least two of the nine hanged afterwards were English. Some writers have assumed the convicts wished to raise an Irish republic, phoenix-like, on the ashes of the overthrown British colony. But the real goal was simply to return home: the rebellion was absconding on a grand scale and its ringleader, Phillip Cunningham, had already felt 100 lashes for trying to flee the colony.

Cunningham arrived as a life prisoner on the *Anne* in 1801, a veteran of both the Irish Rebellion and the failed *Anne* mutiny. He was supposedly an ex-soldier, born in Kerry. By 1804 he had been working as a stonemason at Castle Hill for about a year, and had built himself a sturdy hut. His lieutenant in the uprising, William Johnston, was also a Kerry man with a military background and rebel credentials.

A tantalising scrap of evidence suggests John Place was one of Cunningham's earliest recruits, helping him muster support in the Hawkesbury district. Early in 1804, Place began to visit and occasionally stay at the Hawkesbury farm of Martin Short, where Cunningham also lodged only days before the uprising. A former Dublin carpenter, Short shared with Place the horrific experience of a 500-lash sentence, a consequence of the Irish conspiracy trials in 1800. Short's property was notorious as 'a receptacle for the most disloyal and abandoned description of Irish', who accepted the embittered Place as one of their own.

On Thursday 1 March, two of Cunningham's followers obtained passes from Castle Hill to work at Hawkesbury, intending to smuggle written instructions to signal the beginning of the uprising. On the way they tried to recruit a pair of Irish convicts who were thatching a building at the whimsically named stopover There or Nowhere (now the Sydney suburb Kellyville). But the workmen would have no part of it, and over the weekend went to Captain Edward Abbott, the Corps commander at Parramatta, telling him they had suffered enough during the rebellion in Ireland and wanted to prevent further bloodshed.

While lunching in a tavern that Sunday, Irish exile Joseph Holt was warned by a fellow overseer that the authorities knew about the rebels' plans. Holt immediately went home to safeguard his farm and had nothing to do with what followed. On the same day an unusually low turnout at Castle Hill's divine service spooked the minister, Reverend Hassall. Hawkesbury magistrate Thomas Arndell also twigged what was afoot and wrote a hasty note to his superior, Samuel Marsden, begging for ammunition.

Cunningham went ahead as planned on Sunday evening, not knowing or caring his plot had leaked like a sieve. At 8 pm a hut was set ablaze at Castle Hill. As the flames illuminated the evening a bell was rung, and amidst cries of 'Death or liberty!' some 200 convicts swarmed from their huts to seize the handful of convict constables. There were no soldiers to worry about; the small unit posted there in the wake of the de Clambe–Bean robberies had been withdrawn after months of relative peace. While searching the buildings with other convict rebels, John Place found the despised government flogger, Robert Duggan, cowering under a bed. Place's hatred must have burned as fiercely as his back when Duggan had scourged him. With the help of Irish convict John Brannon, Place wrenched Duggan outside for a savage beating.

George Harrington, like Place a *Glatton* Englishman, was most active in the assault, shouting 'Damn him, I'll kill him!'

Later, standing guard with a musket on his shoulder at the captured storehouse, Place challenged a constable named Robert Jones, asking him if he was 'for liberty'. When Jones replied he was not, Place immediately raised his musket to shoot him, but it snapped without firing.

After securing Castle Hill, raiding parties went looking for arms and recruits, aiming to rendezvous at Sugar Loaf Hill between Parramatta and Toongabbie. Cunningham planned to draw the government troops from Parramatta by torching a farm east of town. A rebel contingent would then storm Parramatta Gaol and light another fire. This would signal the main attack force, bolstered by recruits from Hawkesbury, to sweep into Parramatta and march onto Sydney, where they would commandeer the port and sail home to Ireland in triumph. But the fires were never lit, and someone slipped away during the taking of Castle Hill to alert Captain Abbott at Parramatta. Couriers were sent in a headlong ride to warn Sydney, and by 10 pm Parramatta was secured, with several local families sheltering inside the barracks.

Various rebel units ranged across the countryside that evening, raiding farms for ammunition and rallying converts to the cause. De Clambe's farm was a prime target, and not just for its proximity to Castle Hill. Rumours had been circulating for months that the Irish convicts wanted de Clambe dead. His testimony had helped hang the runaways Gannan and Simpson and, moreover, Irish sympathies lay very much with the French Republic — to many Irish rebels this Royalist refugee was a contemptible traitor to Liberty, Equality and Fraternity.[4] But with his genius for avoiding trouble, the old soldier was absent a second time. In a virtual replay of the previous raid, convicts seized his arms and alcohol. Some time after midnight the rebels regrouped on Sugar Loaf Hill, toasting their freedom with plundered grog, singing rebel songs and pondering their next move. They gave up on Parramatta, realising the barracks were fortified against them, and decided to march on Hawkesbury where they hoped to gain recruits. The specifics now had to be played by ear, but the general idea was unchanged. As Cunningham put it that night during a stirring address to his ragtag army: 'Now, my boys, liberty or death!'

Just before midnight, a breathless messenger burst into Government House at Sydney to wake King with the bad news. The governor dressed immediately, rode to alert Major Johnston and continued to Parramatta, arriving at about 4 am after a tense sixteen-mile night ride. Johnston came in a few hours later with his troops. On the steps of Parramatta's Government House, King unleashed the Corps' dogs of war, declaring that Parramatta, Castle Hill, Toongabbie, Prospect, Seven Hills, Baulkham Hills, Hawkesbury and Nepean were in a state of rebellion and therefore under martial law.

Johnston divided his force to track the rebels along the two main routes from town. One half tramped along Castle Hill Road, where they arrested some stragglers. The other unit, under Johnston's command, took Toongabbie Road accompanied by sixty-seven civilians, Trooper Thomas Andlezark from King's convict bodyguard and Father James Dixon, a transported Catholic priest. By the time they reached Sugar Loaf Hill, the rebels had already left for Hawkesbury. Johnston marched his men another ten miles north. At about 10.30 am, with the rising heat of the day compounding their weariness, they spied the convict army clustered on a wooded hill just beyond Second Ponds Creek.

Johnston rode ahead with Andlezark and Father Dixon to call on the rebels to surrender. Some of them invited him to talk, but he refused to ride within pistol range. Instead he made a calculated appeal to their bravado. Johnston reported himself as saying 'that it was in their power to kill me, and that their captains must have very little spirit if they would not come forward to speak to me'.

Cunningham and William Johnston fell for the bait and strode towards the mounted major. Armed only with cutlasses, they naively expected a parley. Playing for time, Johnston warned them to surrender again, promising he would mention them favourably to the governor. Cunningham refused. 'Death or liberty, and a ship to take us home,' he boldly demanded. Noting the approach of the infantry and militia, Johnston sprang his trap. Whipping out a hidden pistol, he clapped it to his rebel namesake's head, while Andlezark did likewise to Cunningham. Helpless, the two Irishmen were delivered up to Quartermaster Thomas Laycock. Johnston then ordered his redcoats to attack. As the firing commenced, Laycock felled Cunningham with a ferocious slash of his sword. The rebel leader collapsed, blood streaming, and was left for dead.

The Battle of Vinegar Hill — as it later became known — was little more than a rout. The convicts, hardly returning the first volley, soon panicked and fled in all directions. The soldiers chased them through the woods, shooting and slashing, ferreting out stragglers until nightfall. That afternoon Johnston reported his troops had killed nine convicts, captured seven and wounded 'a great many; the number we cannot ascertain'. Four days later he revised this to twelve killed, six wounded and twenty-six taken prisoner.

Cunningham was found in the woods the day after the battle, badly wounded but still breathing. Taking advantage of the suspension of civil law, Johnston had him hanged from the staircase of the public storehouse at the Hawkesbury village of Green Hills (Windsor). Later that day he boasted in writing to King, 'I never saw more zeal and activity than what has been displayed by the officers and men of the detachment for destroying or securing the runaways'.

Mopping up was virtually complete by Wednesday. On Thursday, 8 March, Captain Abbott convened a court martial at Parramatta to make examples of some captured rebels. Of the 200 or so brought in or surrendered, ten were selected as the 'most forward'. John Place was one of these men. Surviving ringleader William Johnston was another. The charge was that they, with others, did 'riotously, tumultuously and traitorously assemble at Castle Hill and various other places in the Territory, armed with guns, pistols, cutlasses and other offensive weapons with an intent to overturn His Majesty's Government in this Territory'. They also stood 'charged with resisting, opposing and attacking His Majesty's Forces'.

William Johnston's leading role in the uprising was well-attested. Charles Hill, Samuel Humes and John Neale had all captained sizeable rebel contingents. The other defendants had all been seen bearing arms or ammunition. Various witnesses deposed that John Brannon, George Harrington, Timothy Hogan and John Place had fired muskets either at Vinegar Hill or during the seizure of Castle Hill. John Burke had been 'very active' during the final battle, although no one actually witnessed him shooting. The weakest case was against Bryan McCormick, who had been seen carrying a powder horn in an eight-man gang with only a single musket between them. Seven of the ten pleaded they were forced to join the rebellion. This was hardly an option for Johnston, who proudly threw himself on the mercy of the court. Neale admitted to joining the rebels, but denied other parts of the charge. Only John Place, accused of two specific acts of violence — the attempted shooting of Constable Jones and the assault on the flogger — denied all charges laid against him. It was his final act of defiance.

Each man was sentenced to death, and the court martial dissolved. At 6 pm that same day Humes, Hill and Place were executed at Parramatta, all three allegedly acknowledging 'the justice of this sentence' before they swung. Johnston, Neale and Harrington were taken to Castle Hill to suffer the same treatment the next morning. On 10 March the last four men faced the gallows in Sydney, although Burke and McCormick were respited at the last minute. Another nine convicts were flogged for lesser roles in the revolt. As principals, Johnston and Humes were reserved the special ignominy of being hung in chains. When the *Sydney Gazette* published obituaries of Cunningham, Place, Humes and Hill on 18 March, the two-time runaway's exploits received another airing:

> John Place was the only survivor of the three [*sic*] who embark'd in
> the fatal enterprise of crossing the Mountains, under the whimsical

and ludicrous supposition of an unknown Settlement there existing, and was pardoned on account of the pitiable and deplorable plight in which he was found. He was afterwards corporally punished for a second time absconding in order to subsist in the woods, and his restless and relentless disposition at length drew down upon him the provoked vengeance of the Law.

The gibbeted bodies of Johnston and Humes, left to dangle and rot as hellish warnings to the likeminded, appear in the well-known contemporary illustration of the Vinegar Hill fight. This remarkable blend of naturalism and symbolism boasts a passable likeness of Major Johnston, the correct number of soldiers and a close approximation of the 233 rebels that King reported had been there. The few discrepancies include the mounted Father Dixon on foot, and Johnston arresting Cunningham instead of his namesake — which was how the *Sydney Gazette* reported it, contradicting the Major's own report to King.

The unknown artist's masterstroke is a distortion of time, hardly perceptible to the casual viewer, presenting key aspects of the battle simultaneously. Commencing with the arrest of the rebel leaders in the foreground, the incidents depicted generally move ahead in time the further the viewer delves into the background. 'Croppy lay down,' says Andlezark, brandishing his pistol at William Johnston, who laments, 'We are all ruin'd'. Phillip Cunningham appears twice, balancing the left and right foreground. One Cunningham is being arrested; he declares 'Death or Liberty Major' as Johnston replies, 'You Scoundrel I'll liberate you'. The other Cunningham cries 'Oh Jasus' in a mock-Irish accent as Laycock cuts him down, cursing 'Thou Rebel Dog'. In the background the battle rages, a line of troopers firing on at the rebel horde. Most convicts flee for their lives up the hill. Five lie sprawled in their own gore. Only four return fire, reflecting the four rebels — Harrington, Hogan, Brannon and Place — hanged for firing weapons during the uprising. At the edge of the carnage, Father James Dixon begs the convicts to surrender: 'Lay down yr Arms my deluded Countrymen'. Beyond the woods in the far left, reprisals have begun and the ringleaders' bodies, labelled 'Humes' and 'Johnston', swing from makeshift gallows in eerie silhouette.

The strangest part of the drawing occurs in the sky, which occupies a full third of the composition and is often cropped in reproductions. Looming above in the clouds — whether the artist intended it or not — is a huge ghostly simulacrum of a crow or raven. The image is straight out of Irish myth, the Celtic war goddess Morrigan presiding over the chaos of battle in her death aspect. And eight birds wheel in the shadow of her raised wing; eight rebels executed by court martial, soaring above the wall of wilderness to an undiscovered country beyond the chains and cats, free at last.

CHAPTER THIRTEEN

Daemons and chimeras

May the annalist whose business it may be to record in future
the transactions of this colony find a pleasanter field
to travel in, where his steps will not be every moment
beset with murderers, robbers and incendiaries!

DAVID COLLINS, 'ACCOUNT OF THE ENGLISH COLONY
IN NEW SOUTH WALES', 1799

OUTRAGED AUTHORITY GAVE THE LOWER ORDERS FEW OPPORTUNITIES
to repeat the events of March 1804. King saw the downside of
concentrating the disaffected on one large farm and scattered them as far
as he could throughout the settlements, ordering that potential troublemakers be watched closely. Some of the most problematic convicts were
sent to the Hunter River, where they would mine coal and burn lime
under atrocious conditions. A plan was hatched to murder the soldiers
accompanying them there, but it came to nothing and ended in more
floggings.

This dispersal of Castle Hill's government men certainly stemmed
both rumour and seditious conspiracy, but the fact that an armed rebellion

took place at all suggests faith in nearby sanctuaries had already declined. Historians have often wondered why it took so long for the transported Irish rebels to rise. One theory is that news of Robert Emmet's short-lived rebellion in Dublin — but not his surrender — reached the colony in January 1804 via the *Mary*, an American whaler. Emmet had the usual hopes for French assistance, and the Irish in NSW may have assumed an independent Ireland — or at least a second chance of fighting for one — would be awaiting their homecoming.

Another possibility is that hotheads like Cunningham could not gain the support of the most desperate prisoners until disillusionment with the idea of reaching an overland sanctuary was sufficiently widespread. There are hints of this process at work during Cunningham's trial for absconding seventeen months before the rebellion, when he expressed dismay at his countrymen's misplaced enthusiasm for the New Settlement. The redirection of John Place's frustration from desertion to rebellion is unusually well documented, but not necessarily unique.

Most of the Irish runaways of the de Clambe–Bean affair were back at Castle Hill and certainly participated in the rebellion. Laurence Dempsey appeared at the trial of Joseph Holt, who stood accused of assuring Cunningham that the crew of HMS *Calcutta*, then in Sydney, would mutiny and seize the ship for the cause. The prosecution wanted Dempsey to corroborate this, but he merely recalled Holt's accuser asking him to invite Holt to meet up for a drink, which Holt had refused.[1]

Some French settlers suspected of encouraging republican sentiment were expelled from the colony. Colonel de Clambe continued to enjoy official favour, but he dropped dead — a 'Visitation of God' according to the coroner — only three months after the uprising. A reward he had advertised for the return of a treasured gold watch stolen during the rebellion remained unclaimed. Mary Turley, who as his de facto had no rights of inheritance, was charged with stealing some minor items of his property due for public auction, but was acquitted for lack of evidence.

On St Patrick's Day 1804 a man took his own wife to court for calling him a 'croppey'. The case was dismissed, but it revealed the paranoia sweeping the colony in the rebellion's aftershock. Fear of Irish radicalism also led to the banning of the Catholic Mass after ten months indulgence. King had been the first governor to allow the Mass in the colony, albeit under the watchful eye of armed constables, but he now considered any kind of sizeable Irish gathering too dangerous.

The spectre of the missing outlaw James Hughes also haunted nervous colonists. Seven fugitive rebels 'on the maraud' near Hawkesbury began the scare when they were captured in late March. They declared that the rest of their gang, supposedly eight men including the dreaded Hughes, were well-armed and on their way to Broken Bay to seize a boat and 'commit themselves to the perils of the sea'. The story was a hoax, however, and the later discovery of Hughes' bones in the mountains suggests his real efforts were in the opposite direction.

Newcastle was only the beginning of a wider distribution of convict labour. Assignment of convict labour to settlers became the norm, and as the new century progressed, the convict workforce increasingly spread across an expanding patchwork of landholdings. They were never able to organise a mass rebellion again. Large concentrations of government men were soon the exception rather than the rule, and these were generally confined to remote places of secondary punishment like Newcastle and Norfolk Island. By August 1805, Castle Hill's convict labour force had dwindled to seventy-four men and four women. In 1811 the penal farm was finally closed by Governor Macquarie and the barn converted into a lunatic asylum.

It is an irony often commented upon that the colony's second armed rebellion was led by Major Johnston himself. On 26 January 1808 he suddenly deposed King's autocratic successor, William Bligh, under circumstances still widely disputed 200 years later. For two years New South Wales was administered by a series of Corps officers, beginning with Johnston, whose six-month rule was dominated by ex-Corps officer John Macarthur as self-styled colonial secretary. After a year spent chafing under house arrest, Bligh escaped to Hobart where he licked his wounds and generally wore out the welcome afforded him by a sympathetic David Collins, by then lieutenant governor of Van Diemen's Land. Lachlan Macquarie, Bligh's legitimate replacement, finally arrived in December 1809, bringing his own regiment to supersede the problematic NSW Corps.

A second, lesser known double-irony of the convict rebellion lay in the exile of the most unruly Irish to Newcastle. First, they were sent to establish a 'new colony' in a region approximating the first supposed location of the overland China. Second, their objective in running was now overwhelmingly to get back to the more settled districts, where the increasing numbers of emancipist farmers were often willing to risk the fines imposed for taking on workers without checking their status. This preference for returning to the devil they knew was a game made more dangerous by Newcastle's Aboriginal population. Although Aborigines sometimes helped the starving desperates steadily trickling into their midst, rewards increasingly induced them to wing and return whoever they found. But if a runaway could run this gauntlet unscathed, an ex-convict farmer willing to hire labour with no questions asked was now the best option available.

There was no road to Newcastle. All official traffic was by sea, a seventy-mile trip. The hard slog through thick bush to Sydney was considered almost as suicidal as any attempt on the mountains. A typical case occurred in September 1804, when an Irish trio fled Newcastle with a small quantity of flour and salt and 'a romantic and in all respects absurd design of crossing the country for these Settlements'. They were twice intercepted by Aborigines. The first lot speared one runaway in the right temple; the second showed them to the coast where they lived on shellfish until they could surrender to a passing ship.

At this time Newcastle held a captured runaway named James Field, whose appalling condition led to him being retained as a kind of half-dead anti-escape exhibit. With two others, Field had taken a boat from Sydney just before the convict rebellion. Three months later, naked and bearded, he turned up alone by the Hunter River in a state 'too deplorable to be described or imagined'. It was several days before he could be identified. Speared through the right shoulder, Field had a crushed right hand and held a scrap of bark against three ghastly head wounds. When he finally spoke he said he envied the 'peaceful condition' of his dead companions, fatally speared by Aborigines after a gale smashed their stolen boat to splinters and washed them ashore just north of Port Stephens.[2]

The *Sydney Gazette* thought Field's suffering should prove the final solution to escape, arguing that 'if example can deter, surely none will leap headlong into the destructive vortex, through the want of unhappy instances to warn them of the certain danger'. The vortex still beckoned, however, refreshed by a new sighting of the white colony which enlivened the newspaper's edition for Sunday, 9 December 1804:

In the course of Thursday evening and Friday morning a report was generally current, that *several persons* accustomed to the woods had by accident fallen in with an imaginary settlement, the extravagant pursuit of which has presented an untimely grave to many.

This latest rumour had reached the ears of Governor King, who probably ordered the article published as a warning to potential runaways. Ruling that 'the dangerous chimera should be traced to its infamous source', he immediately asked Surgeon John Harris, who had been appointed superintendent of police, to investigate. The answer came in a matter of hours. The culprit was one James Houlding[3], a man for whom the *Gazette* had few kind words:

A mean and contemptible offender, whose larcenies have frequently immured him within the walls of prison, and whose *experience* in the interior of the country led no further than the outskirts of various settlements when induced by conscious guilt to abandon labour, and trust for a wretched subsistence to his pilfer about the outer farms.

Harris only had a name, however, as the storyteller had already made himself scarce. The *Gazette* really went overboard this time, bewailing that anyone could swallow a story so outlandish, particularly from someone as depraved as Houlding. It was assumed he had spoken out of pure malice, intending to induce the gullible into the ultimate horror, an unmourned death in the middle of nowhere:

> Upon such authority it cannot be supposed that any man in existence, be his condition what it may, would give the smallest credit to the preposterous assertion, originating in an incurable propensity, amongst other blots in his composition, to infamous falsehood. It is unfortunately certain, however, that similar rumours that have been propagated heretofore, have been as fatally successful in their consequences as the daemons that contrived them could have hoped: Yes! many have been prevailed upon by the deceitful story to pile miseries upon their heads, and wantonly to abandon certain security — to wander through the trackless woods, to labor on the verge of mountains proved to be impassable, to endure the complicated terrors of cold, fatigue, and famine — to curse the propagators of a weak device — to repent too late of their own rash credulity — and then, exhausted, to perish miserably, without a friend at hand to pour the balm of Christian consolation into the tortured bosom, without the very prospect of interment after death!

The newspaper implored its readers to assist in bringing Houlding to account for his deadly fairytales. Unearthed on a Prospect farm in February 1805, he was sent to the gaol gang until further notice but escaped about a year later. On 5 January 1806, a three-pound reward was offered for the capture of 'James Holden' and five others. He was brought in before the month was out and given 200 lashes for bushranging.

Far from being the 'daemon' of the *Gazette*'s lurid overstatement, there is no evidence that Houlding inspired a new wave of seekers. The relative dearth of Irish convict newcomers may help explain this absence of enthusiasm. In the six years following the arrival of the *Rolla* in May 1803, only one Irish transport arrived (the *Tellicherry* in February 1806), whereas in the six years beforehand there had been eight. Besides, the most recalcitrant convicts were now at Newcastle, where absconding was continuous and the role played by the bush legend in buoying their hopes is unknown.

However, evidence that the overland option was by now either discredited or in the too-hard basket is reflected by a fresh upsurge in boat thefts, as noted by David Dickenson Mann. In April 1806, for example, six prisoners stole a boat from Newcastle 'with a trifling quantity of provision and with no other prospect than of perishing on the coast,' and this does seem to have been their fate. The major escape of this period was the theft of the brig *Harrington* from Sydney Harbour's Farm Cove on the evening of 15 May 1808. Led by a former naval lieutenant, Robert Stewart, the scheme was thoroughly grounded in reality: the *Harrington* was outfitted for a voyage to Fiji and Stewart's convict helmsman, William Jackson, was a sailor experienced in the Sydney–Canton run. A bigger seizure than the *Norfolk*, it shows that as the colony grew, so did opportunities to snatch bigger and more seaworthy vessels. Nevertheless, the overland myth was still occasionally put to use. As Stewart plucked the *Harrington* from under Sydney's nose, a fifty-year-old Irishman named James Tracey was deep in the woods, bound for the phantom colony after seven years' servitude in New South Wales.

The Bench of Magistrates, now headed by Captain Edward Abbott since the NSW Corps' takeover of the colony, heard Tracey's case on 11 June. He was charged with 'absenting himself from his master early in May, and continuing absent until within few days since'. With two unidentified companions, Tracey apparently set out to cross the mountains 'in quest of a hitherto undiscovered settlement; the chimerical existence of which has proved fatal to many ignorant and credulous adventurers'. He told the bench his party crossed three ridges of mountains and three rivers, existing on a small supply of flour which they mixed with water before eating. His master attended the court and attested to Tracey's good character. Abbott and the other magistrates accepted this as a mitigating factor in determining his punishment, but they also ruled it necessary 'by example to deter others from similar misdeeds', so Tracey still ended up getting 100 lashes.

The most remarkable aspect of Tracey's case is his longstanding residence — by comparison most absconding believers were pretty much straight off the boat. Sentenced to seven years' transportation at Wexford in March 1800, Tracey arrived in the colony a year later aboard the *Anne* with Phillip Cunningham and other Irish rebels. When he set his sights on the Blue Mountains his sentence had expired, yet he was still working as a farmer's convict servant. As the *Anne* indents were outrageously late, not arriving from Ireland until 1819, his likely motivation in absconding was frustration at being kept in penal servitude past his release date. Tracey had plenty of time to hear talk of the phantom settlement. Did he believe the stories without wishing to risk the search until denial of his rightful freedom made him sufficiently desperate? The *Sydney Gazette*, the sole record of Tracey's adventure, recorded no such appeal to the court — but then it was a government-censored publication. Unfortunately the court minutes are not extant. Possibly his time was extended for some unrecorded colonial offence, but he was not a troublesome individual if his master's good account of him means anything. Indeed, he was given a technically redundant pardon only five months after the trial, and in 1810 received one of the very first certificates of freedom issued by Governor Macquarie.[4]

Whether Tracey's fellow travellers fell prey to their chimera is unknown. There is no evidence they ever returned, although perhaps only their trial records were lost. Did Tracey invent them? Without knowing the circumstances of his departure or capture it would be unwise to be too conclusive about this case; the *Gazette* published nothing to corroborate Tracey's story of entering the mountains. Was he rescued in the bush half-famished, or did he return to his master able-bodied with an outlandish lie to cover his absence? If so, why would he think presenting himself as a failed deserter would earn more sympathy than a confession of shirking or working illegally? Far from prompting pity, Tracey's mistaken mountain jaunt actually persuaded the magistrates a flogging was required to deter imitators. Only his employer's high opinion of him limited his lashes to 100.

Felonry and officialdom seemed to forsake their twin designs on the mountains almost simultaneously. When the authorities cited 'mountains proved to be impassable' to dissuade convict wanderlust, they meant it literally. Barrallier's inconclusive mountain forays had been followed by two expeditions by the botanist-explorer George Caley, who returned thoroughly defeated by terrain he dubbed the Devil's Wilderness. A passage through the Blue Mountains seemed every bit as unlikely as a white civilisation beyond them. In 1805, Governor King's gloomy conclusion to London was that 'persevering in crossing these mountains, which are a confused and barren assemblage of mountains with impossible chasms between, would be as chimerical as useless'.

There were to be no more serious attempts for the best part of a decade, although David Dickenson Mann made his own dilettantish effort in 1807. Taking another European and three Aboriginal guides, Mann spent four days tackling 'four or five stupendous acclivities' before wisely deciding to leave the task to 'some person more qualified, mentally as well as physically'. The believers in phantom colonies seem to have reached a similar conclusion by the time Mann departed for England in 1809. In his *Present Picture of New South Wales*, published in 1811, the last occurrence of note is the de Clambe–Bean incident of February 1803, when 'fifteen convicts once again ventured into the woods from Castle

Hill, in search of this undiscovered country'. As far as Mann could tell, the myth's era had passed:

> Many of these bigotted fugitives were subsequently re-taken, after enduring every fatigue and privation which human nature is capable of sustaining; after bearing the complicated hardships of want, weariness and pain; their feet blistered and bare, their hopes destroyed, their perseverance completely worn out, and their restless dispositions perfectly corrected into submission.

From 1809 the *Sydney Gazette* published regular and ever-expanding wanted lists of absentee convicts, but none with any discernible yearnings for phantom colonies. In some cases they only went into the mountains by accident. When Samuel Waters, John Maxwell and Joshua Baither (or Joseph Bathers) were tried at Windsor on 6 February 1813, they confessed to having 'lost their way, and getting into the mountains wandered three weeks without the hope of ever reaching any of the Settlements'. Two others didn't survive this escape; one was lost in the bush and a fifth man fatally speared by Aborigines.

Absconding was a perennial colonial headache, but unlike his predecessors Governor Macquarie never found it necessary to issue an official denial of a phantom colony — his biggest problem with runaways was settlers sheltering and employing them. He periodically announced strict measures to counteract those who 'for the purpose of benefiting by their labour, connive at their delinquency'. On 24 July 1813 he forbade any worker — bond or free — from travelling out of the district 'he or she may belong to' without a written pass from their employer, countersigned by a magistrate.[5]

Escape mythology still had its corners to hide in, however. Encounters between Aborigines and bushranging convicts were always likely to produce new twists to the tale. Then there was, at last, the first officially recognised crossing of the Blue Mountains. Far from knocking the last nail into the myth's coffin, the opening of the western interior helped resuscitate the belief. Aspirations for overland sanctuary returned to defy the official geography at the very moment of its first significant expansion. To some minds attuned to escape, the apparent absence of an urban civilisation across the mountains was less significant than the sudden presence of a track over the ridges, a track which promised to point the way to new versions of the old chimera.

CHAPTER FOURTEEN

Boundless regions open to our sight

Behold, where Industry's encourag'd hand
Hath chang'd the lurid Aspect of the Land;
With Verdure cloathed the solitary Hills,
And pour'd fresh Currents from the limpid Rills;
Has shed o'er darken'd Glades a social Light,
And boundless regions open to our sight!

MICHAEL MASSEY ROBINSON, CONVICT POET

GOVERNOR KING WAS WRONG ABOUT THE BLUE MOUNTAINS, OF
course, though it wasn't until 1813 that the 'impossible' crossing was
achieved. Want of grass rather than land spurred the renewed effort
— overgrazing, footrot, drought and caterpillar plagues had combined
to create pressure for the establishment of interior sheep and cattle runs
during the early years of Macquarie's administration. As it happened, the
long-sought-after goal was attained more or less as soon as it became an
economic imperative.

On 11 May 1813, Gregory Blaxland, William Lawson and William Wentworth set out for the mountains from Blaxland's South Creek farm, armed with the accumulated knowledge of a quarter-century of European experimentation, including two bids by Blaxland himself. Accompanying the famous 'Three Explorers' was a trio of anonymous convict servants and the Irishman James Byrnes, an emancipist kangaroo hunter who already knew the way to the top of the first ridge. Following a ridge route well known to countless Aboriginal generations and perhaps to John Wilson back in the 1790s, the party reached the western extremity of their journey on 31 May. From the heights of what is now called Mount Blaxland, three pairs of greedy eyes feasted on land 'sufficient to feed the stock of the colony, in their opinions for the next thirty years'.

The Three (or more democratically, Seven) Explorers fell short of the true interior, as the Great Divide lay to the west of Mount Blaxland on the other side of Cox's Valley. But they were the first Europeans to demonstrate a route over the Blue Mountains plateau leading to somewhere of immediate practical benefit to the colony. Later that year, Assistant Surveyor George Evans finished the job by crossing the Divide, reaching about 180 miles west of Sydney. On first sighting the inland plains, Evans momentarily mistook the rippling grass for the waves of an inland sea. Exulting over thousands of fertile acres, he named a plain and river after a delighted Governor Macquarie, whose announcement in the *Sydney Gazette* early in 1814 jumped to an extraordinary conclusion:

> This River is supposed to empty itself into the Ocean on the western side of New South Wales, at a Distance of from 2 to 300 Miles from the Termination of the Tour.

Typographic error can be ruled out. The notice ran for three weeks from 12 February without correction and it's a safe assumption that Macquarie read what was printed. The governor had every confidence in Evans' wildly amateurish estimates of distance. Evans declared himself 'happy and ready to . . . attempt a journey to the western coast, which I think this river leads to'.

Inevitably, some convicts shared this sentiment. Evans had unwittingly confirmed what the felonry long suspected, that the country was not nearly as large as their overlords had maintained. This doesn't mean Macquarie and Evans were ignorant of Flinders' circumnavigation of the continent. Macquarie may have envisaged his new river meeting an inland sea, beyond which lay what we now call Western Australia. Or perhaps it was a bungled description of a supposed outfall south-west of Sydney in the Southern Ocean. Whatever he meant, he had said — with all the authority and gravity of his position — that there was a seacoast over the mountains, only a couple of hundred miles west along the Macquarie River.

The authorities never seemed to realise how their inland sea myth supported convict escape mythology. To them it was a line of scientific enquiry, unrelated to an apparently irrational fantasy of criminals. But aside from the chance of a new sea route home, a false west coast only brought the phantom colony that much closer, or at least limited its ultimate distance.

Evans also boosted convict aspirations in another, more prosaic way. The track he was able to blaze across the Great Divide made escape seem easier to realise than ever. The temptation was too much for a gang of seven English transportees who, as the *Sydney Gazette* reported

> . . . formed the absurd and extravagant plan of crossing the Blue Mountains, and travelling thence to the Western Coast of this Territory, with a view to build a vessel to convey them from thence to the Island of Timor.

Boat-building may have been no more than the newspaper's presumption as a logical requirement for a trip to Timor. One of the escapees, John Ablett, later said only that he 'took to the bush', and bids by later runaways suggest that Timor was not an island to them. Ablett, an assigned servant with the Hawkesbury settler Robert Jenkins, was accompanied in the venture by fellow farmhands John Berwick and John Hall, former shipmate Richard Fryer, and three other convicts named John Barrington, John Bullock and Thomas Buck, an ex-London pawnbroker. All had been in the colony under four years except Barrington, who arrived on the *Glatton* back in 1803 and may have nursed escape fantasies for over a decade.[1]

The seven headed west from Windsor into the mountains in late May 1814, three months after Macquarie published Evans' findings. A week later, provisions exhausted and west coast nowhere in sight, they were forced to eat one of the dogs brought along to help them hunt game. After deciding to turn back, they veered south and managed to find Evans' track. This took them to Emu Island (Emu Plains) about thirty-six miles west of Sydney, just east of the foothills on the Hawkesbury–Nepean River. Following the river downstream as it curved northwards led them to the settled district of Richmond, where they surrendered on 9 June after about three weeks at large. They had been three days without food, having devoured their last dog.

The *Sydney Gazette* deplored this 'visionary, wild, and impracticable' attempt to traverse 'a Continent of not less than 500 miles across, through country hitherto wholly unexplored by any European'. While berating the convicts for their ignorance, the newspaper was blithely unaware it had underestimated the distance to the actual west coast by over 1500 miles.

The Hawkesbury Bench of Magistrates took care of the offenders. As ringleaders, John Berwick and Richard Fryer received 100 lashes each and twelve months labour in the gaol gang in irons. Bullock, Buck and Barrington, 'appearing to have been deluded into this ridiculous project', were acquitted. John Ablett also escaped punishment, despite being named as a ringleader by the newspaper.[2] Jenkins refused to have him back, however, and he was reassigned to a larger Hawkesbury property, Clarendon, owned by an ex-NSW Corps lieutenant named William Cox. The seventh man, John Hall, was remanded on further charges but kept in Jenkins' service. As far as the voice of authority was concerned, the runaways were their own worst enemies and deserved everything they got:

> Although their sufferings were such as to excite commiseration in the mind of humanity, yet with the fatal example of others before them, who deluded by similar absurd and visionary schemes, had fallen victims to their temerity and folly: and where neither example or precept, or the common calculations of reason could avail, the voice of pity is silent, and the criminality of such desperate adventurers becomes a subject of severe censure and reprehension.

Thirty-nine days after the surrender of these renaissance runaways, work commenced on the first proper road across the Blue Mountains. William Cox was handed the responsibility, and a crack team of well-behaved convicts was recruited for the real work. The route closely followed the one taken by both Blaxland and Evans. Cox reported the road finished six months later in January 1815, though major work was still being carried out in March. It was a phenomenal feat of labour, with the convicts' enthusiasm maintained by the dangling carrots of conditional pardons promised upon a swift completion. There was no surge in westward migration, however; Macquarie forbade unauthorised travel along the road.

Cox was richly rewarded with 2000 acres of the new lands. The Three Explorers received generous offerings as well, though only Lawson took up his western portion. Blaxland bleated for more, but Macquarie was reluctant to indulge the pastoral elite or 'exclusives' with unlimited grazing tracts, instead preferring to parcel out smaller lots to agriculturists.

Macquarie embarked on a personal tour of the interior, which he officially dubbed West-more-Land. If read as a pun on the English placename, it had an awkward logic, but the region became generally known as the New Country. The stately progression set off on 25 April, numbering some fifty people including Cox, Evans, Surveyor General John Oxley and an artist, John Lewin. A fortnight later Macquarie formally inaugurated the first inland settlement — Bathurst on the Macquarie River, 130 miles west of Sydney. It was a grand gesture for what amounted to six convicts planting crops and six soldiers guarding them. The delegation of Wiradjuri Aborigines witnessing the event had little idea their universe was about to shatter. After Macquarie marched back over the mountains, Evans stayed to investigate the westerly course of another newly discovered river, the Lachlan.

Several convicts travelled in the governor's party, including John Ablett, now working as William Cox's groom. Ablett had prior experience with horses; he'd been shipped out on a life sentence for stealing one back in his native Suffolk. Pleased with his service on the inland trip, Cox recommended him for liberty and Macquarie obliged with a ticket-of-leave. As Ablett said later, 'I don't know of any other of his servants who got their liberty in the same way'. It was a complete turnaround for a man who, only a year before, had been reduced to eating his dogs while trying to beat an escape route through the bush to Timor. He made no more attempts to run, but after returning to duty at Clarendon he may well have inspired imitators.

The *Gazette* showed remarkable amnesia when reporting the next attempt by convicts to walk their dogs to a western sanctuary. As far as the newspaper recalled, escape mythology had been dormant for the best part of a decade. Its reanimation was both unwelcome and confusing, particularly since there was now a demonstrably real road and town across the mountains without a China or white colony in sight.

This new attempt was also launched from the Hawkesbury district. Its seed probably germinated at Clarendon, where one of the culprits, Richard Kippas, had just arrived to help build a barn. Kippas, a waterman hailing from Penistone in Yorkshire, was described as having a ruddy complexion, sandy hair and hazel eyes. Reaching Sydney in April 1815, he was sent to the Windsor wharf, where he worked three months before his carpentry skills caught William Cox's attention. Just eight weeks later he took to the bush. Harsh as convict life was by modern standards, ill-treatment was not likely to have been a factor. Cox was well regarded as a master and even paid his convict workers, which was optional, giving Kippas nine shillings per week.

Kippas and seven others left Windsor on 1 October 1815, taking with them food, blankets, tin pots, an axe, musket, two pistols, some gunpowder, some extra clothes and four dogs. A fortnight later it was rumoured they had stolen five muskets from a guardpost along the Western Road. Their goal was still unknown, but the initial assumption they had 'betaken themselves to the mountains, with view, perhaps, of subsisting on the cattle that have been driven thither for the benefit afforded by a better pasturage', shows the relative infrequency of myth-inspired escapes at this time.

The *Gazette* recorded afterwards that Kippas and his companions had 'supposed it possible to effect their escape from hence to New Guinea, by the way of the newly discovered Country to the Westward of the Blue Mountains'. Five years later Kippas gave a statement which suggests he thought of New Guinea as an overland Dutch colony:

> Before I went to Bathurst and after I had been in the country five months, I and seven other convicts ran away from Windsor and got beyond Bathurst 150 miles. We hoped to get to the other side of the country, and make our escape under a belief that we should find a Dutch Settlement.

When Kippas said this in November 1820 he had been free six months and had no reason to lie. It's a rare prize: an escape myth described directly by an absconding believer. Instead of an over-ambitious bid to reach Melanesia, Kippas reveals a belief fully consistent with the 'white colony' of the 1790s — a cross-country white settlement. The goal of Ablett's expedition was probably similar: Timor was, after all, a Dutch possession.

The western place name New Holland probably influenced this line of thought, but there is another possibility. At least four Dutch ships were wrecked on the New Holland coast from 1628 to 1728, with some two hundred people stranded ashore and never seen again. With the foundation of English colonies in Western Australia in the 1820s, tales of lighter-skinned Aborigines soon arose, some supposedly bearing traces of Dutch vocabulary. In 1834, an English newspaper claimed that an inland expedition from the Northern Territory's Raffles Bay outpost had encountered a white, Dutch-speaking colony which kept apart from Aborigines and lived by growing maize and fishing from a river. Perhaps, then, tales of lost colonies founded by shipwrecked Dutchmen had an earlier folk currency than records attest. Such stories may have encouraged the convicts who seized upon Aboriginal evidence of white colonies in the 1790s, as well as Kippas and other later adventurers.[3]

The guardpost robbery was idle gossip. Kippas and his companions avoided the road for fear of detection. Nevertheless they made use of it, tracing a parallel route through the thickly wooded heights. Exhausting themselves by 'frequently letting each other and their dogs down abrupt precipices', it took them six days to cover forty-four miles. The eighth day finally brought their first success when they passed the Blue Mountains plateau, descending Mount York into Sidmouth Valley. Here they caught some calves with the help of their dogs, their first meal for three days. They also met and spoke with some convict stockmen, who reported the encounter to their overseer. Four days later the overseer drove a dozen head of oxen over the mountains and personally informed Governor Macquarie, who was inspecting stockyards at Emu Plains. By the time Macquarie received what he recorded in his diary as 'disagreeable intelligence', the subjects of this consternation were nearing the lonely infant outpost of Bathurst. The fresh beef had supplied them for two days, after which they killed more calves — enough, they estimated with deadly naiveté, to see them to the west coast.

Slipping into the hills to pass the soldiers at Bathurst unnoticed, the convicts camped by the Macquarie River only three miles outside town. Sneaking into Bathurst that night, they stole the halyards from the flagpole to make a fishing line. Two went fishing while the others took the dogs kangarooing, but no one caught anything. This was all one man could stand. Late one night he crept from the camp as his companions slept. He took as much as he could carry, though he left them the guns. At Bathurst he told Superintendent Richard Lewis that his mates had only three pounds of salted meat left. An armed party was sent to fetch them, but they had already cleared out.

Fearing the deserter would give them away, the gang fled in a north-westerly direction, following the Macquarie River to their imagined 'Western Coast'. Four days later, still unable to catch any food, they were forced to eat their dogs. Leftovers were used as fishing bait, but without success. Now living solely on 'mint tea' (possibly sarsaparilla, or sweet tea) and plants they described as nettles, the seven men were weakening steadily. After striking rich grasslands twenty-four days beyond Bathurst they saw 'land turtle' in abundance, but lacked the strength to trap any. Another dozen miles along the river, which took three days, saw the lightly timbered country give way to open grassed plains with no nettles in sight. With no idea of how to feed themselves, they realised their only option was to turn back to Bathurst.

At this point the runaways suddenly realised they were not alone. A group of ten Aborigines — men and boys — approached them. This was one of the earliest encounters between Europeans and the Wiradjuri, then masters of an area of western New South Wales larger than England, including almost all land between the Lachlan and Murray rivers. In December 1813, George Evans had briefly encountered two women and four children further south — who collapsed to the ground trembling with fear — but the Wiradjuri had really only known Europeans since Macquarie's visit the previous May. Now, six months later, seven ragged runaways were only the third lot of Europeans known to venture into Wiradjuri territory, and the first to follow the Macquarie River any sizeable distance. When Surveyor General John Oxley made the first official European footsteps north-west along the Macquarie in 1818, he observed of the Aborigines that 'it was evident from the whole tenor of their behaviour that they had previously heard of white people'. Unmindful or ignorant of the convict venture that preceded him, Oxley supposed the Wiradjuri must have been familiar with the distant Newcastle settlement.

The two groups — starving fugitives and curious locals — tried to communicate with improvised hand signals. The convicts conveyed their hunger by frantically pointing to their mouths. The Wiradjuri offered a fish and two turtles for a shirt and other small articles. It was quite an amicable meeting; the Aborigines stayed with the unexpected visitors until nightfall. The next day another Wiradjuri man, also accompanied by some boys, swapped two roasted possums and some pieces of cooked fish for a blanket and rug. Again the Aborigines kept the convicts company until sunset.

The dismal crawl back to Bathurst began the next morning. Although saved from immediate starvation, they were rapidly running out of trade goods. Soon, too weak to eat the nettles, they were existing solely on mint tea. Two days of this diet left one man, John Haigh, too sick to continue.[4] Leaving him in the care of the strongest man, the five others struggled onwards. Shortly afterwards they had their last meeting with Aborigines, who swapped a few possums for a hat. Berries sustained them for the next three days, but they could only stagger two or three miles a day before collapsing with exhaustion. On the third day, while lying on the ground half-dead from hunger and exposure, they had the lifesaving vision of a horseman riding towards them, accompanied by another man on foot.

The search party offered their grateful captives bread, which they could barely eat. A cart had to be fetched to carry them into Bathurst, where they had a surprise reunion with the man who had stayed with Haigh. After two days of watching his companion weaken, neither of them having anything to eat, hunger forced him to leave the dying Haigh and make for Bathurst on his own. Clearly he was the strongest of the group, having travelled further in one day than the others managed in three. Taken back over the mountains to the hospital at Windsor, they lingered in very frail health. On 2 December the *Sydney Gazette* reported their recovery was still very much in doubt. While the convicts' descriptions of large tracts of fertile soil interested the authorities, their 'continuing miserable weakness' precluded them from supplying intelligence of practical benefit.

This time, outrage at the criminality of the 1814 attempt was now replaced by overt sympathy. Again the *Gazette* assumed the runaways were hopeful of sailing to their destination, but Kippas' own statement shows they believed it lay overland, on 'the other side of the country'. At least this time the newspaper had a less confused grasp of the Australian mainland's dimensions:

> Thus has ended the most chimerical and absurd attempt that gross ignorance almost ever suggested to man, for when we consider the vast extent of an hitherto unexplored Continent, from hence to the Western Coast (surpassing any distance that the Continent of Europe itself affords), and the total impossibility, if even this difficulty were surmounted, of procuring a vessel on the Western Coast to convey them a distance of 1500 to 2000 miles to the nearest or most southern extremity of New Guinea. We cannot sufficiently express our surprise and regret, that any persons would have suffered themselves to be so deluded into so hopeless and calamitous an attempt as it must ever prove. The result of the present attempt will probably deter others from exposing themselves to similar distresses; and if this should be the case, however we may regret the loss of one fellow creature, and the sufferings of the survivors, we will be consoled in the reflection that the knowledge of their sufferings and distresses will deter others from ever making a similar attempt for the future.

The survivors were not punished, but they endured a long convalescence. Kippas went to Bathurst with William Cox in January 1817, where he was kept busy building stockyards and sheep hurdles. He wasn't the only convict dreamer pioneering the interior. In March 1818 John Ablett joined the very first party of permanent settlers at Bathurst, granted fifty acres on the Macquarie River's east bank.

The Macquarie River became the subject of Surveyor General John Oxley's attentions later that year, when he was sent to determine whether, as Evans had postulated, it emptied into 'the long sought for Australian sea'. Richard Kippas was selected for the expedition as 'rough carpenter', but doesn't appear to have gone, possibly because of a broken leg he suffered around this time. Instead of retracing the steps he had taken as a runaway, he returned to Windsor and opened a wheelwright business.

However, myth–inspired deserters did not go unrepresented on this first official European exploration along the Macquarie River. Ablett's one–time accomplice John Hall, now working at Bathurst, was recruited as a servant and courier. Oxley left Bathurst in May 1818, walking to a depot in the Wellington Valley and then proceeding by boat. On 23 June, Oxley sent Hall and a soldier named Thomas Thatcher back to Bathurst with an account of the first, rather uneventful month in the field. Hall asked for mitigation of sentence for this service and was conditionally pardoned almost immediately. He spent time in Cox's employ at Windsor, then returned to the New Country to work as a herdsman.

The colonial careers of men like Ablett, Hall and Kippas show how Governor Macquarie's relatively enlightened policies helped rehabilitate some of the more reckless convicts. Ablett's travelling companion John Berwick did well, too, receiving a pardon from Macquarie just six months after completing punishment for leading his escape venture. Settling at North Richmond, the very district he was once so determined to abandon for Timor, Berwick married an Australian–born woman and raised four children. John Ablett came back over the mountains in 1824 and continued farming until his death in 1831. John Bullock set up shop as a tailor on Sydney's George Street. The opportunities Macquarie tried to foster for emancipists undoubtedly helped diminish longing for better worlds, although cruel treatment from individual masters made the assignment system a rather harsh lottery and kept absenteeism a major concern.[5]

Unfortunately, Macquarie's willingness to issue pardons as an inducement to good behaviour, together with his belief that ex-convicts should not be debarred from any aspect of colonial life, brought him into conflict with the wealthy 'exclusives', who pressed for social strictures to satisfy their prejudice against emancipists. Macquarie's 'absurd and mischievous policy', as John Macarthur described it, was of a nation of small farmers, with ex-convicts the social equals of free settlers. Instead, Macarthur and other exclusives yearned for a colonial aristocracy, wanting their vast estates serviced by a transported helotry who would remain serfs even after expiry of sentence. This never transpired, but their influence in England proved Macquarie's undoing. In 1821 he was subject to severe criticism and replaced as governor by Thomas Brisbane. Fearing that transportation had lost its teeth, the new regime toughened up the system with harsh penalties for offences committed in the colony. Such added pressure helped ensure escape mythology was not a spent force.

Ten days after Oxley sent Hall back, he found the Macquarie River channel spreading out into marshes, which forced the expedition backwards in search of dry land to camp on. Abandoning the river course, they turned east to cross the Liverpool Plains and survey the north coast region later home to the convict outstation of Port Macquarie. This was Oxley's second encounter with one of the few patches of marshland in New South Wales. The year before he had run against other swamps (near present-day Forbes) while following the Lachlan River. The coincidence convinced him he had discovered 'an inland sea, or lake, most probably a shoal one, which was gradually filling up by immense depositions from the higher lands, left by the waters which flow into it'. Oxley's conclusion won general acceptance; it seemed that the interior was indeed a vast sea.

A decade later Governor Darling, reporting the explorations of another believer, the botanist Allan Cunningham, informed the Colonial Office that faith in this 'favourite hypothesis' was 'general from the reports of the natives'. The first signs of the dry reality emerged in 1830, when Charles Sturt traced the Murray–Darling River to its outlet in South Australia, and in 1836, when Thomas Mitchell confirmed that the major west–flowing watercourses drained into this river system. Sturt's discoveries were the beginning of the inland sea's end, but of all people he clung to the dream longer than almost anyone. Speculating that the continent was a former archipelago dotted with pockets of remnant ocean, he carried a boat north from Adelaide into the central deserts as late as 1844, sure that 'the interior was occupied by a sea of greater or less extent'.

Although Oxley thought an inland sea meant the Australian interior was uninhabitable marsh, other believers held hopes for fertile soil and a hospitable, Mediterranean climate. The almost mystical fervour with which the sea gripped Charles Sturt's imagination was revealed when Poole, his rather appropriately named lieutenant, reported seeing it from a peak during a spot of forward scouting. Poole's phantom extended along the horizon, strewn with islands. Unable to contain his excitement, Sturt rhapsodised in a letter to a friend in Adelaide:

What is all this? Are we to be prosperous? I hope so, and I am sure you do. Tomorrow we start for the ranges, and then for the waters, the strange waters, on which boat never swam, and over which flag never floated. But both shall ere long. We have the heart of the interior laid open to us, and shall be off with a flowing sheet in a few days. Poole says the sea was a deep blue, and that in the midst of it was a conical island of great height.

Of course, a mirage had beguiled Poole, and Sturt's boat never swam over 'the strange waters', which flowed only in his heart's desire — an interior sea indeed. Errant hopes for the sea finally evaporated for all time when John McDouall Stuart raised the Union Jack in the centre of an arid continent in 1860. Sturt was already against the main tide of opinion in 1844, but as the 1820s got underway amidst a steady European trickle into the New Country, the theory remained buoyant. In turn, further down the food-chain of the colonial imagination, the unknown interior similarly fed other hearts' desires. The convicts' parallel conception of bountiful places across the mountains continued to have influence.

While the shrinkage of New South Wales implied by the inland sea gave shape to a smaller world with vague South Seas place names like Timor and New Guinea within reach, the absence of hard data about the west allowed convicts to make all sorts of global connections between their unthinkably remote exile and the outside world.[6] Peter Cunningham, a Scottish surgeon who supervised five convict voyages to Australia, recorded some of this reasoning. Bemused by the escape myths, Cunningham found believers speculated all manner of countries were accessible overland, except one:

> I wondered, at first, that none had hitherto ventured toward the East
> Indies on foot, till I found they reasoned very justly, on this point, that,
> as the East Indies must lie to the *east*, in which direction the colony
> is bounded by the sea, they knew they could proceed thither only in
> a vessel; but the names of the other countries not indicating their
> position, they had hopes of the reports being true of their joining the
> colony.

Cunningham was enjoying himself at their expense, but amid his sarcasm a plausible, if misinformed, rationale is clear. His understanding was that they ran 'sometimes south, and sometimes west' to reach China and

Timor, but always headed south for Ireland. Why? Because 'as Ireland is a *colder* country than New South Wales, and that the cold winds blow here from the south, *therefore* Ireland *must* lie in that direction'.

The delusion that Ireland itself was nearby appears only in Cunningham's 1828 memoirs, *Two Years in New South Wales*. This enthusiasm, he writes, began in 1821, when an Irishman on one of Macquarie's tours of duty 'first ascertained the proximity of Ireland by detecting the blue mountains of *Connaught* in the distance beyond a river of red water which put a stop to their journey'. Several large parties immediately took off, only to surrender or be recaptured after getting lost or running out of food. New life was then breathed into the idea by an Irish convict assigned to a bookseller, who, after tearing the picture of a compass from the page of an atlas, attempted to navigate some of his countrymen home. 'With all his learning,' Cunningham deadpans, 'this attempt proved quite as unsuccessful as the former, the paper compass losing, somehow or other, its magnetic properties on the route'.

It is difficult to assess how far Cunningham is merely enjoying himself with the sort of black humour that escape mythology was apt to provoke. The convicts' rationale rings true, but the escapes are unverified and there is a strong whiff of Irish caricature in the telling. One party known to have headed south in this period was a gang of eleven who caused 'considerable alarm' when they escaped into the Cookbundoon Ranges south of Sydney in late 1821. A team of constables and soldiers went after them; two runaways left the others to surrender to the local magistrate, Charles Throsby, at Bong Bong. They hadn't eaten for four days and told the usual tale of privation. Some of their companions had deserted various Sydney work gangs, but most were from Grose Farm (now the site of Sydney University), where an unusually large group of 138 prisoners may have assisted the flow of rumour. When the *Sydney Gazette* covered the incident on 10 November the nine others were still at large, but the duo in custody made an interesting confession which partly recalls Cunningham's deluded bookshop worker:

It will hardly be believed that these infatuated men had been led to imagine that New Holland is not an island, and that they could, by the aid of some charts they had obtained, find their way to a country where they would be better fed and treated than in New South Wales.

Here is the same conspiracy theory William Noah heard two decades before, the rejection of the colony's apparent separation from the outside world. How these charts sustained their hopes can only be guessed at. They may not have been real maps at all; perhaps they had been sold false information by an unscrupulous opportunist, or maybe a believer had committed the longstanding convict folklore to paper in some form. In any case, refusal to trust the official geography was equated with irrationality; hence Cunningham's facetious portrait of a colony filled with convict Micawbers, strolling to their deaths in the expectation that something — or rather, somewhere — would turn up. Yet despite his impression that any number of destinations drew them, the handful of detailed 1820s case histories shows the convicts' mythic somewhere increasingly narrowing to one place — Timor.

CHAPTER FIFTEEN

Full march for Timor

Beyond the cultivated districts you might almost
think you had taken a trip to some other planet.

JOSEPH MASON, CONVICT, 1838

SURGEON PETER CUNNINGHAM HAD LITTLE RESPECT FOR THE
unguarded optimism of escape mythology. However, in the interests of
balance, he also offered his version of 'the most sensible of any land–
journey that has yet been taken'. Masterminding this trip, Cunningham
writes, was a convict sailor who had arrived on the same ship as he had
in 1819:

> Getting a party to accompany him, he secured arms and ammunition,
> working–tools, cattle, and every thing requisite to form a settlement
> in the interior, which he had projected; and his party proceeded
> onward over the Blue Mountains, till, losing themselves among the
> ranges, they were captured by a troop of soldiers and natives sent in
> pursuit.

Cunningham may have been recalling five convicts who ran from Bathurst in May 1822, hopeful, as the *Sydney Gazette* wrote, of 'effecting their escape by the way of Timor, by traversing through the immeasurable forests of New Holland'. Now long forgotten but sensational news in its day, the case featured a seaman, an enormous stockpile of stolen provisions, and a convict shipped out on one of Cunningham's voyages (albeit his second, not his first).

The leader of this venture, William Poole, was an Irishman sent for seven years from Kilkenny in 1820. Although the *Sydney Gazette* states he was a sailor, transportation records describe him as a farmer, forty years old with a dark complexion and greying hair. Reaching Sydney in January 1821, Poole worked on a farm in the Cowpastures before being sent west to the Bathurst property of the famous ex-convict surgeon, William Redfern. Early the following year he convinced another convict servant, Thomas Peacock, to join him in an overland escape. A young farmer from Suffolk, Peacock was sent for stealing twenty-eight pounds of wool and nine fowls. He may have been the man Peter Cunningham remembered from the *Grenada*, conflating him with Poole — both Peacock and Cunningham reached Sydney on this ship in September 1821. Poole's next recruit was fellow Irishman Michael Clancy, thirty-three, from County Clare. Just over two years in New South Wales, Clancy had been assigned to the Hassall brothers' station near Bathurst after a stint at the Parramatta brickworks.

Bathurst had expanded rapidly in the four years since the first agricultural lots were parcelled out. Napoleon's defeat in 1815 had enabled Britain to return its attention to the ends of the Earth. It had to — a soaring crime-rate amidst post-war economic and industrial chaos saw to that. A swift rise in the quality and quantity of shipping vastly increased convict arrivals, many of whom were absorbed into the new inland pastoral industry. By 1822, more sheep grazed in the New Country than any other district, and over 9000 acres had been cleared. The Wiradjuri were still recoiling, but began to strike back that same year with resounding short-term success under Windradyne, a charismatic and able leader who had met peacefully with Macquarie's delegation back in 1815.

Unlike his masters, William Poole had no interest in dispossessing the Wiradjuri. Seeing only in his frontier posting the opportunity to get away, he spent weeks

> . . . storing the minds of his fellow prisoners with not only the probability, but also the possibility and certainty of making their way to Timor, through the trackless interior of New Holland.

There is no evidence that he envisaged a sea voyage. Even the *Gazette* thought Poole's maritime experience had merely convinced the others he was 'an active and clever fellow, and therefore well capacitated to conduct his little party to Timor'. Claiming to be a sailor — thus versed in navigation by sun and stars — may have been Poole's way of gaining the confidence of his recruits.

Taking to the bush on 21 May 1822, Poole, Peacock and Clancy built themselves a hideout about five miles from the Hassall brothers' station. Two more of the Hassalls' servants completed the line-up when Poole and Peacock made an evening visit to the hut of John Wiseman and Robert Campbell. They all agreed to abscond together and took a large number of items (mainly clothing and blankets) back to the bush lair. Campbell, a tinsmith from Dundee, had been in the colony since 1818. Wiseman was a Norfolk farmer of five years' colonial residence, longer than any of the others, and was the only lifer in the bunch. Like Poole, Wiseman was in his early forties, while Campbell and Peacock were only teenagers when sentenced and in their early twenties by the time of the escape.[1]

Over the next few days the gang committed several robberies to supply their flight. During one midnight raid Peacock threatened to shoot a hutkeeper for refusing to hand over his dog, but Poole ordered him not to fire. The authorities were later astonished by the sheer quantity of items the gang made off with. The *Sydney Gazette*, covering their trial, reported that 'enumeration of the articles nearly filled a side of foolscap; and, among the number, the prisoners had provided themselves with a Bible!'

For all this preparation — practical and spiritual — it was lack of equipment that led to their capture. Towards the end of June they made their move. From a camp at Mount Macquarie they travelled directly west for thirteen days, when they found a large river blocking their desired direction. Deciding to improvise a bridge or causeway by felling some trees, they had to retrace their hard-won steps back to the Bathurst vicinity just to obtain an axe. They also resolved to collect twenty bullocks to take along, and on the way back they gave chase to a small herd of wild cattle, which escaped.

Meanwhile, search parties were combing the New Country for what seemed to be a nest of locally based bushrangers. Poole's trek had not yet come to light; if not for the want of an axe it never would have. Upon returning to their old haunts, the runaways stole fresh supplies and horses and resumed dealings with convict shepherds and hutkeepers. On 15 July an eight-man search party under District Constable John Blackman set out from Bathurst 'in quest of the Bush Rangers'. After fifteen days in the field they got lucky. A convict stockman named Darby McCarty admitted he had seen two of the fugitives that very morning. In return for protection, McCarty confessed they had given him a fowling piece lock to be repaired, a sheepskin bag to fill with wheat, and two kangaroo skins as payment. Blackman waited a few days until McCarty was due to meet them about thirty miles outside Bathurst. When Poole and Clancy arrived an hour after dawn they found themselves fleeing arrest. Poole carried a musket, but threw it down and stopped running after being shot at. The two Irishmen had no choice but to lead Blackman's party to their camp, where the others were taken. Blackman noted the runaways were in possession of five dogs, four horses, four books and one Bible.

John Wiseman saved himself by turning informer. The others, tried in Sydney on 7 October, were convicted of stealing three horses from

Samuel Hassall and a mare from Robert Johnston. Thomas Peacock submitted a plea for mercy, appealing to 'Your Honor's Humanity', which may cast some light on Poole's recruitment technique:

> William Poole told me that that he was an old lag and that he went out
> of the country before, and if I would go with him he would take me
> out of it in ten Weeks. I asked him was it Possible that he could take
> me away he said positively that he could to an new Settlement called
> Timor. He went round to the different stations at Bathurst telling
> them the same story to Induce the men to go along with him. I had no
> occation to take the bush for I had a good master. Only being young
> and foolish that I was easyly led away by him. So I throw myself on
> the mercy of this Honorable Court to deal with me as to your Honor's
> Humanity may seem suit.

In truth Poole was far from an old lag, having arrived in the colony only eight months before Peacock and well after his other recruits. He must have been a good talker to convince them he had already been out of the country; was his sailing know-how just more blarney too? Peacock's description of Timor as a 'new Settlement' suggests Poole wasn't literally aiming for the Dutch East Indies — another clue that the phantom white society and a contiguous Asia were not necessarily separate notions. In Poole's hazy geography, a place called Timor and an overland colony probably amounted to much the same thing.

Peacock's plea for mercy was in vain. Two weeks later all four men were condemned to death, along with thirty other convicted bushrangers. Additionally, three Irish stock and hutkeepers were charged as accessories for assisting the illegal travel plans. Hugh McCann, judged the most culpable, received life retransportation and the other two, Henry Webb and Michael Kiernan, were retransported for seven years. The court was unmoved by Kiernan's appeal that he had been forced to help on pain of death.

Newspaper coverage showed that the notoriety of the Castle Hill Irish gang of 1803 still loomed large. The *Sydney Gazette* assured readers that 'this singular case was not unprecedented in colonial annals. Many of our Readers may remember the expedition to China about twenty years since!' Worried that Poole might attract imitators, the editor also warned less adventurous malcontents to keep the peace:

> However apparently deplorable your situations may be, oh wretched men! remember that such is the reward of crime; miserable as you are, only try to cast off the yoke yourselves, by thinking to make your situation less irksome, and that instant you render your return to society, and to happiness, more uncertain, if ever to be hoped for. Let the occurrences that continually pass before you serve as a warning; and endeavour, however fallen you are, to begin (even now) to practise honesty and virtue; and who will presume to aver that all may not, in due time, be well.

Only three of the condemned bushrangers were hanged. Poole, Peacock, Clancy and Campbell were among twenty-three retransported for life to Port Macquarie, a north coast penal station opened the year before as a tougher alternative to Newcastle. Eight others were sent to Macquarie Harbour in Van Diemen's Land. John Wiseman was excused, but had plenty of hard times ahead. Transferred to Campbelltown, he was flogged for 'suspicion of theft' in 1824 and later worked in a road gang. In 1837, aged sixty, he was still assigned to a settler as a convict labourer.

On 19 November, Poole, Peacock, Clancy and Campbell were embarked on the brig *Lady Nelson* with forty other convicts. As ringleader, Poole was kept in the scaffold's shadow by a harsh qualification to his respite. If he ever left Port Macquarie without lawful cause his death sentence would proceed, no matter how many years had elapsed. But Port Macquarie proved so bad that Poole quickly decided that running was worth the risk of the rope. Peacock and Clancy took off as well.

Whether or not they still dreamed of Timor, this second shot at freedom was short-lived and by the following March all three men were lodged in Sydney Gaol.

At first Peacock and Clancy were ordered to be flogged 100 times on the 'breech' and sent back, but two weeks later the grim order came to transfer them to Macquarie Harbour.[2] A scurvy-ridden, rainswept outpost on the west coast of Van Diemen's Land, this was one of the worst penal stations ever to operate in Australia. Exiled there for re-offending in the colony, life prisoners endured a brutal routine of tree-felling in dank rainforests and rolling logs through icy water to the shipyard on nearby Sarah Island. Harsh discipline, Antarctic winds, starvation rations and disease piled torment upon torment.

Meanwhile in Sydney Gaol, Poole's odd circumstances were vexing Provost Marshal JT Campbell, who had to confirm his identity before he could hang him. This was normally a formality, with condemned prisoners arriving directly from court. But Campbell couldn't recall seeing Poole before and was, unusually, afraid of executing the wrong man. Seizing his last chance, Poole insisted he was really 'Joseph Poole'. Compounding Campbell's misgivings was the absence of the commutation papers, which made him doubt the execution was legal even if the correct Poole was in custody. He begged the colonial secretary to sort out this 'melancholy and fearful subject'. Unfortunately for Poole he did and the hanging went ahead on 23 May 1823.

As a government mouthpiece, the *Sydney Gazette* wrote approvingly that 'JUSTICE and MERCY were never more strikingly exhibited' by the execution. Poole threw his own life away by 'contemptuously' disregarding a 'wise display of Royal Clemency'. While convinced that Poole's death would save many lives by example, the editor was mystified that some prisoners didn't wish to prolong their lives in chains at any cost, and felt moved to some decidedly cosmic musing:

Why should men, however hardened they may be in principle, be so daring as to court the deprivation of temporal existence, which may be only the prelude to death eternal?

It simply didn't register that places like Port Macquarie helped death eternal shape up pretty well against temporal existence. Faced with a future of utter hopelessness, Timor-in-the-bush was a chance William Poole simply wasn't about to pass up.

Down at Macquarie Harbour, Thomas Peacock took his own final shot at liberty, taking to the bush in December 1824. Apprehended by a convict constable named George Craggs, Peacock managed to stab his captor fatally in the left side, saying he would now die happy for having killed him. Months later he was executed for murder in a multiple hanging at Hobart Gaol's 'new drop'. The *Hobart Town Gazette* interpreted Peacock's loud sobbing on the gallows as an outpouring of penitence, and praised the parson for reclaiming men so 'depraved' and 'misguided'. All five offenders, the paper was pleased to relate, declared 'this awful moment was the happiest of their life'.

While Poole, Peacock and Clancy lay in Sydney Gaol after running from Port Macquarie, the colony was rattled by another outburst of myth-inspired bushranging. On 7 April 1823, two suspicious characters were seen prowling about a hut at Wilberforce in the Hawkesbury district. After a brief chase one of them, Ralph Dean, was captured and taken to the local chief constable, to whom he made a full confession. Dean's accomplice, Ben Cross, was shortly arrested at nearby Churchill's Lagoon with two other runaways, Samuel Phipp and Thomas Belcher. Assigned servants of a local farmer, Thomas McKenna, the four convicts had been missing exactly one week.[3]

This escape was the brainchild of Cross, a twenty-eight-year-old groom from Bedfordshire, who persuaded his friends to attempt 'the old tale of escaping to Timor, though utter strangers to every part of the country'. The transcript of Dean's confession ends with this curt one-liner: 'Cross was to have taken them to "Timor"'. The inverted commas indicate the contempt the authorities had for the convicts' idea of their destination.

Cross mooted the plan during the quartet's voyage from England aboard the *Eliza*, which reached Sydney in July 1822. The gang let their shipboard scheme gestate for nine months until the morning of Monday, 31 March 1823, when they deserted McKenna's farm with their weekly rations. But they had no intention of plunging into the unknown so poorly equipped, as the *Sydney Gazette* related:

> They were, for a while, to take to the road, and plunder the carts going to and fro' the market, from which source clothes, ammunition and money were to be derived. When they had obtained what might be considered a sufficiency to warrant the prosecution of their journey, with the possession of a geographical work, they were to set out; and in order to render failure impossible, it was their intention to keep the beach as soon as the sea-shore was gained, shooting birds, kangaroos &c. for their support!!

Cross seems to have imagined Timor with a seacoast but otherwise, like Poole, he placed it overland from the colony. Seeing the need for a map shows unusual foresight, though examining an accurate one — if he knew how — would have probably been quite a rude shock.

The temporary bushranging career required guns. Unfortunately they only had one old musket between them, which Phipp and Cross stole from the hut of an Indian settler named Sabea during the first evening out. Camping at Churchill's Lagoon, a billabong off Portland Head Creek only six miles from McKenna's land, they lay in wait to bail up travellers.

The first week of freedom ended without a single cart rolling by. All the would-be bandits did was demolish their provisions. They stocked up for the weekend by slaughtering a sheep and taking some corn from a nearby field, but on the Monday they had to go foraging again, which ended in Dean's arrest and the capture of the others soon afterwards. Dean was accepted as an informer and not charged, but the others were tried in Sydney on 29 April and sentenced to death, with Sabea's musket and the skin of the stolen sheep damning evidence against them.

According to Dean, an Irish ex-convict farmer named Henry Denny had promised to help them cross the Hawkesbury River on the evening of 10 April. He was also to provide the precious 'Geography and Compass', along with guns and ammunition, in return for a share of the bushranging spoils. Denny was in custody for employing a runaway convict, so he may have been rounded up on Dean's evidence and then held on that charge.[4]

After the court recommended the death penalty be commuted to 'transportation for the respective terms of their natural lives', the three runaways followed Poole's gang to Port Macquarie. Dean, reassigned to a settler at Newcastle, ran again two years later and was punished with 50 lashes. Phipp also attempted another escape, which saw him become one of the first new exiles to Norfolk Island. After twelve years inoperation, this offshore gaol reopened in 1825 as the last link in a chain of punishment for colonial reoffenders. As Governor Brisbane put it, Port Macquarie was for 'first grave offences; Moreton Bay for runaways from the former; and Norfolk Island as the *ne plus ultra* of convict degradation'. To convicts it was the 'Ocean Hell' which turned the mainland into an ironic 'Heaven' by comparison. Nine hundred miles out to sea, convicts faced conditions so savage and debased that some would murder other inmates just for the trip to the court and gallows at Sydney.

Phipp fell into this abyss after briefly absconding from Port Macquarie and mugging a constable for his gun while at large.[5] Many would have preferred the gallows, but the hardy Phipp survived his tour of Ocean Hell and finally won his freedom in 1841. By this time the era of escape mythology seems to have passed. Evidence for it in the 1830s is all but non-existent. Even so, the *Sydney Gazette* expressed astonishment at the tenacity of the delusion as late as December 1828:

It really is surprising how infatuated too many of the unfortunate prisoners of the Crown become with respect to the hopes of discovering some part of the world which might not only relieve them of the bonds in which they are placed, but introduce them to a community in which they might anew commence their pursuit of crime. How it can ever possibly enter the heads of beings, supposed to be invested with some degree of rationality, that they might penetrate to China through the interior, or succeed in reaching New Guinea, appears to us one of the most comical jokes that could possibly be palmed on the human understanding; but so it is.

The belief which spurred Poole and Cross to take to the bush was probably shared by many more of their contemporaries than history records. By the 1820s the assignment system had virtually negated the risk of a mass uprising or escape. The time when governors were anxious to disabuse believers was long gone; authority no longer cared why convicts ran. If a runaway committed capital crimes while at large — and hunger meant they often did — then the trial usually concerned nothing else. Dean's story that they intended emigration rather than full-time bushranging could not have had — and indeed did not have — any mitigating effect. If Cross and Poole hadn't been betrayed by informers who mentioned Timor, their bushranging would have been indistinguishable from the many instances where runaways charged with similar offences maintained solidarity. And vast numbers of lesser offenders flogged for absconding left no record of their precise motivation.

In this era, evidence that escape mythology was still a lure is usually extant only where court minutes or newspapers preserve information volunteered by the runaways themselves. A rare revelation of this sort appeared in the *Australian* on 31 October 1828:

Four or five prisoners of the crown, in the employment of a respectable settler on the Wollombi, have lately taken to the bush from mere desire of roaming. They were met going over the ridge, leading down to Liverpool Plains, and stated that they were on full march for Timor, which place they expected to reach in five days!

This seems to be the same convict bushwalk to Timor (or New Guinea) discussed at length in the *Sydney Gazette* a few weeks later on 19 December. Inviting 'the attention of the prison population to a careful perusal of what follows', the paper presented the harrowing deposition of William Sergison, apparently the expedition's sole survivor.

A tobacconist from Whitehaven, Sergison was transported for stealing a hat, his third conviction. Shipping indents describe him as a 'sulky looking' eighteen–year–old, illiterate, 5 feet 5 ½ inches tall, with a dark ruddy complexion. His right arm was tattooed with an anchor and stars, with another anchor near his left thumb.

Upon arriving in February 1828, Sergison was sent up to Segenhoe, a vast 20,000 acre property in the upper Hunter region near the present-day town of Scone. European settlement was only three years old in the area and Segenhoe was still the most remote grant along the Hunter River, the colony's north–western frontier. There, Sergison and others came under the spell of James Hill, a convict farmhand who promised 'that he would conduct them in safety to Timor, or New Guinea'.

Hill, thirty–three, a former brickmaker from Hampshire, had been transported in 1826 for housebreaking in Oxford. He was a widower with a child back in England. Four others joined Hill and Sergison in the escape. Bristol–born Richard Smart Jenkins, twenty–five, a silk–wool dyer by trade, had been among Segenhoe's first convict assignees. John Budge, convicted of rape in Cambridge, was one of the tiny minority shipped out for a violent crime. Daniel Lantwheeler, born in London and caught housebreaking in Edinburgh, was a tailor about twenty years old and just over 5 feet 2 inches in height. John Spring, twenty–seven, a stonemason from Wales, was also a convicted housebreaker.[6]

One evening in early October 1828, they met in a sheep paddock to prepare their departure.[7] At Jenkins' suggestion they robbed a hut first, gaining two pistols, a musket, tea, sugar and flour. The next morning they crossed the ranges to reach the vast, sparsely timbered expanse of Liverpool Plains. Once there they attempted to head west. Provisions were soon exhausted — Sergison claimed after 200 or 300 miles, surely a wild overstatement. They spent three torturous days without water. Hill tried to keep spirits up, insisting New Guinea couldn't be far because they were already 'in the trade winds'. But the wind wasn't enough to reassure them, and a fourth day without water convinced the entire party to turn back. Towards evening Jenkins lay down, unable to continue, begging his companions to leave him and save themselves. The next day Lantwheeler collapsed. His tongue was too swollen for speech, but he managed to signal the others to go on without him. Sergison had no idea that Jenkins recovered and somehow made his own way back. Lantwheeler was not so fortunate, and Sergison may have known more about his fate than he dared confess.

Another day reduced the four survivors to drinking their own urine. An early start under moonlight the next morning saw them reach, by daybreak, a river they had crossed a week beforehand. Here they shot some birds, their first meal for five days, and rested two days before wading across and continuing. Five days later Budge 'threw himself down on the banks of a beautiful running river', too weak to continue. Spring was next to fall by the wayside, three days after Budge. That morning he was energetic, 'walking very hard' and making encouraging banter that Liverpool Plains was only two days away. But at about 3 pm, 'while a little ahead of the other two, and walking smartly, he suddenly dropped down, and could neither sit nor stand, nor speak'. Hill and Sergison watched over him all night, but he had worsened by morning and at his own urging they left him to die. Spring's orientation had been sound; they reached the cattle runs of Liverpool Plains only a day later than he predicted. Here the ravenous pair gorged themselves on some 'muscles' found in a creek.

It was an unfortunate feast; Hill sickened and died after lingering several days. Sergison wrapped him in a blanket and found some stockmen who promised to bury the body. The next day he surrendered to Nicholas Connor, a convict overseer, who took him to Peter McIntyre, local justice of the peace and Segenhoe's manager in the owner's absence. McIntyre took Sergison's statement on 26 November and sent it to the *Sydney Gazette*, hoping to dissuade likeminded prisoners.

Sergison probably never knew that a second version of events emerged to furnish a surprising postscript. He had returned just in time to be listed in the 1828 census as 'picked up in the bush having absconded', and, as luck would have it, so did John Budge. Years later, while working as a bullocky, Budge managed to disarm two bushrangers who bailed up his dray. He kept them prisoner for two hours, hoping for assistance from other travellers, but let them go when it seemed no one would come along the road. Coverage of this incident recalled Budge's overland quest for the 'Dutch settlement at Timour' — a much darker journey than Sergison described.

Budge claimed he left his companions after only three days, after two days with no food, and collapsed while struggling back towards the Hunter River. A stockman out mustering cattle found him near death and brought him in. Eventually, as settlement encroached northwards, human remains were found on the convicts' escape route 'so torn about by dingoes, crows, and hawks, as to make it impossible to identify them'. The bodies — presumably Spring and Lantwheeler — were several miles apart, and it was thought that after Budge turned back a man was butchered to provision the rest. One corpse had been cut up, 'it was supposed for food; but this had not saved the others'. Yet it may have done — Budge was unaware that Jenkins and Sergison had survived. It's worth recalling that Sergison, with no need to lie about it, claimed that Budge outlasted Lantwheeler but not Spring. We'll never know what really happened out there, but if all these statements are accurate it must have been Spring who fell victim to the decision to turn cannibal. As Budge was hardly likely to incriminate himself, Lantwheeler may have suffered the same fate while Budge was still with the party. According to Sergison, both Jenkins and Lantwheeler collapsed within twenty-four hours. The others must have been almost as weak at that point, too, after four days without water, but in the next day or so they summoned the strength to reach a waterway without further loss. Sergison's evidence also suggests Budge greatly understated the time he spent with the expedition — and involvement in cannibalism would have given him a very strong motive for doing so. In dropping out early, Jenkins may have been even luckier than he could have ever known.

The final, strange twist to this tale can be found on any reasonably detailed map of New South Wales, where you will find Timor about fifty kilometres north of Scone. The place name, adopted by the region's first white settlers in the 1830s, was inspired by this escape.[8] And so, with an obscure gesture of ironic black humour, Timor was finally manifested in the bush, thanks to one of the last recorded attempts to reach it. Although failing to reach their promised land, Sergison and his companions left an appropriate epitaph. The alternate geography was on the landscape at last.

CHAPTER SIXTEEN

Mistaken and dangerous men

The sergeant of the horse-police discharged his carbine,
And called aloud onDonahoe to fight or to resign.
'I'd rather roam these hills and dales,
like wolf or kangaroo,
Than work one hour for government!'
cried Bold Jack Donahoe.

BOLD JACK DONAHOE, CONVICT BALLAD

THE 1820S ENDED WITH SETTLEMENT STILL MAINLY WITHIN 100 miles of Sydney, despite the first steps toward extending European dominance across the continent. Stillborn northern settlements near Arnhem Land and a failed southern outpost at Westernport (Victoria) were followed by two lasting toeholds over in Western Australia — King George Sound and Swan River. On the whole, however, as the *Sydney Gazette* pointed out on 7 February 1829, 'the vast country known under the names of New Holland and New South Wales' remained as mysterious to its colonisers as the interior of Africa. This meant, the paper noted, that 'the nature or capabilities of this vast country can be known only from analogy'.

To the authorities, longing for a fertile agricultural paradise, the inland sea remained the fondest hope for this blank slate. In turn, some convicts were still using their own analogies to invest the land with the attributes they wanted of it. The handful of real overland settlements had not yet supplanted the phantom one, but they had forced it further west, where it could still thrive beyond the scrutiny of an expanding colony. Towards the end of 1828, a fierce gunfight between police and escaped convicts in the New Country was a dramatic reminder of the myth's lasting potency as an outlet for desperation and desire. As a member of the police party put it:

> These mistaken and dangerous men were going to make an establishment of their own, about 300 miles in the interior, where, they maintain, exists a settlement of white people.

Bathurst was still one of the outer reaches of settlement, if no longer the most remote. As the frontier encroached inland, encounters with newly contacted Aboriginal groups produced the same old stories of mystery white colonies. This undoubtedly helped rejuvenate the promise of inland sanctuary. But did newly contacted Aboriginal peoples introduce new myths, or were they merely confirming rumours carried westward by whites? While both scenarios are likely, it's worth mentioning that the American frontier had a similar myth — the lost tribe of so-called 'Welsh Indians' — which tended to go west by the latter method.

The Welsh Indians were reputedly the descendants of medieval colonists from Wales who landed at Mobile Bay, Alabama, in the twelfth century. They proved very mobile indeed, ranging over a far longer period and wider territory than the Australian myth ever did. First reported in South Carolina in 1686, their rumoured location shifted many times, always tantalisingly just ahead of European frontiers. Evidence for their existence cropped up repeatedly, always collapsing upon close examination. It usually derived from amateurish observation of newly contacted tribes — individuals with comparatively light skin or hair, words that seemed to sound Welsh, etc. The *Sydney Gazette* devoted a two-part feature to the subject in February 1813. No aspect of exploring the American West, it said, excited 'more general attention and anxious curiosity, than the opinion that a nation of white men, speaking the Welch language, reside high up the Missouri'.[1] The newspaper was never so open-minded about the convicts' white colony, but as a government mouthpiece it was hardly likely to be. The American myth, while it was at least backed by a flimsy European tradition, was never much more than an intellectual and emotional curiosity, lacking the Australian variant's subversive potential. As the enthusiasm of social inferiors whose very presence in New South Wales marked them as criminals, the convict myth had little currency amongst free settlers. Yet James Hassall, the landowner who reported the gunfight between the police and visionary bushrangers to the *Sydney Gazette*, was an unblushing exception:

> The same Correspondent most solemnly assures us, that he is quite convinced of the existence of an interior settlement of white people!!! The blacks speak of it with certainty.

Hassall had joined the police manhunt after the bushrangers raided his station. One of the 'mistaken and dangerous men' he sought to arrest was a young Dubliner, a former errand boy named John Donahoe whose rebellious streak and briefly charmed life would soon transform him into an all-time convict hero. By the 1830s Donahoe was 'Bold Jack', the dead star of numerous ballads and even a five-act play.[2] As Australia's foremost folkloric convict-bushranger, Donahoe is still remembered as the rebel who 'would rather roam the hills and dales like wolf or kangaroo'. It is not so well known that his bushranging career was kick-started by convict escape mythology. The irony is that Donahoe, posthumously mythologised into the archetypal 'wild colonial boy', was at least partly produced by the premier convict myth of his own lifetime.

Originally transported for life for 'intent to commit a felony', Donahoe had been missing for six months when he attacked Hassall's property. An unlikely escape from custody had already won him minor celebrity. Under sentence of death for his first known highway robbery, he somehow disappeared between the courthouse and the condemned cell on 1 March 1828, despite being heavily ironed. One of his accomplices (both were hanged) had already given warning that the little Irishman was wily and tough beyond all expectation — 'the very devil himself' — and would escape if the gaolers weren't careful.

A twenty-pound reward described Donahoe on 2 May: 'native of Dublin, 22 years of age, 5 ft 4 inches in height, brown freckled complexion, flaxen hair, blue eyes and has a scar under his left nostril'. Eluding pursuit by crossing the Blue Mountains, in the wilds of the New Country he fell in with James Holmes, who led a mob of convict fugitives. Pale and pock-pitted, Holmes (alias Letters and Parsons) was in his mid-twenties, 5 feet 7 inches with brown hair and hazel eyes. He was reputedly an ex-soldier, although shipping records list his occupation as carter. Born in Bombay and convicted in Glasgow, upon reaching the colony in 1823 he was assigned to a farm at Bringelly, south-west of Sydney. Sometime afterwards his master returned him to government labour, but in April 1827 he escaped from Sydney's Hyde Park Barracks and went bush. Just over a year later, Holmes and other runaway convicts began plundering outback farms, intending to supply a trek to join a mysterious white society that inland Aborigines, presumably Wiradjuri people, had spoken of.

Holmes and Donahoe hit the squattocracy hard: their victims included the landholders Arkell, West, Armstrong, Harris and O'Brien. Just after dark on 22 August they targeted James Hassall's Bolong property, seventy miles south of Bathurst. Three other runaways accompanied them. Pockmarked and tattooed, Thomas Wiskin was a

Cockney butcher in his mid-twenties, originally transported for horse theft. William Owens, a coalminer from Lancashire, had escaped an iron gang. Sent for life from Stafford on a housebreaking charge, Owens left behind a wife and two children. The fifth man, Phillips, may have been the twenty-one-year-old Dubliner Patrick Phillips, wanted for fleeing the Australian Agricultural Company earlier in the year.[3]

Finding Hassall's storehouse locked, the gang started shooting at the door. Three men working inside, who were also armed, returned fire. The bushrangers then marshalled seven convict farmhands from a nearby hut to use as human shields. The besieged storehouse workers heard one bushranger invite them to shoot their mates. Another threatened to burn the building down. After the workers surrendered and were tied up, arguments raged about what to do with them. Holmes strongly vetoed a proposal to shoot them; one victim recalled Holmes telling his bloodthirsty associate that 'he would lose his life if an attempt was made to hurt a hair of our heads'. Instead Hassall's men lived to boil tea and cook lamb chops for their captors. The booty was considerable — all the hats, linen, tea, sugar, tobacco, salt, soap, boots and guns; nearly all the knives and razors; flour, packsaddles, horse hobbles, and some sheep and horses. The bushrangers also took all the books except the Bible, which they made a point of leaving 'for the use of the parson'. This sounds like a joke directed at James Hassall, whose eldest brother Thomas was a well-known colonial chaplain.

Hassall was eighty miles away at a neighbouring sheep run when the attack took place. After a messenger brought him the bad news he hurried home to Bolong (a two-day trip), arriving to find mounted police preparing for a manhunt. A farmhand, forced to help the bushrangers remove their plunder, supplied valuable information about their movements. A stockman had also gone off with the gang to help drive the stolen bullocks. The next day (28 August) the police party, led by Sergeant John Wilcox, set off accompanied by Hassall and another settler, Walker. They had a major stroke of luck on their second day out when an Aboriginal man volunteered his tracking skills. The next day he located the gang's trail and five more Aborigines joined in, eager to hunt the 'croppies'. Proceeding at a rate of four miles an hour, they spent two days tracking them to a shepherd's hut on land owned by Surgeon John Harris. Holmes had taken a sheep and three of Harris's convict servants, who threw in with the gang. Continuing to O'Brien's property, the search party found Holmes had recruited a second trio of convict stockmen, and commandeered three sheep, a bullock and various provisions. At noon on 3 September, the trackers found a newly vacated campsite. Warm ashes remained on the fireplace and a stolen kangaroo dog slept nearby. The party continued in tense silence. By mid-afternoon the Aborigines were announcing various discoveries — 'smoke', 'bullock', and finally, 'make a light, croppy sit down'. The bushrangers were camping near a rock outcrop just ahead.

Although Sergeant Wilcox expected to encounter a greatly expanded gang, only Owens and Wiskin were in camp, absorbed by a game of cards as a pot of mutton cooked on the fire.[4] The police rushed them and they ran off, but not far. Wounded by musket fire and sword cuts, Owens and Wiskin quickly surrendered. Owens confessed the gang was down to nine; the other seven were off raiding Mein's station. Dividing his troops in two, Wilcox lay in wait for an hour before the rest of the bushrangers appeared, driving a bullock laden with plunder, a pack of kangaroo dogs trotting at their heels.

There was no ambush. 'There's the bloody old sergeant!' one bushranger shouted. Holmes threw up his hat, calling defiantly that they were 'ready'. Gunfire rang out as the seven fugitives ran for cover up a rocky precipice, where the mounted police could not follow. Hassall later recalled the bushrangers' poor marksmanship. Donahoe, he said, 'placed himself where he could not be got at, and fired much quicker than the rest, but he always loaded his piece lying on his belly, and it is to this that his constant missing may be attributed'. As soon as the bushrangers were flushed from one hiding place in the rocks they found another. The deadly cat-and-mouse game lasted two hours, stopped only by nightfall. After hurriedly boiling up some tea, the police put their fire out and huddled behind trees. Taunts from the bushrangers rang out in the darkness, Donahoe shouting 'Come on now, we're all ready!' A downpour at midnight added to the misery. At first light, Wilcox found the bushrangers had slipped away, with the rain obliterating their tracks. He decided to visit Mein's and see what the damage was. On the way they chanced upon Holmes, shot through both legs and abandoned by his men. He asked for mercy and admitted he was 'captain of the gang', which he boasted numbered twenty men. The shirt he was wearing — stolen from Hassall's store — had been seen on another bushranger, whom Holmes confirmed was killed in the fighting and buried overnight.

This wasn't quite the end of the affair. Two days later, policemen from the same party caught up with Donahoe and Phillips after Sergeant Wilcox temporarily divided his team. Phillips was shot dead by a Corporal Prosser, but Donahoe outran the two-man mounted patrol and disappeared into the scrub, wounded in the arm.[5] Then Holmes and Owens managed to cut their irons and escape from the Bathurst lockup. Knocking the gaoler down, they fled town but their leg injuries stopped them getting too far away. Quickly overtaken, they were sent to Sydney to stand trial on 8 December with Wiskin. All three pleaded not guilty but offered no defence. A week later they were sentenced to hang by the neck until their 'bodies be dead' for 'stealing in the dwelling house of Mr James Hassall, of Bathurst, and putting persons therein in fear', and also for stealing sheep from O'Brien's station on 1 August.

The execution was set for Monday, 22 December 1828. Four others were to hang with them — two bushrangers, a burglar and the chief mate of a whaling vessel convicted of committing 'the unnatural crime' with a boy. At least one of these other bushrangers, John Walsh, had been with Holmes at the gunfight. A Dublin lad said to be only sixteen years old, Walsh was wounded by Wilcox's mounted police but escaped. A few weeks later he was arrested after committing a highway robbery with

William Bain, now about to hang alongside him. Whether Bain also hailed from Holmes' gang is uncertain, but quite possible. A twenty-two-year-old Irishman who arrived on the same ship as Donahoe, Bain had been several months at large in the New Country, having fled Samuel Hassall's service after a robbery.[6]

At 9.10 am, the seven condemned men were led from their cells to the gaol courtyard where a scaffold stood before a small gathering of spectators. Young John Walsh, crying his eyes out, was too upset to walk unassisted and had to be supported up the gallows steps. His case was particularly hard. On a life sentence for housebreaking, the former 'errand boy' had only been in Australia since June and, in line with Governor Darling's cruel new policy, had gone straight into a road gang — very rough work previously reserved as a punishment for colonial re-offenders. Unable to endure it, Walsh took off in a matter of weeks, only to find his short life now already at an end.

A trio of ministers stayed with the prisoners until 9.45 am, when the sheriff cleared the platform and ordered the trapdoor bolts released. After hanging 'for the usual time, the bodies were lowered down and put into shells for interment by their friends'.

Donahoe, his notoriety now cemented by escaping his accomplices' fate a second time, forsook Holmes' vision of reaching the phantom colony. Joining forces with a pair of road-gang escapees, John Walmsley and William Webber, he began a two-year spree of highway robberies and homestead raids around the fringes of settlement. The price on his head went skywards after the murder of a traveller during a hold-up in March 1829. By September it was fifty pounds, and the following May an absolute pardon and the choice of passage to England or a land grant was thrown in. But Bold Jack remained untouchable for some time yet, enjoying sympathy and shelter from a scattering of ex-convict settlers. His infamy helped prompt the hated Bushranging Act of April 1830, which permitted the arrest and detention of anybody unable to prove they were not an absconder. This was especially tough on freeborn locals and immigrants who, unlike ex-convicts, had no identity papers to confirm their status. In one outrageous instance, an Australian-born man spent seven weeks of three months marching in handcuffs between police stations, simply for identification purposes.

Donahoe's luck finally ran out on 1 September 1830, amid a hail of police musket-fire in the bush near Bringelly. He died cursing his tormentors with obscenities and insults, bragging he'd 'beat' the whole colony. The *Sydney Gazette* sighed with relief that New South Wales was rid of 'one of the most dangerous spirits that ever infested it', touching upon Donahoe's subversive popularity as well as his extensive criminal activities. The net began to close in on his mates, and Walmsley and Webber were captured separately early in the new year. Webber refused to give information in return for a capital reprieve. He said he could only gain a life sentence on Norfolk Island and would rather be hanged, which he was on 11 July. The less resolute Walmsley capitulated, revealing a network of ex-convict sympathisers who had acted as bush telegraphs and fences for the gang. Among the six retransported for this offence was Michael O'Brien or Bryan, a fifty-three-year-old Irishman who had arrived in one of the convict transports central to our story, the *Atlas I*, back in 1802.

Surviving contemporary ballads provide an inkling of how Donahoe achieved cult hero status within his lifetime. *Jim Jones at Botany Bay* ends with the convict protagonist's vow to take to the bush and 'join the brave bushrangers there/Jack Donahoe and Co.' Another, the blatantly Irish republican *John Donahoe and His Gang*, is often attributed (with no real justification) to Donahoe himself. Better known is *Bold Jack Donahoe*, a lament for his death reputedly suppressed in some public houses under threat of loss of licence. This song eventually evolved into the world-famous *Wild Colonial Boy*, which retains the original's defiant chorus lyric: 'We'll scorn to live in slavery, bound down by iron chains'. Nine years after Donahoe's death came *The Convict's Tour to Hell*, a Swiftian tour de force by the Irish convict balladeer Frank 'The Poet' MacNamara offering a cameo of Bold Jack in Heaven!

George Boxall's *The Story of the Australian Bushrangers* (1899) — the first comprehensive account of this topic — describes stories the author learned from old hands about a hideout Donahoe used in the Burragorang Valley. Located in Gundungurra territory beyond Nattai, fifty-four miles south-west of Sydney, the valley's first official European explorer had been Francis Barrallier in 1802. Despite a survey party's visit in the early 1820s it remained a lonely and remote spot in Donahoe's day. Today it is underwater, a bushranging Atlantis, flooded in the late 1950s to create Warragamba Dam. The sanctuary was enclosed by steep cliffs, accessible only by a narrow opening easily blocked with a few branches — ideal both as a hideaway from authority and a container for stolen stock. Known variously as the Camp, the Shelter or the Pound, lurid stories about evil doings there eventually won it the nickname Terrible Hollow, which Rolf Boldrewood used for a fictional robbers' roost in his novel *Robbery Under Arms* (1888). Its downfall may have been Walmsley's confession; an official notice (dated 3 August 1831) in the *Sydney Gazette* shortly afterwards announced that 'His Excellency the Governor has been pleased, at the suggestion of the Magistrates of the District, to direct the discontinuance of the Pound at Burragurang'. According to Boxall's sources, the phantom white colony was responsible for the discovery of this bushrangers' haven:

> Precisely how the entrance to this extensive enclosure was first found is not known. It is believed, however, that it was discovered by a party of bushrangers, who endeavoured to discover a road over the Blue Mountains, in order to reach a settlement of white men, which was popularly supposed to lie somewhere in that direction. Whether this supposed settlement was Dutch or English does not appear, but as I have already said, there was a widespread belief that some of these settlements were no very great distance from Sydney, and could be reached overland.

Runaways hiding in or near the Burragorang as far back as the 1790s, perhaps drawn south by the prospect of living off the wild cattle, may have formed the original 'white colony' themselves without realising it. In 1798 John 'Bun-bo-e' Wilson revealed familiarity with the region.[7] In 1804 George Caley, exploring nearby in the Cowpastures, was alarmed to hear a European voice in the wilderness, perhaps a runaway with a secret new life. The bush haven of those mysterious renegades Fox, Pitt and Burke (see Chapter 7) — said to be a valley fifty miles from Sydney, beyond the Razorbacks — closely matches the Burragorang. It may even be more than coincidence that the white colony myth did not long outlast the Pound's closure.

Another source for later escape myth permutations was George Clarke, alias 'The Barber', who lived with Aborigines for five years in the north-west after absconding from a remote property in 1826. Building stockyards out on the Liverpool Plains, he began stealing cattle with other bolters and local Kamilaroi Aborigines, including two women said to be his wives. This 'degenerate', the explorer Sir Thomas Mitchell wrote, disguised himself as a black by darkening and scarifying his skin so he could approach farms without fear of detection. In hindsight, however, it seems clear he was adopted into the tribe.[8]

The Barber was more than just a starting point for fresh rumours himself. Captured in 1831, he claimed to have reached the sea a great distance to the north-west by following a large river called the Kindur. There he saw an island from which, Aborigines told him, 'a race of light-coloured men came in large canoes for a scented wood'. Here was a bushranger's tale with something for everyone, combining the longed-for western sea with a mystery non-Aboriginal people. Much of it was probably Clarke's own invention, or obtained second-hand from the Kamilaroi, but in November 1831 Mitchell was sent to trace Clarke's route in the hope his story would lead to the inland sea. Sturt also discussed the Barber's claims in detail, though he was sceptical and indeed, the Kindur was never found.

The extent to which escape myths sustained bushrangers of the 1820s is difficult to measure, because evidence had little means of coming to light. The intention of Holmes was only preserved by a passing remark in Hassall's letter to the *Gazette*, and such a detailed account of a police pursuit is very rare. Neither Holmes nor any of his associates appear to have mentioned the myth at their trial; it was irrelevant to the charges and could have had no ameliorating effect. But if Holmes and Donahoe were amongst the last to dream of the phantom white colony, then at least they gave it a fiery last hurrah. Their activities shook the colonial frontier not too far from where some of the original believers had first located the sanctuary. In this retreat westwards, the dream would find its own sunset. Soon the convict myth would meet an unheralded oblivion, in the footsteps of so many of its seekers.

CHAPTER SEVENTEEN

Buckley's and none

He seemed as one not belonging to our world.

JAMES BONWICK, 'BUCKLEY THE WILD WHITE MAN' (1863)

ON SUNDAY, 6 JULY 1835, THREE EUROPEAN MEN AND SEVEN SYDNEY Aborigines were camped near the entrance to Port Phillip Bay on the remote southern coast of the Australian mainland. They had crossed the Bass Strait from Van Diemen's Land, intending to settle a region rejected by colonists over thirty years before, the homeland of half a dozen Aboriginal peoples. As far as the white trio knew, they were the only Europeans for hundreds of miles, certainly the only ones in this part of the wild, windswept south.

Imagine their astonishment when at 2 pm on that Sunday afternoon an extremely tall white man strode into their camp. Their first impression, according to a contemporary report, was 'that this giant would put one of them under each arm, and walk away with them'. But the stranger seemed very pleased to see them. He was dressed in animal skins, his hair and beard spread 'as large as a bushel'. For a time communication was impossible, but when the man was offered bread he suddenly recalled the English word for it. The newcomers took him into their tent and dressed him in their spare clothes, which he must have had trouble fitting into. Measuring the stranger, they found him almost 6 foot 6 without shoes and eighteen inches around the calf and upper arm.

Who was the mystery giant? Tattoos on his arms — a mermaid, a sun, a crescent moon, a monkey, seven stars and the initials WB — suggested a stranded sailor. At first he could only repeat the questions put to him, but eventually enough of his native tongue returned and he identified himself as William Buckley, an English soldier shipwrecked en route to Van Diemen's Land many years before. He maintained this story for three weeks until admitting the truth. Buckley was a runaway convict, left behind when the original Port Phillip colony removed to Van Diemen's Land back in 1804. This 'modern Robinson Crusoe', as the *Sydney Gazette* styled him, had lost track of European time and supposed twenty years may have passed. It was actually almost thirty-two.

In one sense Buckley, the 'Wild White Man', was the most wildly successful of all convicts who took a chance on escape mythology. Although failing to locate his outback China, the home he found met the myth's basic criteria — freedom from authority, no compulsion to labour and minimal involvement in the quarrels and politics of relatively generous hosts. He was also lucky enough to receive a pardon upon his rediscovery, due as much to the imagined value of his local knowledge as the extraordinary elapse of time. Buckley is usually said to have returned to civilisation, but it would be more accurate to say that civilisation returned to him.

William Buckley was born in 1780 near Macclesfield, Cheshire, and apprenticed to a bricklayer at fifteen. Four years later he joined the Cheshire militia, transferring to the King's Own Regiment of Foot in time to fight the French in September 1799. Some time after returning from Holland, wounded in the right hand, Buckley entered a shop in Warnham, Sussex, with one William Marmon and stole two pieces of Irish cloth. Soon arrested, they were sentenced to death at the Sussex Summer Assizes on 2 August 1802, reprieved on condition of life transportation and transferred to a hulk in Langstone Harbour, Portsmouth. Almost a year later they were embarked on the HMS *Calcutta*, bound for the south-eastern edge of Australia, where it was hoped a new penal colony would stave off French interest in the region.

The first site chosen was on the eastern head of Port Phillip Bay, about 500 miles directly overland south-west from Sydney. David Collins, returning to Australia as lieutenant governor of the new colony after seven lean years in England, named it Sullivan Bay. The storeship *Ocean* arrived on 7 October 1803 and the HMS *Calcutta*, carrying 307 convicts, followed two days later. Soon the arc of the beach was filled with clusters of tents — Collins and other officials at one end and the hospital at the other, with the soldiers and convict labourers in between. The forty-nine free settlers were permitted to build huts just beyond the camp perimeter, together with convicts who were mechanics (tradesmen). As a bricklayer Buckley was amongst these, which made escape even easier.

It was a miserable spot: hot, without abundant fresh water, and near a dangerous tidal rip that menaced shipping. Collins quickly sought permission to relocate. Meanwhile, some convicts began relocating themselves without permission. Assuming they were heading overland to Sydney, Collins issued a notice on 10 November warning others that 'independent of the risk they run in being killed by the natives, it is impossible for them, with any quantity of provisions they could carry, to endure the fatigue of penetrating a thousand miles through the woods of this country'. A week later five were captured by soldiers and flogged. The next day three more returned in terrible condition, abandoned by comrades who gave them the slip, taking the group's remaining provisions. Collins had been wrong about their intentions. It emerged the real plan was to skirt the coast in the hope of being picked up by whalers or American traders rumoured to be in the South Seas. Absconding abated after the floggings but was renewed on 12 December, when two convicts, George Lee and David Gibson, stole a gun and took off. Later that same morning the *Ocean* returned from Sydney, bearing permission from Governor King to abandon the mainland for the Derwent River in Van Diemen's Land.

Also arriving with the *Ocean* were back issues of the *Sydney Gazette*, including coverage of John Place's recent 'Fatal Excursion'. Deciding that the grim details of this failed escape might make a useful discouragement, Collins had a full extract printed on 23 December, accompanied by the following Public Caution:

> The LIEUT GOVERNOR, understanding that there are, at this moment, people who are desperate enough to entertain a resolution of quitting the Settlement, previous to the removal of the Establishment, hoping and expecting to find means of subsisting hereafter, think proper to publish the following account of an attempt to escape from Port Jackson, which was made by four prisoners who arrived there in His Majesty's ship *Glatton*, which he has extracted from a Newspaper published at Sydney, by authority of the GOVERNOR, and which he hopes will have the effect of deterring any of the Prisoners under his direction from following so pernicious an example.

An outline of Place's first adventure followed, beginning with the explanation that he and his fellow travellers resolved to 'pass the Mountains' under the impression they would 'get to China, by which means they would obtain their liberty again'. While it is feasible that some convicts brought the China myth with them from England, the first evidence for it at Sullivan Bay closely followed the news of Place's journey.

Despite the harrowing deaths of Place's companions, Buckley and other convicts may have been more worried about being removed to an island, where escape might prove impossible. Buckley had kept out of trouble so far, occupied with building a magazine and storehouse. But it was a life of quiet desperation, and Buckley was not one to miss his chance of freedom, however slim. Several men ran with him, but Buckley only ever named two — his former partner-in-crime, William Marmon, and George Pye. On a life sentence for stealing a ewe, the thirty-one-year-old Pye was allegedly part of a professional sheep-stealing gang in Nottinghamshire.

Four others were implicated in Buckley's escape. Daniel Macallenan, a small dark Irish sailor in his early twenties, was servant to the colony's minister, the Reverend Robert Knopwood. Caught stealing silverware from a London coffee shop, he had been given seven years transportation. Thomas Pritchard, native to Buckley's Chester, and Charles Shaw, of Box in Wiltshire, were both punished for insolence during the voyage out, with Shaw being double-ironed. Pritchard, twenty-two, was serving fourteen years for selling a stolen gelding. Shaw was about thirty and doing seven years for stealing his neighbour's chickens. Thomas Page, a framework knitter also about thirty years of age, already had a criminal record for poaching when he got life transportation for highway robbery. Curiously, Page crossed the globe from one Melbourne (near Derby) to the future site of another, the capital of the as yet unrealised colony of Victoria.

As Buckley recalled it, they decided to run on the first dark night, taking with them a gun and 'as much provisions as we could muster'. Early on Christmas morning Macallenan played Santa Claus in reverse to Commissary Leonard Fosbrook, creeping into his tent and stealing his fowling piece and a pair of boots from the side of the bed as he slept. It was not the only theft of the evening. Someone also entered the hospital tent and stole food intended for the patients.

Collins set up a five-man night watch and offered conditional emancipation in return for information. This brought immediate results. On 27 December an informer — almost certainly Thomas Page — told him the Christmas crimes were down to two men, 'one of whom had been for some time in the woods; the other went off the night he committed the robbery'. Armed and well-shod, Macallenan was now certainly well-equipped to join Pritchard, who had taken to the bush on 19 December. Five others, Collins was told, were intending to join them that night.

Instead of making immediate arrests, Collins decided to catch the runaways red-handed and sent an armed party to ambush them at a place he learned they would pass. The information was solid. At 9 pm Buckley and his companions[1] made their move. Three miles from camp, they were seen travelling along the beach and called on to surrender. Shots were fired after they ignored a third warning. Shaw fell with a musket slug in his belly. Page was also taken, though his arrest may have been a sham to allay suspicion.[2] The rest escaped into the night, soon to be lashed by a ferocious electrical storm.

At 1 am one of the soldiers reached camp to notify Collins. A cart was called to fetch Shaw, who was suffering terribly. He also refused to 'utter one syllable that would lead to a discovery of his associates'. On 30 December a camp sentry was fired upon by an unseen gunman. It was an unsettling period all round; fearing his grumbling marines were on the verge of rebellion, Collins resorted to arming a small militia of trusted convicts.

The first sign of the runaways came four nights later on New Year's Eve[3], when 'great fires' across the bay were correctly surmised to be their distress beacons. More convict-built fires were seen on 3 January. A dawn trip to the harbour's mouth on 6 January failed to spot them, but later that day David Gibson returned, 'a mere skeleton' emaciated almost beyond recognition. He staggered in with the first news of a freshwater river (the Yarra) at the northern end of Port Phillip. His companion George Lee was still up there. Early the next morning another search party marched an estimated fifty miles in a last-ditch effort to find either Lee or the larger mob. When they returned empty-handed Collins gave up all pursuit, but tried to prevent further escapes by stopping the issue of new shoes.

No one expected to see the deserters again. However, in the stifling midday heat of 16 January[4], a bedraggled Daniel Macallenan materialised in Collins' garden. He claimed to have spent five days tramping '100 miles' around Port Phillip with the others, living 'chiefly upon gum and shell-fish', before giving up and spending a fortnight finding his way back alone. He brought back the stolen gun — which he had clearly kept charge of — and the revelation that 'his companions intended to proceed to the mountains, which are to the westward of Port Jackson'. This was the route to John Place's China, unknown at Sullivan Bay until the *Gazette* extract arrived. They also seem to have adopted a familiar tool, perhaps mindful of Place's concern for navigation. A month after Macallenan returned, the colony's surveyor George Prideaux Harris wrote to his brother about the 'daring fellows' who took to the woods:

> These infatuated wretches all declare on their return that they intended
> to go to Port Jackson! Or to China!!! And so ignorant were they that
> some had a compass drawn on a piece of paper, by which they meant
> to steer their course!??

John Pascoe Fawkner, in 1803 the 11-year-old son of a convict at Sullivan Bay, recalled the affair in his later years. Although clouded by time, his lasting impression was that Irish escapees had aimed for China. Macallenan may have sprung to mind when Fawkner wrote the following for the *Launceston Advertiser* (17 August 1829):

> Many prisoners ran away from the settlement. Some (Irishmen)
> professing to be bound overland to China, others (runaways) started
> for Sydney. Only one that I can remember came back.

In fact only two Irishmen absconded from Sullivan Bay — Lee[5] and Macallenan. It is hard to believe that the former, possessed of a classical education, had fallen for any kind of escape myth. Collins even assured Governor King that Lee, 'a man of a cast (in point of abilities and education) superior to the rest', was not likely to 'attempt to cross the

country to Port Jackson, as I think he has more sense'. Fawkner returned
to the subject in 1865, again distinguishing between two kinds of escapee:

> The prisoners were, many of them, possessed of an idea that they
> could travel overland to China; these were mostly from Green Erin.
> Others took to the bush to try to get away to Sydney, ignoring the
> fact that they would be put to work there, if they reached it, and also
> flogged for running away.

At first glance, Fawkner seems guilty of national prejudice in assigning
the most fantastical goal to the Irish, but this may only be because it
was the party's sole Irishman who revealed the intended destination.
Macallenan may have not have believed in it himself — and he did have
the sense to turn back early.

China was unquestionably a mad pipedream to Fawkner and Harris,
but in puzzling over the attractions of Sydney they missed a key subtlety of
the convict myth. The destinations amounted to the same thing; Sydney
was a logical signpost to 'China' for an escapee starting out from Sullivan
Bay. John Place's example suggested that attaining China involved
keeping westward of Sydney's mountains, or crossing them once Sydney
was reached. The imminent removal to Van Diemen's Land lent urgency
to the idea. If Sydney was near China, then the mainland offered a better
crack at liberty than an island across Bass Strait.

No stranger to escape mythology, Collins knew only too well how
difficult it was to oppose. His previous attempt to discourage desertion
involved broadcasting not only the suffering of Place and his companions,
but also their apparently absurd rationale. Clearly it hadn't worked. His
next pronouncement (dated 20 January) shows a reversal of tactics;
there would be no devils in the detail this time. Collins now declared utter
mystification at the motives of recent runaways, as if mindful his target
audience had taken the wrong message from his last warning. In short,
Collins decided he better stop spreading the overland China rumour:

The LIEUT. GOVERNOR hopes the return of Daniel M'Allenan will have convinced the Prisoners of the misery that must ever attend those who are mad enough to abscond from the Settlement. To warn them from making any attempt of a similar nature, they are informed that, although this man left his companions on the fifth day after their departure hence, they all began to feel the effects of their imprudence; and more of them would have returned, had they not dreaded the punishment which they were conscious they deserved. Their provisions were nearly expended, and they had no resources. They lived in constant dread of the Natives, by whose hands, it is more than probable, they have by this time perished; or, if this should not have happened, how is it possible that strong, hearty men, who were always able to consume even more than the liberal allowance of provisions, which is issued to them, can exist in a Country, which no where affords a supply to the traveller.

The LIEUT. GOVERNOR can by no means account for this strange desertion of the people. Were they ill treated, scantily fed, badly clothed, or wrought beyond their ability, he should attribute it to those causes; but as the reverse is the case, he is at a loss to discover the motive.

He thinks it necessary to advise them, not to harbour, or supply with their provisions any people who may quit the Settlement, as it is his fixed determination to punish them with greater severity than he would the infatuated wretches themselves.

He is concerned that the several Prisoners who are now absent must be left to perish, as, by *M'Allenan's* account, they are beyond the reach of any effort he might make to recall them to their duty.

John Jones, a Welshman in his early fifties described by Collins as 'an infirm old man', was the final runaway from the moribund settlement. Taking off on 3 January 1804, he wandered the bush for three weeks before returning to die of 'fatigue' at Sullivan Bay on 17 February, too unwell to sail with the first transfer of convicts. Whether he was another

'Chinese traveller' is unknown, but he was the only other convict known to have taken off after Place's Blue Mountains adventure became general knowledge. Another death during this period was Thomas Page, from unstated causes, on 27 January. Was he murdered for informing on his fellow runaways? Evidence is lacking, but the timing of his death — shortly after Macallenan's unexpected return — is rather suspicious.

The last news of Buckley came from William Marmon, who made a surprise reappearance at Sullivan Bay sometime between Collins' departure for Van Diemen's Land on 30 January and the final transfer on 15 May. Lieutenant Sladden, left to supervise the final withdrawal from the mainland, made one last-ditch effort to rescue Marmon's lost companions, as Collins informed Governor King by dispatch from an embryonic Hobart Town:

> He [Marmon] stating, upon his reaching the Camp, that they were not all dead when he determined on leaving them, a Party was sent out in hopes of discovering and rendering them assistance if not too late; but they returned, having travelled a considerable distance around the Harbour without meeting any Trace of them, and leaving no doubt of their being no longer in Existence.

What befell the runaways after they left Charles Shaw bleeding on the sand? The information Buckley supplied thirty-two years later came in understandably vague snippets, generally painting the escape as an attempt to walk to Sydney spurred by the decision to relocate off the mainland. The earliest of these accounts come from two of Buckley's discoverers, Andrew Todd and JH Wedge.

Buckley gave Todd a patently false story about jumping overboard when the *Calcutta* put in for water sometime before the landing at Sullivan Bay. Nevertheless, his memory of Shaw looms large in this invention, with an unnamed fellow escapee shot dead as they swam from the ship. Two others, Buckley claimed, were killed by the same Aborigines who took him in. Wedge's version, while closer to the known facts, makes no mention of a comrade falling to a soldier's bullet. Buckley told him he 'absconded with two men named Marmon and Pye' just before Collins abandoned Sullivan Bay — the only time he named his companions. The difficulty in finding food, with cockles and mussels picked up along the beaches forming their chief subsistence, closely matches the description Macallenan gave of meagre seaside foraging. According to Wedge, Pye left the others before they reached the Yarra River, and Marmon turned back at Indented Head. Both were presumed killed by Aborigines.

George Langhorne, a missionary who briefly employed Buckley as an Aboriginal interpreter, heard a very different story. Buckley fed him a line about jumping ship after being embarked for relocation to Van Diemen's Land. In this version Buckley leaves his two companions after arguing about the direction to Sydney, unable to convince them to head north — although agreeing it 'could not be far distant', an insight into the futility of Collins' exaggerated assurances that it was a 1000-mile trip. In any case, his resolve soon crumbling, Buckley retraces his steps to the coast and lives off crayfish while trying in vain to spot the departed transport. Then, six months after being adopted by local Aborigines, he finds one of his former companions, now living with an Aboriginal family along the coast. They join forces, but Buckley soon asks him to clear out, explaining that 'from his reckless conduct with the women and dissolute behaviour, I was fully convinced that if he remained one or both of us would be murdered'. Later a rumour reaches him that this man had indeed worn out his welcome and been killed by his hosts.

Buckley's reluctance to talk is most evident in the diary entry of the explorer Phillip Parker King on 14 March 1837, which reads in part:

> Buckley relates that, having heard there was such a place as Sydney, he and two others, whose names he forgets, absconded with provisions enough, as they thought, to carry them to Sydney, of the situation of which with regard to the new colony they had not the least idea.

Yet another variation, appearing in the *Sydney Gazette* (10.9.1835), suggests that four men had eluded the soldiers' bullets to reach the woods: 'He [Buckley] says he does not know what became of the other three runaways'. After this handful of contradictory disclosures, Buckley kept silence for some fifteen years. Finally, in 1852, he allowed a retired newspaper editor named John Morgan to ghost-write his memoirs. The result was *The Life and Adventures of William Buckley, Thirty-Two Years a Wanderer Amongst the Aborigines of the then Unexplored Country Round Port Phillip, Now the Province of Victoria*. Easily the most detailed account of his life, it is now a minor Australian classic, still regularly reprinted. Morgan put many words into Buckley's mouth, but he curtailed Buckley's escape plan to one sentence: 'I determined on endeavouring to make my escape, and to get, if possible, to Sydney'. The following reflection, ascribed to the notoriously inarticulate Wild White Man, reads more like Morgan's own attempt to make sense of Buckley's intention:

> How could I have deceived myself into a belief of ever reaching Sydney, and particularly by travelling in that direction, is to me astonishing; and even if I had found it possible to do so, of course I should, on my arrival there, have been confined as a runaway, and punished accordingly. The whole affair was, in fact, a species of madness.

It was a different species of madness altogether. The actual goal of Buckley's escape — the Blue Mountains near Sydney — lay forgotten but preserved in Collins' fifty-year-old dispatch to England which outlined Macallenan's confession.[6] By the time of his rediscovery Buckley had forgotten or was embarrassed by it, though somehow it crept into West's landmark *History of Tasmania* (1852, page 31), which came out the same year as Morgan's book: 'Buckley, a man of gigantic stature, and two others, set off, it was said, for China!'

As Buckley related to Morgan, after the 'last man of the four of us' was shot down — fatally, he presumed — the remaining trio ran for three or four hours before stopping to rest. He made no mention of the lightning and heavy rain. Here they took stock of their provisions; some tin pots, an iron kettle, the fowling piece and a few days rations. The next evening they reached within twenty miles of the site of present-day Melbourne. Provisions ran out soon afterwards and they went to the foreshore to scavenge for shellfish. Eventually reaching Indented Head opposite the settlement across the mouth of the bay, they began to regret their flight and lit the signal fires recorded by Knopwood on New Year's Eve.

It's hardly surprising that Macallenan, Page and Pritchard are missing from Buckley's thirty-two-year-old recollections. Perhaps Marmon and Pye stuck in his memory by staying with him longer. Wedge's understanding that Pye turned back before the Yarra River, apparently reached on the second day out (29 January), might better account for Pritchard or the armed Macallenan — which in turn might explain the sentry being shot at on 30 January, though the previous deserter Lee was also armed. In any case the evidence for Pritchard's involvement is minimal, resting on his supposed collusion with Macallenan in the Christmas robberies. Morgan thought only two men besides Shaw escaped with Buckley, and implies they stayed together until 13 January. This is a feasible date for the beginning of Macallenan's return journey, although the Irishman's confession infers he turned back on 1 January, which was the day after the first signal fire was lit.

Morgan describes the runaways' anxiety when the rescue boat approached them (6 January) only to turn back halfway across the harbour. After six more days of heartbreaking failure, he writes, Buckley's two companions saw 'no probable relief, gave themselves up to despair, and lamented bitterly their helpless situation'. Fearing starvation, they began walking back the next day. Only Buckley held fast, 'determined to endure every kind of suffering rather than again surrender my liberty'. And so, by mid-January the Wild White Man was left to his own devices on Beangala (Indented Head) — the loneliest man in the world:

I thought of the friends of my youth, the scenes of my boyhood, and early manhood, of the slavery of my punishment, of the liberty I had panted for, and which although now realized, after a fashion, made the heart sick, even at its enjoyment. I remember, I was here subjected to the most severe mental sufferings for several hours, and then pursued my solitary journey.

Lonely as Buckley was, he was far from alone. Numerous Aboriginal clans lived around Port Phillip Bay, and the day after Buckley parted from his companions he blundered across an encampment of about a hundred people. He was spotted but fled for his life and it was some time before he was discovered by other locals. He took to wandering the beaches, living off plants and shellfish in the vicinity of Karaaf (Bream Creek) just west of the ocean side of Indented Head.

Morgan's book is the only detailed source of information for Buckley's new life, though he had also briefly recounted to Langhorne his adoption into the Wattewarre clan of the Wathaurung. At Maamart, the swamps west of Lake Connewarre, Buckley happened upon a gravesite, where he removed a piece of spear placed upright in the burial mound. He intended to use it as a walking stick, but two days later it saved his life in a most unexpected manner. Resting against a tree, faint with cold and hunger, Buckley found himself surrounded by Aborigines who took him by the hands and walked him back to their camp. He thought he was being led to his death, but in fact it was the very opposite. He didn't know it, but he had undergone a transformation of identity, essentially the same rebirth that gave new hope to Turwood's gang at Port Stephens:

They have a belief that, when they die, they go to some place or other, and are there made white men, and that they then return to this world again for another existence. They think all the white people previous to death were belonging to their own tribes, thus returned to life in a different colour. In cases where they have killed white men, it has generally been because they have imagined them to have been originally enemies, or belonging to tribes with whom they were hostile.

Still carrying the spear he had plucked from the grave, Buckley was taken for the buried man returned to life. The soldier, thief and bricklayer from Cheshire was now Wathaurung kin, the reincarnation of a man killed along with his daughters during a recent tribal skirmish. 'To this providential superstition,' Buckley recalled, 'I was indebted for all the kindnesses afterwards shown me.' He was dubbed Marrangurk, either the dead man's name or a title for reincarnated persons. As he entered the camp women wailed and tore their faces and hair, lamenting his suffering. The following night was spent celebrating the miraculous return with hours of dancing around a great fire, the women naked and the men adorned in streaks of pipeclay. Buckley was initially afraid they intended to roast and eat him, but gradually realised he was the guest of honour. The night concluded with the assembly giving 'three tremendous shouts, at the same time pointing to the sky with their sticks'. They each shook Buckley 'heartily by the hand, again beating their breasts as a sign of friendship'. By the time he came to sleep Buckley was so relieved in his newfound safety that he 'enjoyed a sleep undisturbed by dreams, either of the past, the present, or the future'.

The Wathaurung led a semi-nomadic existence, moving between various food sources within a fairly limited territory. The peace of this hunter-gatherer lifestyle was periodically shattered by outbursts of extreme violence, usually the result of abductions and desertions of women to rival groups. Buckley lost his closest friends and adopted family in an ambush, and he occasionally attempted living alone to avoid being swept up in revenge killings. This is not to say Buckley wasn't content with his lot; Morgan emphasised the violent interludes of an otherwise pacific existence. He also claimed that Buckley endured celibacy, fearful of involvement in the jealous disputes over women. But in 1836, while guiding colonist Joseph Tice Gellibrand on a surveying trip, Buckley pointed out an Aboriginal woman who was his daughter, and admitted to having two or more wives in the tribe. The truth was Buckley regretted returning to European civilisation. When he first heard that white men had returned to the area, he had hesitated for some time before making contact. He had known about and avoided the failed colony at Westernport, which was abandoned after two lean years in 1828. According to Morgan, Buckley only made contact to save the explorers from an Aboriginal scheme to kill them for their provisions. Langhorne commented how 'discontented and dissatisfied' Buckley was after his return, of how 'it would have been a great relief to him had the settlement been abandoned, and he left alone with his sable friends'.

Buckley's second biographer, James Bonwick (1856), deplored that instead of attempting to evangelise the heathen Aborigines, Buckley was content 'passing his time unmolested and unmolesting, impressionless and unimpressing — a mere vegetable existence'. Bonwick's motivation was to debunk Morgan, whom he accused of inventing detail that Buckley, a gentle giant of few words, could not possibly have supplied. 'All whom we have consulted,' Bonwick wrote, 'who knew Buckley both in Port Phillip and in Hobart Town, agree in saying that the man was so dull and reserved that it was impossible to get any connected or reliable information from him'.

Bonwick was an absurdly harsh critic, outraged that an Englishman should opt for 'the dirty, lazy life of the barbarian'. This was partly sour grapes, as Buckley had refused to talk to him, but the attitude was common during Buckley's lifetime. Dismissed as a freak or a disgrace, his intelligence was underestimated and his survival instinct unappreciated. Part of the problem was a reluctance to divulge information about the Aborigines that could be used against them. Another was the language difficulties and culture shock that clearly bewildered him for years after his return. He had undergone a double dislocation, from England to the most remote convict camp in the world, and from there to an Aboriginal world totally removed from his experience. Although noted as literate at his trial, thirty-two years in the bush removed most of his spoken English, which he had to relearn at fifty-five years of age. John Pascoe Fawkner, who as a child had known Buckley at Sullivan Bay, utilised the old convict's long dormant bricklaying skills by employing him to build his house, one of Melbourne's first. He also tried to pick Buckley's brains about the wilderness years, only to find that he 'would get angry, and walk away, or else begin to jabber to himself in the native language'. This led to the usual unfair dismissal of the Wild White Man as 'a lump of matter, too mindless to yield any very useful information'.

Other would-be interrogators fared no better. Bonwick listed a dozen eminent colonials who failed to win Buckley's confidence, including Governor Bourke. A man who lived six months with Buckley in 1836 claimed he 'scarcely ever spoke to him at all, and never gave the least information about his thirty years' bush life'. The more sympathetic JT Gellibrand commented on Buckley's 'harmless and gentle nature, if unblessed with the force of mental character', although conceding his 'nervous and irritable disposition', which he had the sensitivity to realise was a product of Buckley's 'peculiar situation'. Even the lucky few that Buckley did confide in had trouble fashioning his disclosures into a coherent story. It was a source of great frustration for those who hoped to use him as an Aboriginal go-between on their own terms.

Buckley deserved better from the founders of Victoria. His very presence in the colony made him a de facto Aboriginal diplomat, without whom European settlement could not have proceeded as speedily or as easily as it did. His skilful mediation helped avoid conflict on several occasions, and he retained the affection and trust of his adopted clan well after his return to white society. When he visited an old friend named Nullaboin, Gellibrand, who accompanied him, saw men, women and children mobbing the Wild White Man, clinging to him with 'tears of joy and delight running down their cheeks'. Another, less happy example of Buckley's high standing occurred when a young Aboriginal girl fled to his protection after escaping from a shepherd intent on raping her.

Buckley complained on her behalf and the guilty party was removed to Van Diemen's Land. After working as an interpreter for the government and missionaries, with mixed results, Buckley was attached to the Police Magistrate at Geelong as a guide. There is some pathos in the reflection that the white man most sympathetic and sensitive towards the Aboriginal Victorians should unwittingly smooth the way for their dispossession.

Part of Buckley's mythology was that like Ishmael, he alone survived to tell the tale. He had no way of knowing that some of his companions had made it back alive with accounts of their own comparatively modest adventures. By 1835 no one else seems to have remembered, either. William Marmon, conditionally pardoned in May 1816 and fully freed two years later, advertised his intended departure from Van Diemen's Land in 1821 and probably returned to England soon afterwards. Daniel Macallenan continued in Knopwood's service in Hobart, but three years later tried to escape again by participating in the seizure of a vessel called the *Marcia*. He was tried in Sydney in February 1808 with others, but was pardoned. Charles Shaw, whose gunshot wound troubled him for years afterwards, drowned in a shipwreck off the South Cape of Tasmania in October 1815.

Of all the convicts who may have taken their chances with Buckley, only Pritchard and Pye were swallowed by the landscape. Some of Buckley's detractors, such as Fawkner, made dark hints that he had swallowed them himself, saving himself by turning cannibal. But there is not the slightest evidence that Pritchard or Pye were eaten, despite the curious synchronicity of the latter's surname. Buckley's earliest recollections were that some of his companions had been killed by Aborigines, and there is no reason to doubt him. Certainly it wasn't his nature to speak ill of the locals.

Buckley's name was mud in the colony from August 1836, when he was heard laughing at the funeral procession of two settlers killed by Aborigines. These men were not suspected of any atrocities themselves, but a pair of shepherds had recently been killed for raping Aboriginal women and serious conflict was beginning to escalate. Other Aborigines joined the colonists in a revenge massacre against the perpetrators, who were old tribal enemies. Amidst this chaos came tall stories that Buckley was about to go bush and marshal further attacks on Europeans. Inevitably, whispers followed that he could do worse than leave the infant colony.

Buckley resigned as Interpreter to Aborigines on 9 October 1837 after a year's service, announcing his intention 'immediately to proceed to Europe'. Soon afterwards he requested a grant of land from Governor Bourke in return for his services in 'inducing an amicable understanding' between the Aborigines and Europeans, though also pleading that by joining European society he had 'so far displeased' the Aborigines he could no longer mingle 'with safety, comfort or satisfaction' amongst them. Bourke ignored his request but recommended a pension of 100 pounds per annum. The British Government refused, deciding the interpreter job had been reward enough considering the ex-convict's 'former history'.

Disappointed, Buckley sailed for Hobart on 28 December. Marrying a widow named Julia Eagers in 1840, he worked as gatekeeper at the Female Factory from 1841 until 1850, when he retired on a modest pension. Bonwick gives us an evocative picture of Buckley in his final years, still a stranger in a strange land, a

> ... gigantic figure slowly pacing along the middle of the road, with his eyes vacantly fixed upon some object before him, never turning his head to either side or saluting a passer by.

The man who so successfully spurned urban living was destined to die in that most horribly urban of deaths, a traffic accident. On 30 January 1856, three years after the Morgan book appeared, Buckley died after falling under a cart at Arthur Circus, in Hobart's Battery Point. He was seventy-six years old.

The saying 'Buckley's chance' (or 'hope') — that is, an exceedingly slim one — is popularly thought to refer to the Wild White Man's survival against all odds. Another derivation points to word play on the old Melbourne department store Buckley & Nunn: an unlikely proposition has two chances, Buckley's and none. But this hardly negates the old convict's influence, being exactly the sort of pun his miraculous reappearance would suggest in the first place.[7]

Whatever the truth, the popular explanation is both more satisfying and forever fixed by folklore. Buckley's chance was precisely what all convict bolters took when they ghosted themselves into the unknown. If they are to have any monument, it may as well be that uniquely Australian phrase.

CHAPTER EIGHTEEN

This fancied paradise

No one fancies that the waters of the unknown river bubble up
from hell's fountains, no strange and weird power is supposed to
guide the ice-berg, nor do we fable that a stray pick-pocket from
Botany Bay has found the gardens of the Hesperides within the
circuit of the Blue Mountains. What have we left to dream about?

MARY SHELLEY, 'LONDON MAGAZINE', MARCH 1824

THE CONVICT BUSH UTOPIA NEVER SUFFERED OUTRIGHT DEFEAT.
Without a fixed location, there was no conclusive demonstration of its
absence. Gradually, as geographical awareness rose, escape mythology
fell. By the 1830s it had faded away, a mystery even in its own passing.

The 1820s saw many changes, such as a free press and trial by jury,
heralding the end of the colony's days as a wilderness–walled gaol. A
steady expansion of governmental concerns beyond penal administration
diminished focus on the convict mindset, and equally the days of myth–
induced mass escape were over. Even so, enthusiasm for overland escape
routes still had some grip on the frontier, as the explorer Charles Sturt

discovered during his first major expedition. Setting out to trace the Macquarie River late in 1828, he soon learned he had been preceded by a pair of Irish runaways from the Wellington Valley penal farm. Sturt understood these men 'thought they could make their way to Timor' by following the river. Some 170 miles from Sydney, Wellington Valley then hosted the most remote settlement north-west beyond Bathurst, an outpost for colonial re-offenders.

Taking off with a fortnight's provisions and a couple of dogs, the two convicts reached about eighty miles upstream before running into serious trouble. Near a waterfall in the Mount Harris vicinity, they met some Aborigines and stayed with them several days. Relations were friendly until the two Irishmen decided to leave, only to find their hosts wanted to keep the dogs. As Sturt describes it, an argument broke out and the Aborigines, furnishing the convicts with weapons, 'told them to defend themselves'. One convict was quickly killed and the other, seeing all hope lost, cut the dogs' throats rather than let the Aborigines have them. He was also put to death. Sturt, who learned the story from some of the Aborigines involved, claimed both convicts were afterwards eaten. 'I questioned several on the subject,' he wrote, 'but they preserved the most sullen silence, neither acknowledging nor denying the fact.'

This fatal escalation of a cultural misunderstanding highlights the volatility of sudden intrusions into Aboriginal communities by people alien in almost every respect. It also shows how the piecemeal revelations of European exploration, instead of destroying escape mythology in a series of fell swoops, actually offered short-lived encouragement in the form of presumed routes to the still undemolished (if crumbling) dream-sanctuaries.

In contrast, an escape from the Moreton Bay (Brisbane) penal station in the late 1820s shows how the geographical blank slate that enabled the escape myth was filling. The attempt by George Mitchell and John Graham to reach China overland, although foolhardy, indicates rudimentary knowledge about remote northern Australia. Both men had made separate escapes from Moreton Bay in 1826. When they met in the bush a couple of years later, Graham was living comfortably with Aborigines near Noosa. Mitchell convinced him of a getaway plan inspired by the annual visits of Macassan trepang fishermen to the northern coastline of the continent. He proposed walking to the Gulf of Carpentaria and joining the Macassan fleet when it left to sell its trepang haul in China. Graham agreed, and the pair trudged 350 miles to Shoalwater Bay near present-day Rockhampton — well short of their target — before giving up and retracing their steps.

The 1830s, when ever-rising demand for convict labour brought transportation to its peak, is also the decade when evidence for myth-inspired escapes evaporates. Between 1831 and 1835 almost 27,000 convicts were shipped to New South Wales, more than twice the total landed in the colony's first quarter century. At the same time, free emigration received its first significant boost, with newly subsidised land sales causing a surge of settlement. In 1828, the colony's first census shows a population of 36,598 — almost two-thirds of whom were, or had been, convicts. Less than 5000 were voluntary immigrants. But by 1841 the colony was home to 43,621 free settlers, approaching the overall number of transportees (44,710) and easily outnumbering the 26,453 convicts then under sentence. Immigration diluted the transported presence to thirty-nine per cent of the population.

The impact of this sudden growth upon Australia's isolation seems to have finally made escape myths untenable. Ignorance about the south land amongst the general populace was naturally still widespread; in 1838 the English convict Joseph Mason noted how 'some persons affirm that it is larger than Europe while others say it not so large viz nearly one fourth'. But as real options emerged for runaways, the fabled white colony lost its meaning, overtaken by reality. Within a year of its settlement in 1836, the actual overland colony of South Australia resolved to form a permanent police force due to 'the number of bad characters arriving daily from Encounter Bay and suspected of being runaway convicts'.

Runaways had long preceded legitimate colonists in the region; in 1827 Peter Cunningham described the offshore convict fiefdom of Kangaroo Island, already established at least fourteen years. This outlaw settlement of some forty men, women and children lived by sealing, ruled over by a man known only as Abyssinia.

Rumours evocative of the white colony were still apt to emerge. Joseph Mason, for example, heard in 1835 that 'a burial place had been discovered on the western side of the Blue Mountain where the bodies were lain in rows in caverns and divided by stones'. To Mason this conjured a past rather than a present mystery settlement; he wondered whether 'the country had once been inhabited by a more intelligent race of people that [sic] the blacks are at present'. Intrigued, he tried to track down other accounts, but without success. He decided the evidence was either false or relating to another country. Prejudice blinded him to the possibility of an indigenous antecedent, such as the Aboriginal burial mounds seen by Sturt on his western travels in the late 1820s.[1]

Mason also described 'two spots of ground' supposed to have 'once undergone the opperation of ploughing'. One, 'about thirty miles south of any residence' was known as The Ploughed Grounds; the other was by the Hunter River. Ruling them 'too uniform' to be the natural features they were, Mason wondered if 16th-century Portuguese explorers had raised crops to provision their voyage home. Earlier, unrecorded sightings of these apparantly tilled fields could easily have sown white colony stories.[2]

The idea of a secret overland white society lingered for many years, long outliving its potency for inducing escape. A latter-day instance occurred in 1858, when AC Gregory set out to search for traces of the explorer Ludwig Leichhardt, who had vanished ten years previously while attempting to cross the continent. Renewed interest in his fate had been stirred up by the claim of Garbut, a Sydney convict, that Leichhardt and his men were captives of a hidden colony of convict runaways, who feared detection if they let the expedition go.[3]

One aspect of colonial development that superseded escape mythology was the sense of possession that convicts began to feel for the country thrust upon them. This rising proprietorship was given voice in the late 1820s by a bushranger who was heard to say of free emigrants: 'Bad luck to 'em! What business have they here in the prisoners' country?' The attitude became typical of the colonial working class, which was still mostly ex-convict, particularly in back-country regions. 'Free objects' were figures of fun; the 1820s emigrant Alexander Harris recalled being laughed at for having 'lagged myself for fear the king should do it for me'.

The sudden influx of voluntary immigrants prompted much rivalry and resentment. Having endured the horrors of penal servitude, ex-convict settlers felt they had earned a greater right to the country than relatively privileged 'new chums'. The sentiment was also assisted by the fact that transportation was no longer as dreaded as it was in earlier days. Reforms from about 1814, due largely to the surgeon William Redfern (himself a transported convict) vastly improved conditions on the voyage out, often the worst part of the sentence. Meanwhile, conditions in Ireland had deteriorated to the point where some Irish transportees told ship's surgeon Peter Cunningham 'they had never been half so well off in their lives before'. Of all convicts, it was the Irish that Cunningham found most 'happy and contented with their situation', although 'more loth to leave their country' than the English. Despite such sentimentality, and hardships still frequently encountered, many soon realised their standard of living would rise considerably in New South Wales.

The traditional Australian self-image of an egalitarian, self-reliant bushman is often traced to the anti-authoritarian attitudes of the ex-convict rural working class. Twentieth-century historians, most notably Russel Ward, have described how this self-image was significantly influenced by anti-British Irish sentiment. Irish ex-convicts and emigrants alike, Ward claimed, tended to defy the steadfastly British self-identification of their colonial betters by declaring a sense of belonging to Australia. Escape mythology complements this theory nicely, supplying perhaps the very earliest example of the general convict population adopting a mindset from its Irish minority.

The 1820s, when this identification with the outback became entrenched, also saw the rise of a related trend — the tendency of convicts to glorify the concept of bushranging and make anti-heroes of bandit leaders. Like the old escape myths, bushranging folk heroes invoked an idealised bush life as an alternative to convict drudgery. They performed a similar function in dealing with the most pressing issue for any prisoner — escape. Both dreams were open to the daring; both offered a vicarious fantasy for less adventurous malcontents. But when it came to sanctuary, however, the best bushranging could offer was the uncertain refuge of a bandit brotherhood. This was characterised, as the folklore developed, by the temporary freedom of 'a short life and a merry one' and the chance to 'die game'. Its ballads and tales were a glamorised record of brave individuals striking back at penal overlords, usually at the eventual cost of their lives. This shows a rising fatalism, the convict dreaming shifting from flight to fight. Along with an awakening confidence in their new country came a certain grim realism, an acceptance of its limitations and hardships. This meant a withering of escape mythology's wild, ultimately untenable sense of possibility. Fantasies of rebellion changed from penetrating the bush to seizing it as a platform for going out in a blaze of glory. As expectations for a life on the run narrowed, bushranging balladry seems to have usurped escape mythology's psychological function as a sublimation of rebellion.

In all probability, the folklore of overland sanctuary delayed the celebration of bushranging's comparatively lesser freedoms. For three decades, it seems, the appeal of preying on settlers from bush hideouts was outshone by the prospect of finding refuge across the mountains. Evidence of the shift doesn't emerge until the mid-1820s, when Peter Cunningham noticed that convicts were making up sympathetic songs about bushrangers. He also recalled Riley, the 'captain of the Hunter's

River banditti', bragging that his exploits would 'be long spoken of'. But Riley was forgotten; the first extant ballads date from about 1830 and reserve their pedestal for another Irish recalcitrant, Bold Jack Donahoe. In fact, Donahoe marks the transition period personally. After involvement in one of the last known bids to reach an interior white colony, he became the folkloric emblem of the new way of freedom. Recast as an avenging angel, he struck out at hated authority from his outback retreat until dying in defence of refusal, as his ballad states, to 'work one hour for government'. The bush became his home rather than a gateway to a better place.

Tasmania provides a striking contrast. Lasting antiheroes were produced much sooner than they were on the mainland — within a decade of the island's settlement. Bushrangers were a serious problem from the very beginning there, because dire food shortages prompted Lieutenant Governor Collins to arm groups of convicts and send them on kangaroo shooting expeditions. Many never returned, preferring to establish outlaw fraternities and live by terrorising settlers and Aborigines.

Things got so bad that in May 1814 a general amnesty was offered (in vain) to all bushrangers who came in by 1 December. One of these rogues, Michael Howe, became Australia's first truly celebrated bandit, the subject of a bestselling book upon his death in 1818 and, by the 1840s, hailed as the 'historical great man' of a community dominated by transportees. Howe's stardom in Tasmania long predated Donahoe's mainland glory, but unlike Bold Jack he didn't have the appeal of an escape mythology to contend with. Although the geographical limitations of this relatively small offshore settlement may have prevented the rise of a sanctuary myth, the early existence of a floating community of self-supporting renegades — virtually an actual back-country 'white colony' — probably obviated the emotional need for a false one.

Tasmanian bushrangers were also the first known to present themselves as a colonial counterculture, asserting their freedom in terms which hijacked the language of authority. Howe styled himself

'Lieutenant Governor of the Woods' in a defiant letter to Lieutenant Governor Davey, whom he contemptuously retitled 'Lieutenant Governor of the Town'. Later he apparently promoted himself to 'Governor of the Ranges' when proposing a truce with Davey's successor. Matthew Brady, a runaway from Macquarie Harbour who also became a celebrated antihero, continued this satire when he saw a posted reward for his capture headed 'Government House, April 14th, 1825'. His response was a matching notice from 'Mountain Home, April 20th, 1825', offering twenty gallons of rum to anyone who would arrest Governor Arthur and 'deliver his person unto me'. Written as if between equals, these notes were effectively declarations of independence from self-made kings of the mountains, mocking reminders that the Crown's sphere of influence was not nearly as extensive as it pretended.

Similarly, the shortfall between declared and actual jurisdiction gave escape mythology licence to cause trouble on the mainland. Knowing little more than the convicts about the true nature of the interior, authority's strenuous denouncements of the 'fancied paradise' were tainted by their vested interest in quashing such stories. Assurances that Aboriginal accounts were worthless rang hollow in the face of the interior's apparent blank slate and the overwhelming need to place hope somewhere. The frontier was an imposition and a dislocation for convicts and Aborigines alike. Dialogue between these two lowliest colonial strata on the nature of their common environment was inevitable. The phantom colonies show us one way they came to terms with it.

In this shared dreaming is the first stirring of that pervasive Australian cultural response to the bush which casts it as the 'other', an outside force unsympathetic to European presence and even capable, in fictional treatments, of supernatural retaliation. At first the convict myth seems to be the very opposite, being characterised by hope in the landscape — but the important point is that this hope was misplaced. The deadly lure it dangled gives us the earliest example of a quintessentially Australian theme — people vanishing or coming to grief in the bush. The outback has never since quite shaken its hint of the uncanny. Even today, a single lost bushwalker can attract voluminous media coverage. In Australia, the news value placed on a person swallowed by nature is greater than that of almost any other category of missing person; it equals and sometimes surpasses that of victims of violent crime. This obsession especially relishes the sentimental appeal of lost 'innocents'. First delineated by Australia's literal 'babes in the woods', the three young Duff children nine days missing in Victoria's Wimmera country in 1864, it's now seen in the lasting impression made by the disappearance of Azaria Chamberlain in 1980 near Uluru. Essentially, it is the same grim fascination evoked by those dozens of convict skeletons found scattered in Sydney's bush back in the 1790s. The supreme fictional example is Joan Lindsay's 1968 novel *Picnic at Hanging Rock* (even better known as Peter Weir's haunting film), in which the bush spirits its victims away in circumstances of utter mystery. This familiar cultural motif unearths all the hidden dislocations, identity crises and guilt wrought by colonialism. But its first expression was in the grim theatre of convict escape mythology, when seekers went to find their mirror selves, that enigmatic Aboriginal promise, and found nothing except their own estrangement. This failure echoes in a particular legacy of Australia as imperialist construct — the 'dead heart' unease that non-Indigenous Australian culture is empty inside, neither genuine nor legitimate. And yet more profound anxieties than this are prompted by confrontation with the power of a vast, mysterious, all-consuming landscape. Ultimately it evokes unanswerable questions about our relations with nature and creation, with our place on the Earth. *Do we really belong here?* The theme may be universal; the bush metaphor is peculiarly Australian.

Both the inland sea and the convict myth invested a promise in the interior that was never fulfilled. Both were essentially dreams of oasis, of new beginnings — for the authorities, a new Mediterranean to succour an inland society, and for the convicts an existing inland society with bounty to share. But inland Australia has never been able to sustain a major city. This disappointment anticipated another aspect of the 'dead heart' idea — a land literally barren and unproductive at its centre, a country where Western-style agricultural exploitation demands environmental modification such as irrigation. More recently, as this disenchantment is increasingly dismissed as unreasonably Eurocentric — and the destructive aspects of irrigation and hydroelectric schemes increasingly acknowledged — the outback has emerged as a new kind of spiritual oasis. Nowadays, as we go there in search of inner wellbeing and relaxation, our traditional cultural unease with the bush and central deserts is giving way to respect for their power.

An example of this phenomenon especially close to the themes of this book comes from Barrallier's biographer Andy Macqueen, who has crowned the King of the Mountains 'that spirit, that presence, that sense of whole, that power of creation, which inhabits . . . the southern Blue Mountains.' In Governor King's whimsical image, resurrected as the invisible lord of 'a world of space and contrast', Macqueen has found a potent metaphor for his own wilderness experience:

> The King is elusive. He is there all around, but in hiding . . . I have
> heard the lyre-birds call, and the dingoes howl; the crackling of the
> fire and the drips fallen from the leaves; the roar of waterfalls unseen,
> and the silent sound of the abyss. I have yet to meet the King: but he
> knows I am there and he looks after me because I respect him. He
> refreshes me and gives me life. It is a fulfilling search.

The tourist industry, the environmental movement and the rising profile of Aboriginal culture have all influenced this recasting of wilderness as the place for redemptive immersion in nature's purity. As a symbol, convict escape mythology underscores the reinvention in both directions: the failed vision of European oasis seems to prefigure contemporary Australia's waning Eurocentrism, but the outback's new mainstream mystical resonance is not inconsistent with the convicts' hopeful stumblings toward an imagined personal salvation.

This calls attention to the cultish aspect of escape beliefs. The believers' cynical defiance of official refutations recalls any number of present-day conspiracy theorists. Moreover, expeditions were often led by charismatic individuals offering deliverance to followers prepared to accept their word. The bush was their Red Sea, parted by the mythologising which sustained an illusory route home. For Irish runaways, the apparent failure of Catholic worship, banned in New South Wales for all but ten months of the first three decades of settlement, gave them even less to lose. Seen in this light, escape myths offered believers a quasi-spiritual consolation that, despite losing everything else, they had gained forbidden knowledge of a path to freedom. The truth was out there.

Transportation in the 1790s was, especially for the Irish, an assault on identity. Removed almost as far across the world as physically possible, to slave for a starving shanty town, their paranoia was stoked by abuse on the voyage out, by the suppression of their religion, by the suspicion engendered simply by speaking Gaelic. The power of rumour and superstition amongst the convict class was frequently alluded to, by Collins and others, but without acknowledgment of the wretchedness that forced the natural wish for escape to fever-pitch. As a crutch for Irish hope in what seemed an utterly hopeless situation, escape mythology held out the most appealing of psychological straws, the possibility of returning home via nearby countries free of the British law that condemned them.

Contemporary accounts recoil from the phenomenon as an exasperating offshoot of stereotypical Irish wildness and eccentricity, a natural outgrowth of ignorance and irrationality. Deplored for the concomitant loss of provisions and labour, its true nature remained unexamined. Adherents were scorned as fools and feared as loose cannons, but their behaviour signposted only natural criminality and Celtic superstition. Governor Phillip, confident it was a passing fad, thought the hard luck stories of survivors would provide a speedy and permanent remedy. Hunter felt some pity but defined the myth in the context of 'their natural vicious propensities', the same Irish intransigence threatening the colony in other, more conventional ways. King expected no better from Catholic croppies infatuated with 'death or liberty', and despite the rise of English seekers remained convinced it was an Irish evil. Meanwhile, in the lower orders, the exciting prospect of being within reach of another society provided a platform for intellectual debate, to which unschooled imaginations brought all the resources they could muster. The result was China, Timor, navigation by the sun's position on the shoulder or by wind directions, paper compasses and so forth. Amidst the wishful thinking and flawed premises there was a methodology of sorts at work.

A defining eccentricity of this class of runaway is their fixation on the inland in an era which mostly looked to the sea. All early settlement was underpinned by the necessary maintenance of shipping lanes, and whaling was the leading export industry until the 1830s. For the first quarter century, inland exploration was largely an intellectual curiosity — and what the authorities hoped most to find there was, in fact, a sea. But the need to combat escape mythology supplied a rare concrete short-term objective, thus spurring the most far-reaching of the early expeditions. Although the achievements of Wilson and Barrallier were not immediately followed up, they added to the capital of knowledge which eventually opened the inland to European exploitation. The first interior settlements were also interior in the sense of being deduced by the convict imagination, shadow-refuges rooted as deeply in the psyche as they were positioned in the isolated bush regions that shaped such possibilities.

Transportation to New South Wales all but ceased in 1840, although more convicts landed in 1849 and others continued to be shipped to various Australian colonies until 1868. They also continued to escape, as captives inevitably do, but the phantom sanctuaries of the inland were no longer among their priorities. Much of the rugged bushland that starved and froze convict runaways has long been eaten up by the urban sprawl of contemporary Sydney, although vast pockets remain in an outlying ring of magnificent national parks. There is nothing spectral about the towns now dotting the Blue Mountains along Blaxland's trail, administered as a single city contiguous with Sydney's western outskirts. Near the metropolitan area's geographical centre, the long-vanished penal farms of Castle Hill and 'cursed' Toongabbie are commemorated in the names of the suburbs built over them. We now fly to the real China from Sydney in less time than our convict predecessors took to struggle 150 miles north to the China of their dreams.

Theirs is a hidden history, half-told through government dispatches and the patchy court and newspaper records of the 'successful failures' — those who made it back alive, perhaps disproportionately in the belief's declining years. It's difficult to say how representative these case histories are of the whole, or how reliable individual convict testimonies are in themselves. We can speculate, make educated guesses, pinpoint patterns and corroborations; ultimately, however, all myths retain some mystery at their core.

It is easy to dismiss convict escape mythology as delusion born of desperation, enabled by illiteracy and ignorance. Nevertheless, from the often terse accounts scattered across a handful of 200-year-old documents, one poignant historical truth still echoes across the centuries; the truth of the almost inconceivable hardships that fuelled that desperation. This is perhaps best summed up in Tench's description of the beliefs of the first Chinese travellers. Has anyone else ever expected so little of a Promised Land than it simply be a place where people 'treat others kindly'?

A note to the reader

I have used footnotes to expand on side issues, offer extra detail about convicts whose adventures this book relates, and also to acknowledge where my analysis differs from other writers.

After more than a century in which escape mythology received little more than brief acknowledgment of the adherents' delusion and desperation, there has been some recent attention to the possibility that convicts never really believed such stories at all.

This notion of the myth as myth began with Paul Carter, who views convict escape myths through the prism of his idiosyncratic 'spatial history' in *The Road to Botany Bay* (1987). While accepting some convicts were 'persuaded to believe' their own rhetorical ploy, he suggests the myth was mostly likely a deception which 'concealed, rather than revealed a plot to travel' using 'imperial figures of speech especially concocted for the interrogators' consumption'. As convicts were neither irrational nor irredeemably stupid, the argument goes, they must have had an ulterior plan, an agenda missed by colonial officials because the absurd cover story flattered their ideas of criminal and/or Irish irrationality. But at the heart of this theory is the same dubious certainty dear to old-time governors: that a bush-China or inland white society is a fundamentally irrational concept.

Aside from confusing ignorance with stupidity, surely wishful thinking is at play here — the natural yearning for underdog to outwit oppressor, to place those smug Enlightenment overlords in the dark, blinded by their sense of superiority.

Carter's refutation of escape myths has since been developed further by historian Grace Karskens, although she too concedes it 'likely that some in the community believed such stories'. Nevertheless, she finds those claiming to seek overland places no different to the majority of runaways, aiming either to reach the coast and escape by boat or to live as bushrangers.

Bush-Chinas and white colonies are also sometimes explained as excuses concocted by captured runaways to avoid punishment, bids to win pity by playing the fool. But trial records do not bear this out. Governor Phillip, astounded at the very first walk to China, treated the famished survivors with leniency, but myth-seekers were usually only spared the lash if their bush ordeals left them too weak to withstand it.

Far from deflecting the authorities' attention, peculiar tales of nearby sanctuaries increased focus on convict activity. If this was a cool-headed strategy to mask other escape plans, then it was such a poor one it is difficult to understand why convicts would have employed it across four decades. That, to me, would indicate more idiocy than falling for the spell of better places, which beckoned and gave purpose to a flight into the unknown.

Bibliography

Abbreviations

(used here, and in Sources and Endnotes)

BNL, British Newspaper Library (London); **BT** (Bonwick Transcripts); **CSI**, Colonial Secretary's Index; **HRA**, *Historical Records of Australia* (1.1 is Series 1 Volume 1, etc); **HRNSW**, *Historical Records of New South Wales*; **HRV**, *Historical Records of Victoria*; **JRAHS**, *Journal, Royal Australian Historical Society*; **PRO**, Public Record Office, UK; **SG**, *Sydney Gazette*; **SLNSW**, State Library of NSW (Sydney); **SM**, *Sydney Monitor*; **SR**, State Records of NSW (Sydney).

Original records

(institutions where found in **bold**)

State Library of NSW: *Sydney Gazette*; *Sydney Monitor*; *Australian*; *Sydney Herald*; *Hobart Town Courier*; Convict transportation registers and hulk returns, microfilm reels; Mutch Index of Births, Deaths and Marriages 1787–1814; Bonwick papers microfilm; Musters (i) 1800–2 (ii) 1805–6 (iii) 1811 (iv) 1814 (v) 1822 (vi) 1823–5; Census of NSW 1828; 1837 General Return of Convicts 1837; Convict Pardons 1.1.1810–31.12.1819; *NSW Archives Kit — Convict Arrivals 1788–1842* (microfiche copies of convict indents) and *Index to NSW Convict Indents*.

State Records NSW: Colonial Secretary Index; Bench of Magistrates & Court of Criminal Jurisdiction minutes; index of convict pardons.

Select Bibliography

(years in parentheses refer to original publication dates)

Atkins, Richard *Journal 1792–4* (manuscript at National Library of Australia, Canberra)

Atkinson, Alan *The Europeans in Australia Volume 1*, Oxford University Press, Melbourne, 1997

Barker, Theo *A History of Bathurst: Volume 1 Early Settlement to 1862*, Crawford House, Bathurst, 1992

Barrington, George *A Voyage to Botany Bay* (1793), John Swain, New York, 1801

Bateson, Charles *The Convict Ships 1787–1868*, Brown Son & Ferguson, Glasgow, 1969

Bonwick, James Buckley *The Wild White Man; and the Blacks of Victoria* (1856), Ferguson & Moore, Melbourne, 1863 (2nd edition)

Bowes Smyth, Arthur *The Journal of Arthur Bowes Smyth*, Library of Australian History, Sydney, 1979

Boxall, George *The Story of the Australian Bushrangers* (1899), Penguin, Ringwood, 1974

Brownscombe, Ross *On Suspect Terrain: Journals of Exploration in the Blue Mountains 1795–1820*, Forever Wild, Brighton East, 2004

Caley, George *Reflections on the Colony of NSW*, Lansdowne, Melbourne, 1966

Cambage RH (i) *Barrallier's Blue Mountain Exploration in 1802*, *JRAHS*, vol 3, pp. 10–25, Sydney, 1910

Cambage RH (ii) *Exploration Beyond the Upper Nepean in 1798*, *JRAHS*, vol 6, pp. 1–36, Sydney, 1919

Carter, Paul *The Road to Botany Bay*, Faber & Faber, London, 1987

Chisholm, AH *The Romance of the Lyrebird*, *JRAHS*, vol 43, pp. 175–204, Sydney, 1957

Clark, Ralph *The Journals and Letters of Lt. Ralph Clark 1787–1792*, Library of Australian History, Sydney, 1981

Cobley, John (i–v) *Sydney Cove (Volumes 1–5, 1788–1800)*, Angus & Robertson, North Ryde, 1962–1986

Collins (i and ii), David *An Account of the English Colony in New South Wales* (two volumes, 1798 & 1802), AH & AW Reed, Sydney, 1975

Cotter, Richard (ed.) *John Pascoe Fawkner's Sullivan Bay Reminiscences*, Lavender Hill, Red Hill South, 2002

Cumpston, JHL *The Inland Sea and the Great River*, Angus & Robertson, Sydney, 1964

Cunningham (i), Peter *Two Years in New South Wales* (1827), Angus & Robertson, Sydney, 1966

Cunningham (ii), Chris *The Blue Mountains Rediscovered*, Kangaroo Press, Kenthurst, 1996

Deeks, Richard *Transportees From Suffolk to Australia 1787–1867*, Seven Sparrows, Fressingfield (UK), 2000

Donohoe (i), James Hugh *Norfolk Island 1788–1813: The People and Their Families*, Archives Authority of NSW, Sydney, 1986

Donohoe (ii) James Hugh *The Catholics of NSW 1788–1840 and Their Families*, Archives Authority of NSW, Sydney, 1988

Easty, John *Memorandum of the Transactions of a Voyage from England to Botany Bay 1787–93*, Angus & Robertson, Sydney, 1965

Egan, Jack *Sydney 1788–1792: Eyewitness Accounts of the Making of a Nation*, Allen & Unwin, St Leonards, 1999

Evans–Wentz, WY *The Fairy–Faith in Celtic Countries* (1911), Humanities Press, New Jersey, 1978

Favenc, Ernest *The History of Australian Exploration from 1788 to 1888*, Turner & Henderson, Sydney, 1888

Flinders, Matthew *A Voyage to Terra Australis* (1814), Libraries Board of SA, Adelaide, 1966

Flynn, Michael *The Second Fleet: Britain's Grim Convict Armada of 1790*, Library of Australian History, Sydney, 1993

Glidden, Molly *The Founders of Australia: A Biographical Dictionary of the First Fleet*, Library of Australian History, Sydney, 1989

Grant, James *The Narrative of a Voyage of Discovery*, Roworth, London, 1803

Hall, Barbara (i) *A Desperate Set of Villains: The Convicts of the* Marquis Cornwallis, Coogee, 2000

Hall, Barbara (ii) *A Nimble Fingered Tribe: The Convicts of the* Sugar Cane, Coogee, 2002

Hall, Barbara (iii) *Of Infamous Character: The Convicts of the* Boddingtons, Coogee, 2004

Hamilton–Arnold, Barbara (ed.) *Letters & Papers of GP Harris 1803–1812*, Arden, Sorrento, 1994

Holt, Joseph *A Rum Story: The Adventures of Joseph Holt 1800–1812*, Kangaroo Press, Kenthurst, 1988

Hughes, Robert *The Fatal Shore*, Collins Harvill, London, 1987

Hunter, John *An Historical Journal of Events at Sydney and at Sea* (1793, also titled *Transactions at Port Jackson and Norfolk Island*), Angus & Robertson, Sydney, 1968

Jacobs, Joseph *Celtic Fairy Tales* (1892), Random House, London, 1996 (includes *More Celtic Fairy Tales,* 1894)

Jervis, James (i) *Beginnings of the Settlement in the Parish of Castle Hill, JRAHS*, vol 15, pp. 226–66, Sydney, 1929

Jervis, James (ii) *Discovery and Settlement of Burragorang Valley, JRAHS*, vol 20, p. 164, Sydney, 1934

Johnson, Donald *Phantom Islands of the Atlantic*, Walker & Co, New York, 1996

Karskens, Grace *This Spirit of Emigration: The Nature and Meanings of Escape in Early New South Wales*, in *Journal of Australian Colonial History*, vol 7, Armidale, 2005

Kiernan, TJ *Transportation from Ireland to Sydney 1791–1816*, Canberra, 1954

Knopwood, Robert, *Port Phillip Diary 9 October 1803 –31 January 1804*, Banks Society, Malvern, 2002

Kohen, Jim *The Darug and Their Neighbours*, Blacktown & District Historical Society, Blacktown, 1993

Lang, JD *Botany Bay, or True Tales of Early Australia* (1849), Mulini, Canberra, 1994

Leigh WH *Travels and Adventures in South Australia 1836–1838* (1839, as *Reconnoitering Voyages and Travels*), Currawong, Milsons Point, 1982

Macquarie, Lachlan *Journals of His Tours in NSW and Van Diemen's Land*, Library of Australian History, Sydney, 1979

Macqueen, Andy *Blue Mountains to Bridgetown: The Life and Journeys of Barrallier*, Springwood, 1993

Mann, David Dickenson *The Present Picture of New South Wales*, John Booth, London, 1811

Martin, James *Memorandoms: Escape from Botany Bay 1791*, Mulini, Canberra, 1991

Mason, Joseph *Joseph Mason: Assigned Convict 1831–1837*, Melbourne University Press, Carlton South, 1996

McCrum, Robert, Cran,William & MacNeil, Robert *The Story of English*, Faber & Faber, London, 1992

McDonald, WG (ed.) *Earliest Illawarra By Its Explorers and Pioneers*, Illawarra Historical Society, Port Kembla, 1966

McIntyre Graham & Whitaker *Voyage of the Ship* Friendship *from Cork to Botany Bay 1799–1800*, PR Ireland, Sydney, 2000

McIntyre, Perry & Cathro, Adele *Thomas Dunn: Convict and Chief Constable*, PR Ireland, Sydney, 2000

Meredith, John *The Wild Colonial Boy: Bushranger Jack Donahoe 1806–1830*, Red Rooster, Ascot Vale, 1982

Mitchell, Thomas *Three Expeditions into the Interior of Eastern Australia Volume 1* (1839), Eagle Press, Maryborough, 1996

Morgan, John *The Life and Adventures of William Buckley* (1852), ANU Press, Canberra, 1979; Ares, Hobart, 1996; Text, Melbourne, 2002

Noah, William *Voyage to Sydney in the Ship* Hillsborough *1798–1799 and a Description of the Colony*, Library of Australian History, Sydney, 1978

Nicol, John *The Life and Adventures of John Nicol, Mariner* (1822), Text, Melbourne, 1997

O'Farrell, Patrick *The Irish in Australia*, UNSW, Kensington, 1986

Oxley, John *Journals of Two Expeditions into the Interior of New South Wales* (1820), Libraries Board of SA, Adelaide, 1964

Peron, MF *A Voyage of Discovery to the Southern Hemisphere* (1809), Marsh Walsh, North Melbourne, 1975

Reece, Bob (i) *The Origins of Irish Convict Transportation to New South Wales*, Palgrave, New York, 2001

Reece, Bob (ed.) (ii) *Irish Convict Lives*, Crossing Press, Sydney, 1993

Rees, Alwyn & Rees, Brinley *Celtic Heritage: Ancient Tradition in Ireland and Wales*, Thames & Hudson, London, 1973

Reynolds, Henry *The Other Side of the Frontier*, James Cook University, Townsville, 1981

Richards, Joanna Armour *Blaxland Lawson Wentworth 1813*, Blubber Head, Hobart, 1979

Roberts, Stephen (i) *History of Australian Land Settlement 1788–1820*, Macmillan, Melbourne, 1924

Roberts, Stephen (ii) *The Squatting Age in Australia 1835–1847*, Melbourne University Press, Carlton, 1964

Robson, Lloyd *A History of Tasmania Volume 1*, Oxford University Press, Melbourne, 1983

Roe, Michael et al. *The First Australian Governors*, Oxford University Press, Melbourne, 1971

Rolleston, TW *Celtic Myths and Legends*, Senate, London, 1994

Ross, Valerie *The Everingham Letterbook*, Anvil Press, Wamberal,1985

Rusden, GW *Curiosities of Colonization*, W Clowes & Sons, London, 1874

Scott (i), James *Remarks on a Passage to Botany Bay 1787–92*, Angus & Robertson, Sydney, 1963

Scott (ii), Ernest *Australian Discovery*, London, Dent, 1929

Stockton, Eugene (ed.) *Blue Mountains Dreaming*, Three Sisters, Winmalee, 1993

Sturt, Charles *Two Expeditions into the Interior of Southern Australia* (1833), Corkwood, North Adelaide, 1999

Tench, Watkin *1788*, Text, Melbourne, 1996 (*A Narrative of the Expedition to Botany Bay*, (1789) & *A Complete Account of the Settlement at Port Jackson*, (1793))

Thomas, Martin *The Artificial Horizon: Imagining the Blue Mountains*, Melbourne University Press, Carlton, 2003

Tipping, Marjorie *Convicts Unbound: the Story of the* Calcutta *Convicts & Their Settlement in Australia*, Viking O'Neil, South Yarra, 1988

Todd, Andrew alias William *The Todd Journal 1835*, Geelong Historical Society, Geelong, 1989

Turbet, Peter *The Aborigines of the Sydney District before 1788*, Kangaroo Press, Sydney, 2001.

Walsh, Michael & Yallop, Colin (eds) *Language and Culture in Aboriginal Australia*, Aboriginal Studies Press, Canberra, 1993

Ward, Russel *The Australian Legend*, Oxford University Press, Melbourne, 1966

Watling, Thomas *Letters from an Exile at Botany Bay to his Aunt in Dumfries*, Review Publications, Dubbo, 1979

Whitaker, Ann Maree *Unfinished Revolution: United Irishmen in NSW 1800–1810*, Crossing Press, Sydney, 1994

White (i), John *Journal of a Voyage to New South Wales* (1790), Angus & Robertson, Sydney, 1962

White (ii), Charles *History of Australian Bushranging Volume 1*, Lloyd O'Neil, Hawthorn, 1970

Whitley, Thomas *Reputed Passage of the Blue Mountains in 1798*, *JRAHS*, vol 1, pp. 186–91, Sydney, 1904

Williams, Stephan, *Bold Jack Donahoe*, Popinjay, Woden, 2000

Sources

(Main references used for each chapter. Material referred to is in **bold**.)

Introduction
Convicts lost 1788–90: HRA 1.1 p. 47, Phillip to Sydney 9.7.1788; pp. 144–5, Phillip to Sydney 12.2.1790. Glidden p. 451 (9 missing 7.2.1788)
Dalrymple: Hughes p. 63

Chapter one: The hopeful fraternity
Edinburgh Bee quote: HRNSW 2 p. 786
Queen in Ireland: HRNSW 2 pp. 752–4, 772 (*Dublin Chronicle, Freeman's Journal*); Reece (i) pp. 242–66 (letter to Hood, reports re colony, Thomas St escape 17.2.1791, 'hopeful fraternity' *Dublin Evening Post* 1.3.1791)
Queen convicts: Kiernan; Reece (i) pp. 296–303; *Queen* indent (SLNSW)
Queen arrival, Third Fleet: HRA 1.1 pp. 274, 283–8, 353; Collins (i) pp. 149–62; Tench pp. 204–8; Bateson pp. 131–7; Hunter p. 366
Queen at sea, trial: HRNSW 2 pp. 453–8; Phillip HRA 1.1 p. 274
Colony 1788–91: Collins (i), especially pp. 5, 56, 57; Clark; Easty; Hunter; Scott (i); Tench (Bereewolgal, p.266); Egan (letters by Clark and Rev. Johnson, pp. 78, 164); HRNSW 1 (ii) pp. 212–3 (Ross to Nepean 16.11.1788)
Caesar: Collins (i) pp. 57–9, 73, 76, 80, 319–20, 371–81
Corbett: HRA 1.1 pp. 50, 57–8; Tench pp. 67–8; Collins (i) pp. 25–6
Saunderson: Easty p. 108
Alligator: Bowes pp. 72–7
'Attacking straglers': HRA 1.1 p. 179 (Phillip to Grenville 17.6.1790)

Chapter two: An evil which will cure itself
Phillip to Nepean: 9.7.1788, HRA 1.1 p. 57
Queen runaways: Tench pp. 208–212; Collins (i) pp. 154–164; HRA 1.1 pp. 308–9 (Phillip to Nepean 18.11.1791); Hunter pp. 372–3; Barrington pp. 109–110; Scott (i) p. 68

Turwood (also Tarwood): Collins (i) pp. 112–6, 356–7; Tench pp. 140–1;
    Scott (i) p. 57; Flynn
Bryant: Collins (i) pp. 126–32; Tench pp. 180–3; Flynn; Martin
Wurgun: Collins (i) p. 357

Chapter three: Thoughts of liberty
'Thoughts of liberty': Easty p. 127
Baudin & pre-Cook theory: Scott (ii), Cumpston (Dampier, p. 29)
Flinders' orders: 22.6.1801, Flinders vol 1 bk 1, p. 8
Nicol in China: Nicol pp. 103–104
'World a friend': Holt p. 44
Dublin Chronicle 5.1789: Reece (i) p. 252
Convict daily life: HRNSW 2 pp. 793–7
Phillip requests leave: Phillip to Sydney 11.11.1791, Cobley (iii)
Colonial events 1791–92: Collins (i) pp. 162–74, (ii) p. 57; Hunter pp. 373–5;
    Tench pp. 179–226

Chapter four: The greatest villains on Earth
Boddingtons and *Sugar Cane*: HRNSW 2 pp. 61–3; Atkins; Collins (i) pp. 254–65
Escapes 1794–5: Collins (i) pp. 292, 304, 309, 325–6, 335
Marquis Cornwallis: HRNSW 2 pp. 819–20 (officer's letter to brother 18.6.1796)
Britannia: HRA 1.3 pp. 36–68
Convicts 'turbulent, dissatisfied': Hunter to Portland 15.2.1798 (HRA 1.2 p. 129),
    Collins (ii) p. 42
Irony: Collins (i) p. 176
All convict ships: Bateson

Chapter five: The phantom white colony
1797–98 outbreak: HRA 1.2 (Hunter to Portland 10.1.1798, p. 115; 15.2.1798,
    pp. 128–131; 1.3.1798, pp. 132–134; Hunter's Orders 13.5.1797, p. 79;
    19.1.1798, pp. 209–210). Collins (ii) pp. 42, 54–59, 74–5. HRNSW 3
    (Hunter to Banks, p. 820)
John Wilson: Glidden pp. 388, 451; Collins (i) pp. 41–2, 355, 382–3; (ii)
    pp. 43, 57; trial SR reel 2391 (5/1147B pp. 239–41, 267–71)
Lost cattle: Tench p. 230, Collins (i) p.365

Extra detail, Ramsay's boat piracy: Patrick Clark committal 18.8.1798, SR reel 655 (SZ766 p. 50) & trial (8.11.1798) SR reel 2651 (X905 p. 51). Hunter's *Names of the Men Gone off with Ramsay's Boat* 10.1.1798, CO 201/14 p. 129 (PRO reel 7, SLNSW), Collins (ii) p.38

Turwood: Collins (i); Flynn

Chapter six: Checking this spirit of emigration

Palmer quote: Cobley (v) p. 166

Wilson and expedition: HRNSW 3 pp. 819–823 (Price's journal *Journey into the Interior of the Country New South Wales* and Hunter to Banks 29.7 & 21.8.1801); HRA 1.2 (Hunter to Portland 15.2.1798, pp. 130–1; Hunter's Orders 19.1.1798, p. 210); Collins (ii) pp. 62–6, 75–6; Cunningham (ii) pp.74–85; Cambage (ii); Whitley; Brownscombe pp. 61–7

Gundungurra myth: Turbet pp. 109–10

Chapter seven: The opinion of the common people

Irish escapes, 'prophetess': Collins (ii) pp. 59, 61–2, 77–9; 'completely ruined' (Hunter) HRA 1.2 p. 118

Ramsay's boat piracy: HRA 1.2 p. 135; Flinders vol 1 intro pp. 113–8; Collins (ii) pp. 57, 68, 74–5; Cobley (v) p. 215

Stolen mares: Collins (ii) pp. 43, 75, 91–2

Arson: Collins (ii) pp. 93–4, HRA 1.2 pp. 358–9

Escape myth 1799: 'Opinion of the common people', Noah p. 69; 'Absurd notion', Mann p. 10; Phillip's 'day's work', Hunter p. 373; Hunter's 'comforts', HRA 1.2 p. 131; Marsden quote, Cobley (v) p. 5; Kiddy language, Tench p. 270

Bushrangers: Collins (i) p. 379; state of settlement, Cobley (v) 454–7; King's bushrangers, HRA 1.5 pp. 592–3; Knight, HRA 1.3 pp. 251–2, 465–7; Colin Hunter, SR reel 656 (SZ768 p. 74); Flinders at Lake Illawarra, McDonald p. 11; Little, reel 656 (SZ768 p. 127); Barr/Smith, reel 655 (SZ766 p. 145)

Inland sea: Dumaresq, Thomas pp. 144–5; King, Banks, Maslen map, Cumpston pp. 60–1, 56, 103; Barnes, SG 2.5.1827; Hunter, Cobley (v) 331

Norfolk piracy: HRA 1.3 pp. 14, 38; HRNSW 4 p. 416; Grant pp. 91–99; SR reels 2651 (X905 pp. 481, 5/1149 pp. 6–16a, 20), 2392 (5/1145 pp. 157; 163)

Aborigines: Cosmology, Reynolds pp. 25–33; language, Tench p. 195; greeting procedure, *The Story of Our Mob* (1997) by Sally Dingo pp. 13–15; gratuitous concurrence, Walsh & Yallop p. 186; attitude to Turwood, Collins (i) p. 357; 'boi', Stockton p. 156; 'boee', Tench p. 104

Early 'bunyips': SG 23, 27.3.1823

Chapter eight: Their natural vicious propensities

Yeats quote: Evans–Wentz p. 357

Irish jokes: Cunningham (i) pp. 199–203; Leigh pp. 190–1

Opinions of Irish: Holt p. 68; Tench p. 209; Marsden, Hughes p. 188

Escapes: Daverne, Collins (i) p. 309, Atkins; Prosser, SG 25.1, 1.2.1807

Irish speakers in 1800: McCrum et al. p. 195

Hibernian Journal **19.6.1789:** Reece (i) p. 251

Irish myth: MacConglinney & O'Mulready stories, Jacobs; otherworlds, Cormac, Bran, Evans–Wentz pp. 332–57; fairy abduction to America, Rees; Hy–Brasil, Johnson

Compasses: Atkinson, p. 249

Aboriginal spirituality: Turbet

Irish rebellion: Pakenham

'Strong arm of government': Collins (ii) pp. 102–3

Convict ships 1800–1802: Bateson pp. 158–86; HRA 1.3 pp. 531, 581–4 (King to Hobart 23.7, 30.10. 1802); Holt pp. 39–47 (*Minerva*); HRA 1.3 p. 379 (*Canada, Minorca*); HRA 1.3 pp. 552–4 ('filthy beyond description'), pp. 718–22 (*Atlas I*); HRA 1.3 pp. 535–59 (*Hercules,* Betts tried); HRNSW 4 p. 889 (*Atlas II*); Whitaker p. 78 (*Atlas II* mortality bets)

Castle Hill: HRNSW 4 (King to Portland 21.8.1801, p. 462; King to Hobart 9.11.1802, p. 892). HRNSW 5 (King to Hobart 30.6.1803, p. 163). Peron (visitor, p. 111)

King's 'vultures': HRNSW 4 p. 894

Chapter nine: King of the mountains

King to Cooke 20.7.1805: HRNSW 5 p. 665

John Day: SR reel 656 (SZ768 p. 127)

Bush 'castles': Ross p. 56, Macquarie 1.11.1820 pp. 162–3

Daley: Hunter pp. 57–9, Collins (i) pp. 31–2, 39; Scott (i) p. 86; Tench p. 93; White (i) pp. 162–3

Barrallier's life: Macqueen

King plans to explore interior: HRNSW 4 pp. 668–9, 716, 784; HRA 1.3 p. 653

Paterson–King dispute: HRA 1.3 pp. 646–84; HRA 1.4 pp. 320, 323; HRNSW 5 p. 136 ('King of Mountains'), p. 458

Results of Barrallier's trip: King to Hobart 31.12.1802, HRA 1.3 p. 748

King's orders re runaways: 19.10.1802, HRA 1.4 p. 323; 28.10.1802, HRA 1.3 p. 691

1802 myth & escapes: Peron p. 290; October 1802 trials and Castle Hill work inquiry, SR reel 656 (SZ768 pp. 177–9, 185–8, 193–9); Marsden to King re firemaking, Rusden p. 70; Neale etc. in hulks, PRO Reel 3560 p. 249

Chapter ten: Almost superhuman efforts

'Country of enchantments': Watling

Barrallier expedition: *Voyage dans l'interior de New South Wales*, HRNSW 5 pp. 748–825; *Principal Occurrences in Ensign Barralier's [sic] Journey*, HRA 1.5 pp. 586–9; Caley to Banks 8.11.1802, HRNSW 4 p. 887

Expedition route: Cambage (i); Cunningham (ii); Macqueen; Brownscombe

Barrallier's life: Macqueen (King to Banks re Barrallier, p. 102)

Gogy: 'Gougey' speared, SG 17.3, 31.3, 7.4.1805; 'Cowgye' at Broken Bay and Goondel vs colonists, SG 4.6.1814; 'Gogie' to attend inquiry 11.6.1814, SR reel 6004 (4/3493 p. 187); Macquarie meets 'Koggie', Macquarie pp. 6, 9; 'Goggie' inspected 22.4.1816, SR reel 6065 (4/1798, pp. 43–5)

Gundungurra described: SG 4.6.1814

Koolah: SG 21.8.1803

Chapter eleven: Wild and madlike plans

Castle Hill escapes, 1803: SG 5.3, 19.3 (trial), 26.3, 21.8, 28.8, 18.9, 25.9, 2.10.1803; 19.1.1806. Court records SR reels 2651 (5/1149 pp. 127–135), 2392 (5/1145 pp. 199–201, 223–224). HRA 1.4 (King's order 23.3.1803, p. 337; King to Hobart 9.5.1803a, p. 242; King to Hobart 9.5.1803b, pp. 84–5). HRNSW 5 (King's order 16.2.1803, p. 22; Caley to Banks 31.12.1803, p. 300; Suttor to Banks 10.3.1804, pp. 350–2). Rusden pp. 70–1 (de Clambe letter 15.2.1803, Marsden to King 17–18.2.1803; Arndell to King 19.2.1803)

'Hangman Dog': 11.2.1804 SR reel 656 (SZ768 pp. 438–44)

De Clambe: HRA 1.3 pp. 109, 406; SG 10.6.1804, Peron 308–9, Jervis (i) p. 240

Bean family: McIntyre & Cathro p. 32

Escapees' futures: Doyle, Conway, Ramsey, Ross, Mulcahy pardoned, convict pardons 1.1.1810–31.12.1819 (SLNSW), pp. 47, 56–7; Conroy and Mulcahy, 1823–5 muster (SLNSW); Woollaghan murder trial, SG 4, 18, 29.6; 16, 23, 30.7.1814

Chapter twelve: The fatal excursions of John Place
Place/Hill UK trials: *York Courant* 6.4, 22.6, 20.7, 27.7, 3.8.1801; *York Herald* 18.7, 25.7, 1.8.1801 (BNL)
Place's escapes: SG 26.6, 3.7, 18.12.03; 18.3.1804; trial SR reel 656 (SZ768 p. 421)
Castle Hill: HRNSW 5 pp. 113, 163, 329
Glatton in Sydney: HRNSW 5 p. 209, SG 19.3.1803
Convict rebellion: HRA 1.4 pp. 563–577; Rusden pp. 56–98; HRA 1.5 p. 79; Holt pp. 79–87, SG 18.3, 25.3.1804
Flinders on interior: Cumpston, p. 57

Chapter thirteen: Daemons and chimeras
Newcastle: HRNSW 5 p. 366; HRA 1.5 p. 112
Emmet and rebels: Whitaker pp. 89–115
Post-rebellion: Holt's trial; Rusden pp. 78–85 & Holt pp. 83–7; De Clambe's death, SG 10.6.1804; Turley charged, SG 24.6.1804; man charges wife, SR reel (SZ768 p. 461); Hughes hoax, SG 1.4.1804; Castle Hill, Jervis (ii) & SG 1.6.1811
Houlding: SG 9.12.1804, 17.2.1805, 5.1.1806, SR reel 656 (SZ769 p. 1)
Blue Mountains impassable: King to Camden 1.11.1805, HRA 1.5 p. 594; Mann pp. 31–2
'Bigotted fugitives': Mann p. 10
Newcastle escapes: SG 23.9.1804; 3.3, 7.7, 22.12.1805
James Field: SG 10.6, 1.7. 1804; 13.1.1805; HRA 1.5 pp. 112–3
Newcastle boat theft: SG 27.4, 18.5.1806, Mann p. 12
Harrington piracy: SG 22, 29.5.1808
Escape by Tracey: SG 12.6.1808; pardoned (8.11.1808, 1.3.1810), SR reel 601 (4/4427 pp. 158–9, 482–3); Freed 9.6.1810, CSI. Spelt Tracy in SG and *Anne* indent.
Escape by Waters etc: SG 13.2.1813
Catholic mass: Granted 19.4.1803, HRNSW 5 pp. 97–8

Chapter fourteen: Boundless regions open to our sight

Robinson verse: Hughes p. 300

Blue Mountains crossed: Blaxland's journal, Richards pp. 70–5; Evans' journal, HRA 1.8 pp. 165–77; Evans seeing 'inland sea', attributed to Bathurst's 'earliest settlers' in Ida Lee's *Early Explorers in Australia*, 1925

Escape by Ablett etc: SG 11, 18.6.1814; Ablett's statement to Bigge Inquiry 12.10.1820 (BT Box 10 pp. 4024–5); Ablett's UK crime, Deeks p. 11

Escape by Kippas etc: SG 14.10, 21.10, 2.12.1815; Macquarie pp. 125–6; Kippas' statement to Bigge Inquiry 29.11.1820 (BT Box 10, pp. 4076–9)

Kippas: CSI for arrival (as John Kippas), pardon 31.1.1820, Oxley's carpenter, Cox 1818, Bathurst 1819. Broken leg, Bigge Inquiry 12.10.1820 (BT Box 10 pp. 4022–3). Other detail in 1822, 1823–5 musters, 1828 census

Inland sea: Darling, Cumpston p. 87; Sturt, Favenc pp. 142–3; HRA 1.10 (p. 28, Oxley to Macquarie 1.3.1819)

Other bios: CSI for Bullock mitigation, Buck to marry, Hall with Oxley (also Oxley p. 229) and Cox, Ablett at Bathurst and Evan, pardons (Berwick, Ablett, Hall, Bullock, Barrington)

Chapter fifteen: Full march for Timor

'Other planet': Mason p. 61. 'Sensible land journey', Cunningham (i) pp. 203–4

Escape by Poole etc: SG 11, 25.10.1822; trial notes and statements (taken Bathurst 4.9.1822), SR reels 1977 (SZ798 pp. 492–503) & 1978 (SZ799 pp. 1–46); Poole hanged, SG 29.5.1823. CSI for arrival in colony (Poole, Clancy, Peacock, Campbell), condemned then sent to Port Macquarie, controversy re Poole's execution, Wiseman flogged. Peacock's UK crime, Deeks p.28

Peacock in Tasmania: tried (29.8.1825) & executed (31.8.1825), HRA 3.8 p. 1161, *Hobart Town Gazette* 3.9.1825

Escape by Cross etc: SG 1.5.1823; SR reel 1979 (SZ801 pp. 507–16); CSI for arrival in colony, sent to Port Macquarie, Dean punished July 1825

Pardoned/Freed: Phipp CF 41/1516, 2.11.1841 SR film 1009 (4/4369); Burchall CF 47/0805, 31.12.1847 SR film 1025 (4/4410); Jenkins CP 43/049, 1.1.1842 SR reel 780 (4/4441 p. 305)

Escape by Sergison etc: SG 22.10, 29.10, 5.11, 19.12.1828; Boxall pp. 85–6; 1828 muster; 1837 General Return of Convicts; Jenkins as Macqueen's servant 16.9.1825, SR reel 6015 (4/3515 p. 319); other detail from shipping indents (microfiche, SLNSW)

Chapter sixteen: Mistaken and dangerous men

Holmes gang: SG 8.9, 17.9, 19.9, 22.10, 15.12.1828; SM 13, 15, 20, 22, 27.12.1828; 5.6.1830; *Australian* 11.11, 14.11, 9.12, 16.12.1828

Holmes: assigned 29.8.1823, SR reel 6011 (4/3509 p. 135); servant of E. Wright at Bringelly, 1825 muster; fled Hyde Park Barracks, SG 16.4, 2.5.1827 (age 23); in Sydney Gaol (with 'Whisken', Owen & Walsh), 1828 Census

Donahoe: SG 6.2, 5.3.1828; *Australian* 1.10.1830 ('the very devil'); SG 5.6 (rewards), 4.9 ('dangerous spirit') 7.9.1830; Williams; Meredith (i)

Other Bushrangers: Owen escaped No. 4 Iron Gang, SG 14.4.28; Walsh escaped No. 20 road gang, SG 13.8.1828; Bain fled Hassall's service, SG 14.7.1828; other detail from shipping indents (microfiche, SLNSW)

The Pound: discovery, Boxall pp. 52–6; closure, SG 6.8.1831

George Clarke: Mitchell pp. 1–2, 22, 139–40; Sturt pp. 100–1; Favenc pp. 102–3; *Hobart Town Courier* 7.8, 14.8.1835

Chapter seventeen: Buckley's and none

Sullivan Bay escapes: HRA 3.1 (Collins to King 16.12.1803, pp. 48–50; 29.2.1804, pp. 226–7; 31.7.1804, p. 252; King to Collins 30.12.1803, p. 51; Collins to Hobart 14.11.1803, pp. 37–8; 28.2.1804, pp. 56–59; General Orders 10.11.1803, p. 73; 21.11.1803, pp.75–6; 26.12.1803, pp. 83–4; 20.1.1804, p. 91; 28.7.1805, p. 533; A Public Caution 23.12.1803, pp. 82–3). SG 26.8.1804; 10.9.1835. Knopwood. Todd. Morgan

Buckley: early life & 1835–56, Bonwick, Tipping; life 1803–35, Morgan

Sundry detail: Wedge journal, Morgan (1979) pp. 165–71; Langhorne's memoir, Morgan (2002), pp. 190–200; Fawkner's 1865 memoir, Cotter p. 27; Harris to Henry Harris 11.2.1804, Hamilton–Arnold p. 60; PP King's diary, HRV 1 pp. 111–12; Buckley requests pension, HRV 1 pp. 130–1; *Calcutta* convict bios, Tipping

Chapter eighteen: This fancied paradise

Wellington Valley runaways: Sturt pp. 70–1

Mitchell & Graham: Reece (ii) pp. 114–121

Population figures: Hughes pp. 144, 162, 323; Ward p. 15

Abyssinia: Cunningham (i) p. 206

Joseph Mason: Mason pp. 75, 121–3

From Ward's *Australian Legend*: Irish contented, p. 50, 'Bad luck to 'em' and 'free objects', pp. 58–9 (ch. 3); Howe as 'great man', p. 145; Riley the bushranger, p. 165 (ch. 6)

Outlaw counterculture: Robson pp. 86–8

Brady & Howe: Boxall pp. 17–22, 41–7; White (ii) 28–53; Hughes pp. 226–34, HRA 3.2 pp. 162–3, 194

Garbut: Favenc pp. 194–5

Duff children: *The Country of Lost Children: An Australian Anxiety* (1999) by Peter Pierce visits the cultural resonance of this case

Runaways to Adelaide: Hindmarsh to Colonial Office 1837 (www.sapolice.s.gov.au/operations/history.htm)

King of Mountains: Macqueen p. 11

'Labyrinth': Thomas p. 145

Whaling: *Tyranny of Distance* (1966) by Geoffrey Blainey, p. 115

Endnotes

Chapter one: The hopeful fraternity

1. Collins (i) says 126 male *Queen* convicts arrived (p. 149) and also 122
   (p. 175). As Hunter (p.366) says seven males and one female died at sea,
   122 is presumably the error. Collins says 'several convicts' died at sea.
2. In July 1788 Collins (i) describes an Aboriginal family visited by 'large
   parties' of male and female convicts on their days off, singing and dancing
   with their guests 'with apparent good humour' (p. 29).

Chapter two: An evil which will cure itself

1. Other pregnant *Queen* women were Mary Connor (child born 16.6.1792)
   and Catherine Devereaux (or Devereux), whose son James (born 18.12.1791)
   was fathered by James Kelly, the ship's cook. Dennis Driscoll (tried Cork city
   1790, aged 30, reprieved from death) was buried at Parramatta 18.3.1792
   (Cobley (iii) p. 228). By 1793 Catherine Edwards was living with William
   Yardley (an English convict). They married in 1796, had four children and
   settled at Hawkesbury. In 1805 Yardley was apparently killed in a house fire.
   Catherine (now Mary Yardley) was arrested in March 1806, suspected of
   bashing him to death (his body had head wounds) and burning their house
   down. She was released without charge after weeks of questioning. In
   1818, she was found dead with head injuries. Her son-in-law was tried for
   murder, and acquitted (Flynn pp. 632–3).
2. Tench claims most of the 21 were back 'in the course of a week', but Collins
   implies a longer timeframe. Collins, as judge–advocate, was perhaps more
   involved than Tench, who was not among the soldiers pursuing these runaways.
3. Tench treats this quartet (and their two dead mates) as being among the first
   China bid, but as Collins otherwise accounts for at least 18 of the 21, they
   may have absconded later (Hunter mentions three escapes). When Tench
   has some of the first 21 finding their own way back, wounded by Aborigines
   and leaving dead friends behind, he seems to mean the hospital quartets' story.

Chapter three: Thoughts of liberty

1. Carter (p. 297–303) takes this cue to dismiss overland China stories as 'strategic coolheadedness', citing Tench (p. 93) re convicts inventing stories to fool officials, e.g. pretending discovery of gold or rivers. He ignores Tench's point: authorities quickly learned to be sceptical of such claims. Yet official scepticism regarding convicts' confessed beliefs in bush–Chinas is almost entirely absent — except, tellingly, as this shortlived cynical reaction when the outlandish belief first arose.

2. Six burials 17–28.11.1791 were likely *Queen* convicts: Edward Allen, John Bennett, James (Edward?) Kennedy, Patrick Mooney, Anthony West, Arthur Young. See Cobley (iii).

Chapter four: The greatest villains on Earth

1. Collins claims only 50 male *Queen* convicts were still alive by May 1792 (Collins (i) p. 175). As various records put this closer to 60, he perhaps overlooked the handful (6–10) on Norfolk Island (Donohoe (i)). Burial registers show 14–22 (8 may be namesakes from other ships) of the 126 arrivals buried by 2.5.1792 (Cobley (iii)). Some certainly eluded record, but Collins roughly corroborates the registers' accuracy (he notes a total of 155 male deaths in 1791; registers list 147) and Anglican parish registers kept Catholic records (Donohoe (ii) p. 1). Thus up to 52 *Queen* Irishmen are unaccounted for and may have vanished in the bush.

2. 22–34 men (some ambiguous) and 2 women per *Boddingtons*, and 14–20 men and 6 women per *Sugar Cane* left no trace in the colony. Hall (ii) & (iii).

3. The *Britannia* indent lists 151 men and 45 women (Cobley (v) pp. 497–508), yet the usual figure for arrivals is 134 men and 43 women, with 11 fatalities at sea.

Chapter five: The phantom white colony

1. Yet Governor King used 'Carmarthen Mountains' as late as 1.11.1805 (HRA 1.5 p. 593).

2. The stolen mares were stabled but not owned by the government. August 1797: 15 mares, 3 horses (government); 43 mares, 23 horses (privately owned). Cobley (v) p. 462.

3. Estimated from subtracting 8 possible *Britannia* males buried in 1797 from 134 landed. Cobley (v).

4. Karskens (p. 23) says these men were flogged for refusing to admit their destination, but if their inland myth was a smokescreen for a sea-going escape, as she claims, why didn't they use it? If it helped mitigate punishment, why not avoid the lash with a show of repentance and a nod to Hunter's leading questions? In fact, informers told Hunter of this plot in advance (HRA 1.2 p. 129), and their credibility was proven by the mass arrest they enabled. This suggests a premature revelation of actual intentions, not a strategically leaked red herring.

Chapter six: Checking this spirit of emigration

1. Collins has the expedition announced before the mass arrest, during the magistrate's address at Toongabbie, but Hunter (who omits the magistrate story) is clear (HRA 1.2 p. 130) that he conceived the expedition after visiting the gaoled runaways.
2. Price wasn't identified as Wilson's companion until the 1950s (see Chisholm). In 1895, HRNSW attributed his journal to 'Barracks', who never existed but was believed in long enough to have a Blue Mountains waterfall named after him. The mistake was a confusion with the explorer Francis Barrallier.
3. Collins says they set out on 14 January. This may be wrong; Hunter's order of 19 January seems to launch the trip. Mount Hunter — steep, conical and wooded to the top — gave the best views of the south-west. Tench knew it as Pyramid Hill; it was renamed for the governor in June 1796 but it is now Mount Prudhoe.
4. No convicts named Roe were then under sentence. It may be an alias or mistake. He is Roe only once in Price's journal, and twice 'the other man'.
5. Most writers assert they reached the Wollondilly River by a route traced by today's Hume Highway until Mittagong, then the road west to the Wombeyan Caves. Brownscombe regards the Wingecarribee River near Berrima a more likely terminus. Thomas (p. 130) finds 'the cost of sending Roe and the boy, thereby acquiring a written record, was the premature termination of the expedition'. Yet it ended precisely as Hunter ordered, when the convict participants had had enough.
6. In his 15.2.1798 dispatch Hunter writes, 'I hope the return of the above three and the story they can tell, will serve to make them [convicts] more

contented with their present lot'. If this refers to the discouraged convicts, he lets slip that only three returned early. If he means the exploring trio, it still implies Wilson's party included a convict, as his scheme relied on convicts convincing their fellows that overland escape was futile. Misled by Hunter's contradictions, Collins — certain one convict stayed with the guides — assumes a four-man (three guides, one convict) party, although he later has a trio returning. Price's journal proves it was a three-man team. The absence of the days with all four convicts from Hunter's copy of Price's journal supports the idea he wished to de-emphasise the trip's original intention.

7. Cunningham (ii) argues that Wilson's official trips deserve recognition as mountain crossings, speculating the achievement was realised but suppressed as it defeated Hunter's intentions by unwittingly revealing an easy interior escape route. But Roe and Price had far from an easy time, enduring extreme hardship in fear of their lives. Also, Hunter's stated purpose was to quash the convicts' myth, not to prove the mountains were impassable. That authorities genuinely believed the mountains were impassable is obvious in numerous letters by colonial officials.

Chapter seven: The opinion of the common people

1. Karskens (p. 23) cites this escape to show that China and the white colony were cover stories for attempts to contact ships. Thus, instead of aiming for inland sanctuaries, this Irishman 'travelled eastward to the head of the Georges River' (Prospect Creek junction). But this is actually about six miles almost directly south of Parramatta, or ten south of Toongabbie, his most likely starting points. The east route derives from Collins, who relates the runaway's claim of *reversing* an outbound westerly journey. There is no proof he aimed coastward or finished much closer to the sea than he began; his movements match an aborted bid for the southwest 'white colony'.

2. Again Karskens (p. 23) discerns a seawards goal, claiming they were 'heading east to Botany Bay'. This is from Hunter (HRA 1.2 p. 131), but he presents Botany Bay as plan B, after weeks spent aiming elsewhere: 'after travelling for many weeks through the country [they] made shift to reach the sea-coast, near Botany Bay, but in a part where no boat had ever been'. As they were lost, their location alone proves neither their goal nor where they had travelled.

3. Hall (i) names 6 female and up to 32 male *Marquis Cornwallis* convicts (11 died at sea) absent from colonial records. Of 134 *Britannia* males landed, 64 are in the 1806 muster, 9 burials noted 1797–1801 (Cobley (v), Mutch) and I've located 5 others from various sources, but up to 56 are unaccounted for. Doubtless some died 1801–1806, but the increased Irish presence from 1801 makes burial records too ambiguous for reliable estimation. Also, escapes were much less likely to be recorded 1800–03, the gap between Collins and the first *Sydney Gazette*.

4. Karskens (p. 22) speculates that Noah fell for a tall tale used to tease newcomers, or a loose metaphor for anywhere outside settled regions.

5. Carter (p. 317) likens escape myths to convict slang; just another linguistic mask to hide meaning from authorities. How odd, then, that while Tench describes courts using translators of 'flash' language, in almost forty years not a single informer was available to translate the 'real' meaning of 'China' or other mythic destinations. In fact, informers tended to reveal such plots, not explain them away, and myth-seekers often denied their destination.

6. From Carter (p. 181), quoting JJ Shillinglaw Papers, Manuscript Box 81, Latrobe Library. Flinders' lost Malays may have been inspired by his encounter with Pobassoo, leader of a Macassan fishing fleet, in February 1803. They spoke via Flinders' Malay cook. Hailing from Sulawesi, Macassans harvested trepang on Top End coasts during the wet season until the early 20th century.

7. Did this 'copper-coloured' tribe signify long-gone Asian colonists, a fragment of folk-memory from the Eora's more northerly ancestors? Arnhem Land tradition has the *Baijini* — light-skinned, rice-planting, house-dwelling seafarers — who resemble early South-East Asian visitors.

8. Blaxland found this cairn (a 20th-century reconstruction is near Linden) during his 1813 crossing. At first he thought it marked the furthest point Bass reached in 1796. On 9.5.1815, just 12 days after visiting and naming it 'Kealy's Repulse', Macquarie saw several similar cairns on Mt Pleasant near Bathurst with 'every appearance of having been collected by the Hands of Man', but still made no overt Aboriginal connection.

9. Fox, Pitt and Burke appear in Lang, who semi-fictionalised allegedly true stories to conceal identities.

10. The 1852 memoirs of William Buckley (see Chapter 17) describe possibly earlier sightings, but may be editorial colour; by 1852 bunyips were a popular bogey.
11. Thomas (p. 141) discerns no diplomacy in agreeing with leading questions and denies Aborigines would do it, finding it conjures 'the child–savage who idiotically affirms everything that the white man says, a familiar stereotype in the annals of Australian history'.
12 Collins (ii, pp. 214–5) believed Turwood's example inspired Wilson to pose as a reincarnated Aborigine, but his tribal associations predate Turwood's discovery.

Chapter eight: Their natural vicious propensities

1. *Labouring With The Hoe*, a well-known ballad by 1830s Irish convict Frank 'The Poet' MacNamara, begins: 'I was convicted by the laws of England's hostile crown'.
2. Pointing to the power of symbol and code in Irish underground movements, Atkinson (pp. 249–50) suggests these drawings were actually secret liberational insignia. He notes the figure of a compass enclosed in a heart denoted brotherhood in some Irish revolutionary societies. But he doesn't explain why Hunter saw a paper compass with written directions (see Chapter 5), nor why some English convicts used them (see Chapter 17).

Chapter nine: King of the mountains

1. Probably John Day alias Hill, who got 14 years at Derby (17.3.1800), arrived per *Canada* or *Minorca* (14.12.1801) and was buried in Sydney, 16.9.1802. Another John Day, arrived 1799 per *Hillsborough*, appears in the 1806 muster as a Hawkesbury farmer, free by service. Roger Brigden (life, Middlesex 23.5.1792, age 22) arrived per *Barwell* in 1798. Four James Rileys arrived 1796–1800 on Irish transports *Britannia*, *Marquis Cornwallis* and *Friendship*.
2. King had refused the *Atlas I* permission to land liquor because of the high mortality among its convicts, but later allowed Baudin's visiting French expedition to buy 800 gallons for private use. Harris told King that Corps officers, feeling hard done by, were saying the French had sold some (which they denied). Paterson apparently heard this accusation (he denied it) but didn't tell King, who was furious. Harris was court–martialled on 13.10.1802 for 'ungentlemanlike conduct' in telling King that Adjutant Minchin said

complaints against the French were made in Paterson's presence. Minchin faced the same charge for denying he said it! Both were acquitted. Barrallier was one of the panellists. HRA 1.3 pp. 646–688.

3. Thomas (pp. 142–3) sees the phantom white colony as part of 'a deliberate policy of obstruction' whereby Aborigines delayed white penetration of the mountains for a quarter-century. This surely overstates the case, especially since white colony stories helped draw various Europeans inland, increasing the familiarity which led to the first crossing. But his idea of the myth as an Aboriginal anti-colonial mime (supported by citing their aptitude for mimicry) is an intriguing possibility: when asked about the inland, Aborigines gave whites nothing more helpful than a mirror image of themselves.

4. Four of the five Englishmen were new arrivals. From *Earl Cornwallis*: John Marsh, tried 25.7.1798. *Perseus*: William Clarke (Warwick 23.3.1801, life); John King, 9.3.01; Elbert Neale or Albert Neil and Philip Poore, 7.3.1801. Note: the *Perseus* and *Coromandel* indents were combined, but the 1828 Census notes King per *Perseus*, so Neal and Poore most likely were too. William Clarke was probably also per *Perseus* — of the four convicts in 1802 so named, the 1822–1825 muster lists Clarke per *Perseus* as a sawyer, the runaway's occupation. Marsh, White and King were pardoned by Macquarie between 1814 and 1816.

5. Barely legible trial minutes may read Michael or Daniel McAlister or McAlish — probably Daniel McAllas (Macaleese, Macaliskey), a convict constable at Castle Hill. Sent for life from Antrim in 1797 (age 30), he was a hangman and 'leader of banditti' by one account (Holt pp. 46, 83), although his ship (*Minerva*) indent calls him a gardener. McAllas was Mary Turley's de facto after de Clambe's death (see Chapters 11, 13) and was pardoned for loyalty during the 1804 convict uprising.

6. Walsh, 7 years, tried 1800; Byrne, life, 1801. Joseph Wild, an English convict (Chester 21.8.1793, life) per *Ganges* (1797), was the white discoverer of Lake George in 1820. His entry in *The Australian Dictionary of Biography* states 'he is said' to have been with Barrallier's party. Proof is lacking but it is likely. Although still a convict in 1802, he was already a good bushman, entrusted with shooting game and familiar with the back country. His rescue of Irish runaways within a week or two of Barrallier's trip may have influenced his

recruitment, and perhaps King's hopes that the trip might help disabuse Irish myth-seekers. In 1847 he was gored to death by a wild bull in the Cowpastures, aged 74.

7. White, 7 years, 1800; McCarthy, 7 or life, 1801. Karskens (p. 22) cites this trial to argue that runaways turning up closer to the coast than where 'they said "paradise" lay' (west) suggests 'paradise' was a sham. But none of the four here who confessed the New Settlement gave its imagined direction, so where they aimed is unknown — and surrendering at Hawkesbury or Broken Bay could easily denote failure to attain the mountains beyond Richmond Hill. The Irishmen (who denied seeking paradise) reached the Nepean River, matching a bid for the south-west white colony favoured by Irish convicts about1797. Ideas of how and where to find bush-sanctuaries were likely very fluid, subject to rumour as well as trial and error. Moreover, those reaching where 'paradise lay' were less likely to be recovered and questioned than those who found outlying settlements after giving up or getting lost.

8. The idea of convicts using myth stories to avoid floggings (Karskens p. 22) is not supported by this case, where mitigation was a game of chance and two of the three flogged were among the four who confessed the New Settlement.

9. King to Hobart 9.5.1803 (ii), HRA 1.4 pp. 84–5. Or, as a Dutch settlement, the Cape of Good Hope was conflated with New Holland. For more on whether the 'white colony' was thought to be Dutch, see Chapters 14 and 15.

Chapter ten: Almost superhuman efforts

1. Thomas (p. 143) presents Gogy's troubles arising from aiding a white interloper, ignoring his murder of Goondel's sister. He implies the offer of a wife (to Gogy, not Bungin) was a strategy to thwart Barrallier's progress by removing his only guide. Yet Badbury and others weren't pressured to stop helping him. Gogy's victim was perhaps not literally Goondel's sister; could Barrallier have fully grasped kinship concepts? He calls her both 'soeur' and 'une femme de ce chef'.

Chapter eleven: Wild and madlike plans

1. Mary's 'Balloon' nickname (Holt p. 46) hints she was a bit of a windbag. On 14.2.1804 the courts heard that 'much abusive language' passed between Turley and a man she accused of 'libellous and seditious' words that her

'husband would lose his head' when the French invade. SR reel 2651 (5/1149 pp. 179–80); SG 12, 19.2.1804.

2. All were lifers except Shanks and McDermott (7 years), and perhaps Morgan and Brown. The *Atlas I* had two John Morgans, one from Louth (life), one from Meath (7 years). Brown was either John Brown via *Hercules* (Derry, life) or *Atlas I* (Limerick, 7 years). Conroy was either via *Hercules* (Louth), or James Conway (as court minutes spell it), *Atlas II* (Baltinglass). Trial places: Down (Shanks), Meath (McDermott, Gannan), Cork (Dempsey), Baltinglass (Doyle), Limerick (Woollaghan, Mulcahy, Ross), Dublin (Lynch), Galway (Simpson). SG 19.3.1803 calls Mulcahy 'Malahoy' and Patrick Ross 'Peter Ross'. Gannan also Gannon, Gammon, Cannon.

3. Probably the *Atlas II* lifers William Ramsey (tried Fermoy, Limerick, 1800) and Patrick Ward (Moate, Westmeath), or Patrick Ward (Kildare, 7 years, *Hercules*). The only source naming them (SG 5.3, 19.3.03) calls him 'Richard Ward'.

4. John McCormick, tried Carrickfergus 1800, 7 years, *Hercules*. Rusden p. 71. 'M. McCormick', SG 19.3.1803.

5. Karskens (pp. 24–25) claims they 'probably planned to live as bushrangers' as they 'retreated with stolen weapons and other goods to the plain between the Hawkesbury and the mountains, living near a group of Aborigines'. But there is no proof they camped there more than a single night (after robbing Neale's farm). In eight days at large they moved roughly north-west from Castle Hill towards their claimed goal, the Blue Mountains.

6. SG 19.3.03. Karskens (p. 25) speculates this was a tactical bid for mitigation, which 'probably reduced the number of hangings'. But executing small samples of large gangs was the norm, regardless of courthouse excuses — it was often thought proper to hang only the worst as a warning (e.g. the piracies of Ramsay's boat and the *Norfolk* each yielded just two executions). Also, the mountain-crossing story arose while the gang was still at large; it was not solely a last-minute excuse.

7. Lane's evidence (SG 19.3.03) omits Smith, but court minutes omit Lane, despite listing him as a witness. Both men apparently identified Lynch, Conroy, Brown and Shanks.

8. 55 death sentences (34 commuted) were given in King's six-year term (Roe et al. p. 18).

9. SG 26.3.03. Quote wrongly refers to Gannan, initially confused with Simpson. A correction (same issue) says Gannan 'behaved himself with a penitence becoming his situation, but Francis Simpson died truly impenitent and hardened'. Yet the main report states the 'impenitent' man finally 'died a penitent'.

10. King's reference to 14 capital convictions is not an error; he includes an unrelated case from the same sitting — William Jones, theft (reprieved). HRA 1.4 (p. 337), also SG 26.3.1803.

11. Bryan O'Brien was sent for life from Wexford per *Atlas II*. Hoey and Dowling were later hanged for stealing from houses, Hoey on 26.4.1806 and Dowling 26.8.1809 (SG 27.4.06, 27.8.09).

12. Michael Woollaghan is buried in St John's Cemetery, Campbelltown, along with other local pioneers. His birthplace is noted as Tipperary.

Chapter twelve: The fatal excursions of John Place

1. SG 26.6.1803 gives John Cox and John Phillips, but for their names I've followed the PRO Convict Transportation Register (reel 87B, SLNSW) and the *Glatton* indent.

2. SG 3.7.1803. The 'large lagoons' may be a speculative error rather than misinformation. On his 1807 trip, Mann (Mann pp. 31–32) saw terrain 'relieved by the interposition of pools of stagnant water'; such descriptions may have had earlier currency.

3. SG 18.12.03 has Place's second escape from Hawkesbury; trial minutes say Parramatta.

4. Reverend Marsden wrote (18.8.1803) that de Clambe was 'intended to be murdered when they [the Irish] break from Castle Hill again' (Rusden p. 71). On 30.1.1804, Mary Turley claimed one John Sullivan threatened to cut de Clambe's head off as a 'French traitor' who sold out 'to the bloody English government'. SR reel 2392 (5/1145 p. 235).

Chapter thirteen: Daemons and chimeras

1. In his memoirs, Holt has Dempsey accusing him of agreeing to lead the rebellion, a perjury crushed by Holt's own heroic cross-examination.

2. Field was rescued on 29.5.1804 by the ex-convict pirate Joseph Crafts (Chapters 5, 7), by then master of the government sloop *Bee*. Months later Field ran from Newcastle but was caught by Aborigines.

3. Possibly James Holding, per *Surprize* (1790), 50 years old in 1804, sent for 7 years at the Old Bailey (2.4.1788) for stealing from his employer, a London ironmonger.
4. Tracey's movements at large are unverifiable. Karskens (p. 26) suggests he sought a more agreeable situation with a farmer who sheltered runaways. While possible, this would seem more likely if he wasn't already assigned to a settler, especially one willing to plead for him in court. The 1828 census lists Tracey as 70, free by service, with 100 acres at Wilberforce (20 cleared, 15 cultivated) and 20 cattle.
5. SG 24.7.1813. Macquarie's quote is from a similar order (SG 2.3.1816), when 70 convicts were gazetted as at large.

Chapter fourteen: Boundless regions open to our sight

1. Per *Earl Spencer* (arrived 9.10.1813): John Ablett, age 29, tried Suffolk 23.7.1812, life; John Hall, 24, Stafford 1812, life; Richard Frier, 41, Suffolk 18.3.1812, life. *Glatton* (11.3.1803): John Barrington, Gloucester 25.3.1801, life. *Anne II* (27.2.1810): John Berwick, Chelmsford 1808, life. *General Hewitt* (7.2.1814): Thomas Buck, 36, London 7.4.1813, 14 years. *Admiral Gambier* (29.9.1811): John Bullock, Derby 1810, 14 years.
2. The *Sydney Gazette* claimed 'James' Ablett was punished, but Ablett himself (as John Emblett) denied this to the Bigge Inquiry in 1820: 'I was first assigned to Mr Jenkins of Sidney. I worked for him four or five months and then took to the Bush. I delivered myself up and was not punished, some of the others were.' The 1814 muster (taken 19.10.1814) supports his version, listing Berwick and Fryer in the gaol gang and Ablett working for Cox.
3. Mike Dash (*Batavia's Graveyard*, pp. 238–41, 351–4, citing *Leeds Mercury* 25.1.1834) links this rumoured colony to the Dutch vessel *Concordia*, lost in the Indian Ocean in 1708. Otherwise the report may be fiction inspired by escape mythology. An eyewitness account of 'light-coloured natives' occurred on 7.7.1825, when a boat crew from the brig *Amity*, exploring the Brisbane River, claimed they were menaced by 'a considerable number of natives, of a light-coloured complexion, apparently above six feet in height, and of a robust form'. One was armed with a bow and arrow. The five men responded to doubters by publishing affidavits in the *Sydney Gazette* (24.11.1825). The paper suggested this 'northern copper-coloured gentry' — a phrase evocative of

the Chinese travellers of 1791 — was not a newfound race as, claimed but the offspring of Aborigines and escaped convicts. For early Dutch Aboriginal contact, *And Their Ghosts May Be Heard* (2002) by Rupert Gerritsen.

4. John Haigh (or Hague) and Richard Kippas (as John Kippas) were both tried at York (19.3.1814, life) and reached Sydney per *Indefatigable*, 29.4.1815. Like Kippas, Haigh was assigned to Windsor. Ship indent notes Haigh as 31, a labourer, 5 ft 5, ruddy complexion, brown hair, hazel eyes.

5. Freed in May 1820, Richard Kippas married Mary Hartnett, a convict and adopted her daughter Mary Ann. John Ablett's wife Ann, 33, died a few months after him, leaving five children between 5 and 13.

6. In August 1825 a mass escape plan was discovered which also appears inspired by false ideas of the Macquarie River meeting the coast. Convict servants from Bathurst properties had joined bushrangers in stockpiling tools, seeds and guns, intending to 'move towards the sea-coast' and settle 'until opportunities offered for leaving the country'. Led by William Percival (an ex-soldier) and bushranger Robert Storey, the plot involved some 60 convicts. They planned to kill George Ranken, a 'bad master' for whom some of them worked, steal his cattle, burn his house, 'force his wife and servant girl', then move west to Wellington to steal more cattle. They conceived of creating rather than reaching a sanctuary, but aiming for the sea via Wellington suggests inland sea mythology influenced their plan. In 1829 Sturt found the Macquarie joined the Darling River. SG 20.10, 28.11, 8.12.1825; Barker pp. 77–8; White (ii) pp. 113–4

Chapter fifteen: Full march for Timor

1. Robert Campbell or Cammell: tried Perth 16.9.1818, 7 years, arrived *Shipley* 22.11.1818. Michael Clancy or Clensey: Co. Clare, Lent 1819, 7, *Minerva I* 17.12.1819. Thomas Peacock: Bury St Edmonds 23.10.20, 7, *Grenada* 16.9.1821. William Poole: Kilkenny Lent 1820, 7, *Prince Regent II* 9.1.1821. John Wiseman: Norfolk 22.3.1817, life, *Larkins* 22.11.1817.

2. Police list (20.3.1823) of recaptured Port Macquarie runaways: Thomas Sims, Richard Williams, William Blackburn, Thomas McCarthy, James Cossofo, Michael Clansey, Isaac Cooke, James Mara, Thomas Peacock. Peacock and Clancy departed Sydney for Hobart per *Brixton* 15.4.1823. SR reels 6057 (4/1767 p. 56), 6010 (4/3508 pp. 129, 133–4).

3. *Eliza* indents/PRO records give ages, occupations and trials: Cross: 27, groom, Bedford 14.3.1822, life. Dean: 29, cotton-spinner, Chester 10.9.1821, life. Phipp, Fipps or Phipps: 23, porter, Hertford 7.3.1822, 7 or 14. Belcher or Burchall: 24, carman, Middlesex 1.12.1819, 7.

4. Dean may have falsely implicated Denny to diminish his own involvement, but as approver he had already beaten the gallows and had no need to complicate his story. On 26.4.1823 Henry Denny (per *Three Bees*, 1814) was fined for employing Daniel Dynan, a runaway convict, and gaoled on 10 May, unable to pay. SR reel 6057 (4/1768 pp. 23–24b).

5. Phipp, William (or Charles) Lovell, Edward Mahon, John Brown and William Hennessy planned to sail to Sydney, then steal a larger boat for a longer voyage. On 1.6.1825, armed with knives, they fled Port Macquarie after robbing a soldier and George Stuart, a constable. Stuart's musket accidentally fired; Brown prevented an enraged Hennessy from stabbing him. Soldiers soon arrested them, shooting Brown dead. The others, tried in Sydney 30.9.1825, got life on Norfolk Island. SG 6.10, 17.11.1825; CSI.

6. All except Sergison were lifers. Ships and arrivals: Budge (*Hooghly*, 24.2.1828); Hill (*England*, 18.9.1826); Jenkins (*Royal Charlotte*, 29.4.1825); Lantwheeler (*Guildford*, 25.7.1827); Spring, (*Florentia*, 3.1.1828). Sergison also Sergerson, Sargisson and Sergeantson. His age noted as 34 in 1837 General Return of Convicts. SG 19.12.28 calls Budge 'Bridge'. Only 3 per cent of transportees were sent for 'offences against the person' — rape, murder, assault, kidnapping and sodomy (Hughes p. 163).

7. 4 October (SG 19.12.1828) or 1 October (SG 29.10, 5.11.1828).

8. The name Timor was in use by July or August 1836, the time a court witness later claimed visiting 'fine forest land . . . near a place called Timor' (*Australian* 8.9.1837). The first landholder, James White, had a fitting name for the occupier of somewhere effectively named for the fabled 'white colony'.

Chapter sixteen: Mistaken and dangerous men

1. Mason (p. 120) records an Australian parallel; an amateur linguistic comparison claiming Aborigines hailed from Egypt. Mason's supporting comment is that, like the 'Israelites', Aborigines barred leprosy victims from their camps. Similarly, SH 26.8.1840 speculates on the Jewish origins of Sioux Indians.

2. *The Tragedy of Donahoe* by Charles Harpur, published SM Feb–Mar 1835, was not performed.

3. Holmes: tried aged 19, Glasgow 17.9.1822, 14 years, arrived per *Henry* 26.8.1823. Donahoe: *Anne & Amelia*, 2.1.1825; Owen or Owens: *Midas*, 15.2.1827. Wiskin or Whisken, Wigden, Widgin, Wiscott: *Guildford*, 25.7.1827. Phillips: possibly *Henry Porcher*, 3.12.1825 — my guess at his identity rests on Patrick Phillips being the only gazetted runaway (SG 3.3.1828) named Phillips in 1827–28 apparently absent from later records.

4. SM (5.6.1830) has a jocular dig at its rival by claiming Owens and Wiskin were reading the *Sydney Gazette*!

5. Recounting Phillips' death, SM 5.6.1830 claims he (not Holmes) saved the lives of Hassall's servants.

6. Walsh's age (SM 27.12.1828) may be understated; 1828 Census says he came per *Mangles*, 6.6.1828, aged 18 when tried in Dublin, 30.12.1827. The *Australian* (11.11.1828) links him to Holmes. Bain's connection to Holmes is questionable, but Hassall's hazy recollection (SM 5.6.1830) that five bushrangers were arrested at the gunfight supports the idea that Bain was there — only Owens and Wiskin were taken that day, but Bain makes five eventually caught. Here Hassall names Holmes 'Parsons' — an alias given at his arrest? A Hassall convict stockman, Kelly, was also said to have joined Holmes (SG 8.9.1828).

7. John Wilson's intimate knowledge of the region is revealed in the journals of his 1798 travels, when he claims the Wollondilly River 'runs clean through the mountains to the Hawkesbury'. As Cunningham (ii, pp. 77–78) shows, Wilson knows of the Warragamba 'slot' — then still officially undiscovered — where the Cox–Wollondilly confluence passes through the mountain wall to join the Nepean.

8. Mitchell says 'Barber' was the Aborigines' mispronunciation of 'bushranger', but the indents of Clarke's transport, the *Royal Charlotte*, list his occupation as hairdresser. Clarke was later sent to Norfolk Island, and was hanged in Tasmania in 1835.

Chapter seventeen: Buckley's and none

1. Knopwood's diary and Collins to Hobart 28.2.1804 (HRA 3.1 pp. 56–59) suggest the convicts who ran on 27.12 were Buckley, Pye, Marmon, Shaw,

Page and Macallenan. Knopwood (27.12.1803) says six 'endeavoured to make their escape' at 9 pm. On 31.12 he lists all recent runaways — 'MacAllennan, George Pye, Pritchard, M. Warner [Marmon], Wm. Buckley; Charles Shaw, wounded and brought to the camp; Page, taken same time when Shaw was shot, G. Lee, and Wm. Gibson.' Interviewing Macallenan (17.1), Knopwood says he 'escaped with Pritchard and the party when Shaw was shot'. The informer told Collins that five sought to join Macallenan and one other (Pritchard?). If Macallenan deserted on Christmas Day, then Knopwood failed to note his servant's absence in his diary.

2. Knopwood interrogated Page on 28.12 with no mention of an informer. Collins omits Page's capture, but his dispatch to Hobart 28.2.1804 (HRA 3.1 p. 58) confirms the informer had died.

3. Morgan's edited selection of Knopwood's diary changed this date to 30.12.

4. 13 January (Collins); 16 January (Knopwood).

5. Lee's reputation for cleverness caused a rumour he had 'resources unknown to them to enable him to live independent of the public stores'. Collins was told 'a large party' intended joining him. Nothing connects this to Buckley, except perhaps Pritchard's escape on 19.12 (before Place's story was distributed), but an attempt to find Lee doesn't negate the gang's plans confessed by Macallenan.

6. Collins had forgotten much by 28.7.1805, listing the gang as Charles Shaw, 'Jeremiah' Buckley, George Lee, David Gibson and 'Willm. Veospers' [William Vosper]. Seven convicts were missing when Sullivan Bay was abandoned — Lee, Buckley, Pritchard, Pye and three who ran in November 1803 — Vosper, William Brown and James Taylor. Only Buckley reappeared.

7. Wilkes' *Dictionary of Australian Colloquialisms* (1978) traces written proof of Buckley's chance, hope or show to 1898. It's likely to be far older; examples suggest it was already hackneyed and it may be significant that Buckley & Nunn opened within a year or so of Morgan's book popularising Buckley's story. Often taken to mean no chance, logically it can only mean almost no chance.

Chapter eighteen: This fancied paradise

1. Similar speculation was made much earlier, when 17th century Dutch explorers mistook the limestone columns of the Pinnacles Desert in Western Australia for a city in ruins.

2. Another was Fairy Meadow in the Illawarra region, a 'beautiful little natural meadow in the midst of the tall gloomy forest' which 1820s immigrant Alexander Harris at first found hard to believe 'was not of artificial construction'. Harris, *Settlers and Convicts* (1847), Melbourne University Press, Carlton, 1969, p. 25.

3. The appeal of a lost white colony resurfaced in the 1890s with the vogue for Rider Haggard–style adventure novels about encounters with mysterious outback civilisations. Melissa Bellanta identifies nine published between 1890 and 1908. They include *An Australian Bush Track* (1896) by John David Hennessey, featuring 'Zoo Zoo Land', a remnant Asian civilisation in Queensland; *The Lost Lemuria: A Westralian Romance* (1898) by George Firth Scott; and *The Secret of the Australian Desert* (1895) by eminent historian–explorer Ernest Favenc. 'Fabulating the Australian Desert: Australia's Lost Race Romances 1890–1908', *Philament* 3, April 2004, Sydney University.

Index

Acknowledgments

I'd like to thank my agent Selwa Anthony, who saw this project to fruition over several years. The ever-professional and enthusiastic University of Queensland Press team, including Alexandra Payne, Rob Cullinan and editor Sybil Kesteven, have also been a pleasure to work with.

Josephine Pennicott read innumerable drafts; her writerly eye and belief in the book were invaluable. Angelo Loukakis gave generous and influential feedback on an early manuscript. Others who offered much-appreciated advice and/or support include George & Anne Levell, Selena Hanet-Hutchins, Barbara & Ian Pennicott and my two UQP readers. Grateful thanks to you all.

Thanks also to Bob Rickard, David Sutton & Paul Sieveking, co-editors of *Fortean Times* magazine (UK), who published my original article on this topic in 1999.

Tour To Hell was made possible by resources available to the public at the State Library of NSW, State Records NSW and Fisher Library (University of Sydney).

Comments and questions about the book are welcome. I can be contacted at www.davidlevell.com